SUNR

S. T. SANCHEZ

Cover designed by Courtney Johansson
Edited by Courtney Johansson

Library of Congress Control Number : 2017907741

To my kids
Eden, Maximo and Kyler
For always being my biggest supporters.
Dream Big!

Chapter 1
It's a Girl, sort of

"Just one more big push. You're almost there," the doctor coaxed. He glanced up to check on his patient. Everything seemed normal. He had done home births before, but this was different. He was just as nervous as the patient was, or maybe even more so.

His patient was lying on the bed, her eyes closed and scrunched together. She was trying to focus on her breathing and press through the pain of the contractions. Her normally beautiful black hair was plastered down, sweat rolling down her face. She managed a meager smile when she noticed he was looking at her.

Everything seemed normal, but he felt off. Maybe because he was delivering Elaine's baby. He had delivered hundreds of babies. He was Dr. Adam Marsh, the highly sought-after neonatal surgeon. Normally he wouldn't take on a patient he knew so well. Maybe it was the atmosphere. It was a little eerie. It was like he was in the hospital but, he wasn't. The room had been made up just like a room in the maternity wing at his hospital. Every detail was present, including the lingering smell of bleach. Elaine laid sweating and panting, her feet propped up in the metal stirrups.

She had been very adamant about not wanting to give birth in the hospital, but at home, an alternative that many mothers opted for nowadays, mainly for the comfort and relaxed setting.

1

But that had obviously not been Elaine's reason for choosing this option. She had an IV coming out of her right arm in order to stay hydrated, and all the normal machines had been brought in to monitor the fetal heart rate and contraction strength and duration.

At first glance, it would appear to be a normal hospital room; white tile floors, white walls, bright lights—but for some reason it felt strange. Normally he would have a staff of nurses assisting him. But Elaine had requested—or rather, demanded—,that it be just the two of them.

"Aaahhhh!" Elaine screamed as she struggled through the exhaustion, forcing her little kicker out in a bittersweet moment, grasping the rails of the bed for support. She rested a moment and then wiped the sweat from her forehead with a small washcloth, setting it back down on the small table beside her bed.

Adam guided the baby out carefully. He clamped the cord and cut it. *Normally that would be a privilege reserved for the father, but there was none*, he thought sadly. He moved the baby over to a small table, and switched on the heat lamp. It was a girl. Adam worked carefully and quickly, suctioning and cleaning her off.

"Oh, no!" he gasped.

Elaine glanced over. "No!" Elaine sobbed into her pillow.

He set the infant down in the small plastic portable bassinette. It was identical to the ones used in hospitals. He turned to her, his eyes fighting back the tears. "Elaine. I'm so sorry…I know what this meant to—"

She fought back the tears. "Boy or girl?" she asked, glancing over at the half-bloody infant that lay crying in its bed.

Adam shook his head. "Elaine. Don't you think knowing will just make it harder? I'll dispose of it quickly and then you can put this all behind you." He turned quickly and reached for the baby.

Elaine bolted straight up. "Don't take another step," she ordered.

Adam hesitated. "Don't worry, you won't see a thing. You shouldn't have to watch this." He turned back towards the small bed. Why did this have to happen?

Elaine pulled herself up out of her bed, half staggering, blood trailing down her legs. "Adam, if you lay one finger on my baby, I WILL kill you." Her eyes were half crazed.

Adam stopped, stunned. He had thought she had merely not wanted him to dispose of the creature in her presence. She couldn't really want to keep it. He turned and put his hands up slowly, trying to show her he meant no harm. He walked cautiously towards her, much in the same way a parent approaches a child who is holding something breakable that they don't want dropped, and spoke hesitantly. "Elaine. Please...lie back down. " He warily reached forward and put his hand on her shoulder.

She shook it off violently. "I'm keeping my baby," she insisted.

She had clearly lost it. Adam coaxed her back into the bed and pulled up a chair. He took her hand in his and caressed it slowly. He spoke to her carefully, as if talking to a scared child. "Elaine, I know how much you wanted this. I wanted it too. Of course we all would have loved for a part of Dylan to go on living. I know you miss him. I miss him too. But that thing has to be destroyed. There are laws. Dylan would have—"

Elaine spat back angrily. "Don't you dare say Dylan would have destroyed our child. NEVER!" She shook her head fervently, tearing her hand away from his. "Just because you were his brother doesn't mean you knew everything about him. I know he would have protected our child. We created that baby out of love. It cannot be wrong."

Adam sat quietly beside her, trying to think of a way he could rationally explain things to his sister-in-law, who was obviously not thinking clearly.

"Boy or girl?" she asked softly.

Adam glanced over at the whimpering creature in the bassinet. "Girl." He sighed reluctantly. Maybe if he just gave her a minute, then she'd be able to see things clearly, begin to think rationally again.

Elaine smiled, gesturing to her daughter. "Bring her to me."

Adam shot up out of his chair, nearly knocking it over. "NO!"

3

"Adam, bring her to me or leave. Either way, I will keep her and you will not tell a soul."

Adam regarded her incredulously. He started to speak, but she cut him off.

"You swore to Dylan." She shook her head back and forth. "You swore before he left on his last assignment, that if anything happened to him, you would protect me and our child. This is my miracle, my little piece of him," she reminded him.

Adam turned in frustration and paced beside the bed. "That," he pointed at the crib, "is not the child that he was envisioning!" he yelled. He didn't care anymore. He had tried to be patient and that clearly wasn't working.

Elaine propped herself up in her bed. "And did he specify?" she yelled back. "He knew the risks and still he wanted a child. Did he tell you only to protect the child if it were human? NO! He was prepared for either and so am I!"

Adam slumped back down in the chair, burying his face in his hands. "Elaine, please!" he begged. She was being impossible; the law was clear, the creature had to be destroyed.

"My daughter," she demanded.

He opened his mouth, as if to argue, but sighed instead. He slowly walked back over to the small creature that lay in the bed. She appeared so human. Could Elaine be right? Would Dylan have wanted him to protect this being?

He pulled her out and finished cleaning her off. She would have been beautiful for a human baby. She had the same jet-black hair as her mother, and although most babies' eyes changed color within a few weeks after they were born, he doubted hers would. She had the same dark green eyes as her father. He cleaned out her mouth, avoiding the four prominent sharp teeth.

He wrapped her in a white receiving blanket and brought her to her mother.

Elaine reached for her eagerly and caressed her in her arms. "Hello, Lilly. I've been waiting a long time to meet you."

"You are not naming that monster LILLY!" Adam screamed.

4

Elaine's expression changed to one of sadness, pity even. "Just leave. Come back later or don't. I know this is hard for you. You weren't expecting this." She paused, looking down at her daughter. "Maybe I should have told you earlier that I was planning on keeping my child no matter the outcome, but I wasn't sure you'd help me." She placed her hand over his. "Just leave. You've already helped me. Lil...the baby is here. Just sign the birth certificate and leave. I won't ask anything else of you. You've kept your promise to Dylan. If I had given birth at a hospital, she'd be dead already."

Adam glimpsed down at the piece of paper on the nightstand.

"I can't sign that. She's a monster. I won't lie for you."

"You'll do it for Dylan. You promised him. You promised you'd take care of us. Sign it and then you can wash your hands of us."

Adam sighed in defeat as he wrenched the pen from his pocket. He scrawled his name quickly and spun to leave. She was right. He'd done more than anyone else would have done, family or not. After all, he could lose his medical license, go to jail, or worse. He could walk away, conscience clear. He turned back, leaned forward, and kissed Elaine on the forehead. "Goodbye," he whispered. He walked toward the door. He would not come back. He paused at the foot of the bed. There was blood everywhere. The placenta was lying on the ground on a pile of towels.

He should stay and clean it up. He should, but he couldn't stay here another minute. He felt like he was suffocating. Adam walked swiftly to the bedroom door, swung it open, and then closed it behind him.

He paused, disoriented, glancing around. He was in a small hallway; brown carpet lined the floor. On the wall were framed pictures of Elaine and Dylan, taken throughout the years; wedding pics, vacation pics, family pics. There was a picture of Dylan in his Marine's uniform, taken the day he left. He seemed to be peering down accusingly at him. Adam's eyes locked on his brother's. "I'm sorry," he said, and then stormed out of the house.

*   *   *   *   *   *   *   *   *   *

"Lilly," Elaine smiled and leaned down to kiss her daughter lightly on the top of her head. "I love you."

She cradled her daughter in her arms, attempting to spend a few minutes just enjoying her. She tried to not worry, but there was so much that needed to be done, so many problems to be addressed. It was no use, worry came with the territory now.

This had always been a possibility. She had prepared as best as she could. But now that Lilly was here, there would be a lifetime of concerns.

Lilly cried loudly. Surely she was hungry. Elaine carefully set her on the bed, and awkwardly pulled herself off of it. Pushing her IV stand, she walked to the corner of the room where she had a small, white mini fridge. She opened the door and pulled out one of the plastic pouches.

She returned to the small plastic crib and pushed it back towards the bed, carefully avoiding the mess that was splattered all over the floor at the foot of the bed. That would need to be cleaned up. But first, Lilly was hungry.

Pulling a bottle out from beneath the crib, she opened it up. She cut open the pouch and let the red liquid slide into the bottle, glancing at the label on the pouch. O negative. She hoped that Lilly didn't have any allergies. Could a vampire be allergic to a specific blood type? She wasn't sure. Everyone knew relatively little about them.

She pulled herself back onto the bed and cradled her daughter in her arms. She brought the bottle to Lilly's lips and immediately Lilly stopped crying and started sucking like a pro.

Lilly downed the entire bottle within a few minutes. *Should she have more? How much should she drink? How often?* All of these questions and more swarmed around in her head.

She watched her daughter. The baby seemed happy and content, so Elaine decided to wait before offering another bottle. She cradled Lilly closely and leaned back on her pillow, exhausted.

6

Elaine had blood on hand. She had ordered some from a black market supplier she had found. But blood had a short shelf life of only a few weeks, so Elaine had not ordered much. She hadn't even been sure her daughter would be a vampire, or if she was, how much blood she'd need. It's not like Elaine could ask anyone.

The world had changed so much over the past ninety years. The west coast was completely gone. Overrun by vampires. California, Washington, Oregon—all a wasteland. That is where the world first became aware of vampires, where myth became reality.

Some of the vampires had grown sick of hiding in the shadows, and decided to feed publicly. Panic ensued. Hundreds of thousands of humans were killed, drained of their blood. The government, believing the situation had become so dire and believing a nuke would destroy all the vampires, ordered the strike. So on June 8th, 2025, at 8:01 a.m., the US government fired a nuclear bomb into central California. To be fair, the initial blast probably killed a few vampires. But vampires didn't get sick and die. They existed in a different state than humans. Not alive, like a human would define it, but not dead either. The radiation did nothing to them. It killed millions of humans, between the impact and the fallout from the radiation after, but the vampires emerged unscathed.

The world changed. Walls went up. Smaller cities were abandoned. Vampires came out more openly. Elaine had studied all of this in school. She still had a hard time imagining a world without walls.

Then came the biggest breakthrough, the one that had changed Elaine's life. In December of 2055, a French geneticist named Frédéric Beauvais discovered a gene that created vampires. No one had ever before thought that vampires were born. No one knew how the vampire species had begun, but they knew vampires could change a human into one. Most scientists believed creation came from a bite from a vampire. However, none could explain why it didn't seem to happen every time. But through his research, Dr. Beauvais proved that when a certain gene, which he named the

Sang gene, was present in a human, there was a chance that child would be born a vampire.

Dr. Beauvais' breakthrough was huge. Vampires weren't some kind of demon as others had imagined, they weren't some mutation from being around too much radiation, or eating foods covered in pesticides or pumped with too many hormones, as some had hypothesized. Some vampires were born. They came directly from the human race. They weren't some evolutionary event gone wrong.

It was so rare for a vampire to be born and not created. The majority of the vampire population had been created. The vampire gene that was needed to give birth to one was rare—only one in a hundred million carried it. If a person was a carrier, there was a one in a ten million chance that they would give birth to a vampire.

They even had a test to see who was a carrier, thanks to the breakthroughs of Dr. Beauvais.

Elaine thought back to the day she and Dylan were tested.

*   *   *   *   *   *   *   *   *

They had walked into the clinic, carefree. They were being tested as a precaution, more to appease their parents than anything else. If either of them had felt an inkling of what was about to happen, they would have never gone in. Ignorance is bliss, or would have been. Neither of them really thought there was a possibility that either of them could be carriers of the gene.

The nurse called Dylan first and then Elaine. The test was quick, just a finger prick. The blood was analyzed immediately. It took about five minutes.

Elaine and Dylan were sitting in the waiting room on a comfortable faux leather sofa, sharing a bag of Cheetos they had bought from a vending machine. A nurse walked out, flanked by two doctors wearing gray scrubs. One was older, white-haired and wore dark thick-rimmed glasses. The other was dark-haired, shorter, and most likely Hispanic. The nurse pointed at Elaine and Dylan as she whispered something to the two men.

Dylan and Elaine were ushered quickly into a room where they sat, waiting as the two doctors just stood there staring at them.

Elaine was sure that one of them had the gene. Why else would there be all this commotion surrounding their tests?

"What's going on?" Dylan finally asked when it was clear that the doctors had no intention of speaking.

The older doctor cleared his throat . "Uhh um, pardon me, let me introduce myself. I'm Dr. Wilson and this is Dr. Hernandez. We're just waiting for some equipment to be brought in here, and then we are going to retest you both personally."

Elaine reached for Dylan's hand and squeezed it nervously. "Is something wrong? Does one of us have the gene?"

A nurse walked into the room, pushing a small cart with some type of machine on it. It was big and shiny, with many switches and dials on it. She whispered something to Dr. Wilson and then left.

"Please don't worry. We think the nurse contaminated your tests. She's new and we just want to retest to make sure you both get accurate results."

The older doctor walked up to Dylan and pricked his finger, while Dr. Hernandez pricked Elaine's.

They sat quietly waiting as the doctors ran their blood samples through the machine. The minutes ticked by slowly. Elaine's heartbeat pounded so loudly she was sure everyone could hear it. Sweat beaded up on her forehead. She dabbed at it with her sleeve.

Finally, the machine began printing out a piece of paper. Dr. Hernandez walked over and took the paper. He read over it slowly and gasped.

"NO," Dr. Wilson said, as he rushed over to the machine, ripping the paper out of the other doctor's hand and read it.

Elaine began to cry softly. "No. One of us has the gene, right?" she asked.

The doctors didn't answer at first. Then Dr. Hernandez walked over and put a hand on each of their shoulders. "I'm sorry.

This is unheard of, literally, but you are *both* carriers of the Sang gene. We've run the test twice."

There was silence, other than an occasional sob from Elaine. Dylan hugged her tightly.

"Both of us?" Dylan asked when he found his voice again. "What does that mean? Can we have...kids?" Then in a whisper, "Normal kids?"

The young doctor glanced at Dr. Wilson; the uncertainty was written all over his face.

The white-haired doctor sat quietly for what felt like a long time. He drummed his fingers on the desk. "NVs are very rare. Most of the vampire population is made up of CVs," he began. "The percentage of humans that carry the vampire gene is nominal. Those who actually give birth to an NV is even smaller."

They both sat there, not understanding a word of what the doctor was babbling on about.

"I'm sorry Doctor," Dylan interrupted. "We're a little lost...DVs and CVs...I don't have a clue what you're talking about." He looked at Elaine for reassurance; she nodded in agreement.

The doctor's face turned red. "I apologize. I'm used to speaking with other doctors. Let me try to explain." He reached for an opened bottle of water and took a few swallows. "Are you aware that there are two different types of vampires?"

Dylan nodded.

"Yes, some have always been that way and others were once human but have been turned by another vampire." Elaine responded, more of a question than a statement.

The doctor nodded. "Yes some vampires have been born as they are. We call those NVs, or Natural Vampires, because they are born that way. They are rare, but they are also faster and stronger and usually even more intelligent than those the vampires they create, the CVs. Your odds are definitely higher, given that you both carry the gene, but NVs are so rare that I believe it is highly unlikely that you would actually give birth to a NV," the doctor added reassuringly.

*   *   *   *   *   *   *   *   *   *

Elaine peered down at her very own natural-born vampire. *Highly unlikely. Sure.* She laughed out loud, slightly hysterically.

The world had changed so much. She hoped one day society might learn to accept her daughter. Sixty years had passed since Dr. Beauvais' discovery, and for now the only thing that had changed was that genocide was now not only supported by the government, but mandated.

"I wish you were here, Dylan," Elaine whispered. "Your daddy loved you so much," she added quietly. She leaned down and kissed Lilly on the top of her thick black hair. She was sleeping soundly.

Elaine watched her daughter sleep for some time, amazed at this tiny creature in her arms. She was beautiful. It saddened her that she could not share this joy with her family, or Dylan's parents. They would react like Adam had, that was for certain. Not to mention the fact that it would be such a heavy burden for any of them to carry a secret this big. A secret that would endanger anyone who knew.

The law was clear. If a vampire was born, it was burned immediately. *It went against nature*, they said.

Against nature. How could that be when two people created this baby out of love? Nature created Lilly. It wasn't like she was some test tube baby, or the result of an experiment gone wrong. Elaine loved her child. She would defend her to the death. It didn't matter that she was a vampire. The love would have been the same whether she was human or not. Lilly was her child. She had carried her for nine months, felt her as she'd grown and moved inside her. Elaine had cried when the child was born, not because of the fact that her baby was a vampire, but because she knew this life would be harder on Lilly.

Elaine was still uncertain on how exactly she would be able to keep Lilly hidden, undiscovered. Especially since humans were endeavoring to hunt down vampires to the point of extinction.

11

There was so much to do, but first, she must sleep. She shifted comfortably on her side and cradled Lilly in her arms, then drifted off to sleep quickly.

Elaine awoke famished. Lilly was staring up at her with her dazzling green eyes. She was quiet and seemed content.

Elaine glanced around the room. Lilly had been born at two-sixteen that afternoon and it was still light outside, so she knew that she couldn't have slept too long.

She got off the bed and realized the IV was still sticking out of her arm. The bag was empty so she decided to take it out. She'd drink plenty of water and get some food in her system. She would be fine. She set Lilly in the crib softly and walked to the bedroom door. As she walked around, she was reminded of the mess on the floor. That would be cleaned up after she had some food.

She was in some pain, but not too much. Elaine walked out to the kitchen and opened a can of soup. She didn't even bother reading the label. The hunger was so intense that she didn't care. She grabbed a large green ceramic soup bowl out of the cupboard and poured the soup in. It was chicken something. She walked over to the microwave and punched in a minute and thirty seconds, tossed the bowl in and hit start.

She turned behind her to reach for a spoon in the silverware drawer and froze. Had the microwave clock said eleven something? Surely that was a mistake; she was just so hungry, that she'd read it wrong.

Elaine turned around and hit the end button on the microwave, waiting for the time to be displayed. Eleven-twenty-three. *Impossible*, she thought. Maybe the power went off and the time was messed up.

She walked to the living room. The television remote was on the small wicker table next to the black leather sofa, where she always left it. She aimed it at the television and hit the power button. Elaine scrolled through to the news channel—they always had the time displayed. On the bottom right-hand corner of the TV, the time flashed eleven-twenty-five. Impossible.

Elaine punched the volume up. There was a reporter standing behind a pile of rubble. She was explaining how the Vampire Assassination Squad had just destroyed a clan of vampires late last night, on Wednesday.

Today was Thursday! She had slept all night and half the day away. Lilly must be starving and soaked.

Elaine rushed back into her homemade hospital room. She picked up Lilly. She still seemed content. Her baby wasn't crying. Elaine's worries started to diminish until a new thought occurred to her. What if Lilly was so weak from missing so many feedings that she was too tired to cry?

Elaine rushed to the fridge and pulled out another pouch of O negative. She poured it hastily into a clean bottle, only managing to get about half of the contents inside, while spilling the rest on the floor. She hastily offered it to Lilly.

Lilly didn't seem to want it. Maybe baby vampires didn't need to eat as often as human babies. Elaine then remembered her diaper. She fumbled underneath the crib for a new one, and swiftly had the old one off. It was dry. How could that be? Lilly was almost a day old. Shouldn't she have gone by now? Elaine studied her, concern written all across her face, but Lilly seemed fine, content.

She knew there would be differences between raising a vampire versus a human infant. Maybe this was the beginning.

She decided to wait another day and if Lilly didn't eat or have a wet diaper by then, she would have to call Adam.

Once Elaine was somewhat reassured that Lilly was doing all right, she went back to the kitchen and ate her soup, not even bothering to heat it up this time. She just ate it cold—no, she devoured it.

Then she got bleach out and cleaned up the mess from the birthing process that laid at the foot of the bed,. The placenta was disgusting. The mess wouldn't have been so bad if she hadn't had to clean up the placenta. And because she had slept so long, things had begun to smell.

When everything was finally clean, Elaine felt exhausted all over again. She was about to lie down and rest for a little bit when she noticed she was in the same bloody nightgown as yesterday.

Pushing Lilly in her crib, she walked down the hallway to her room. They were done with the hospital room. She wanted her own bed and her own shower.

She pushed Lilly all the way into the bathroom and up close to the shower door. Elaine cranked the hot water on and stepped in. The water felt amazing. She felt so dirty and grimy from the whole giving birth process.

She reached over to her shower caddy and pulled out a large bottle of lavender shampoo. Pouring a generous amount into her hand, she massaged it through the tangled, matted mess that was her hair. Elaine rinsed her hair through with conditioner and then found her large bottle of body wash. She lathered it up well and scrubbed herself head to toe. When she was finished, she just stood there, letting the hot water envelop her.

Only when the shower doors began to fog, inhibiting her view of Lilly, did she decide to shut off the water.

She pulled on a clean pair of sweats and then collapsed on the bed with her daughter beside her.

"Lilly, if I pass out again, please cry and wake me up if you get hungry," Elaine said in a cute baby voice, letting Lilly hold tight to her little finger. She was strong, much more so than a human baby. Elaine would have to be careful. At just a day old Lilly could already squeeze her finger so much that it was actually slightly painful. In a few more weeks she probably wouldn't be able to let Lilly hold on to her finger.

She held and enjoyed Lilly, talking about Dylan to her. She wanted Lilly to know her daddy. Elaine told her the story of how she and Dylan had met. She told her how they fell in love and sometime in the middle of telling her how much her Daddy had wanted her, Elaine and Lilly floated off to sleep.

Chapter 2
Dinner

Seventeen years later

Lilly grabbed her bag and shoved until her history book overcame the mess inside. "Bye, Mom!" she called as she opened the front door.

"Have a good day at school, tell Lex hello for me," Elaine called from her bedroom.

Lilly skipped down the sidewalk and jumped over the car door into Lex's Maida.

"Probably one of the last days you'll be able to keep the top down," Lilly noted. She noticed out of the corner of her eye that Lex just shook her head and rolled her eyes. "What?"

"I hate you, you know that, right?" She shoved Lilly playfully on the shoulder. "You just seem to glide down the sidewalk all elegant and then jump into the seat so gracefully. If I tried to do that I'd fall flat on my face, or worse," Lex complained.

Lilly laughed. "You know you love me. Besides you can do plenty of things I can't."

"Like what?" Lex demanded as she shifted into first and started down the street.

"Like be so confident. You can tell people what's on your mind, and you have no problem talking to guys. I wish I could be like that," Lilly answered.

Lilly was always too nervous. She was always thinking about all the things that could go wrong. *What would happen if they could tell she was different? What if they couldn't, what if they just thought she was normal? Would her fangs extend if she started kissing a human? Would a human even want to kiss her if they knew the truth? Could she ever tell anyone the truth?* She thought as Lex drove.

Only her BFF, Lex, knew. They had been friends since kindergarten, when Jacob Eaton had pushed Lilly off the seesaw at recess and Lex had made him eat worms as some sort of retribution.

Lilly had waited until last year to tell her. Lex hadn't talked to her for a week, though Lex had made it clear she would never tell anyone else about her secret. She kept quiet, just watching Lilly as she kept her distance. Then after a week had gone by, Lex had walked up to her, apologized, and things went back to normal.

"Whatever, that's nothing special. And I may be able to talk to guys, but all they want to talk to me about is you." Lex reached for the radio and cranked up the volume. "Let's see if they're playing the new Yeyey single."

"Chances are if they're not playing it now, they will be within the next few minutes. You know whenever they dig up a song that's not on file, they play it like a zillion times," Lilly said.

"I know. But it's just so exciting, it's not like they find new music all the time. And besides I only caught the end of it yesterday."

Since the blast, technology had downgraded big time. Vampires had attacked communication towers, satellites, and power plants in retaliation for the nuclear bomb that the government dropped on California. Even after over a hundred years had passed, they were still struggling to maintain life as they had

16

once known it. Energy was to be conserved and entertainment was minimal. There were only two radio stations—one for the news and one for music.

So much music had been lost since the nuke and the events that followed. Now every song that was found was kept in a file on a database somewhere. It was only updated every six months, since cities all had internet and electricity quotas.

Lilly was lucky. Her mom worked for some of the wealthiest companies, and since she worked from home, she had a generous allowance of both internet and electricity.

Lex didn't have to worry either. Her dad was a high-ranking scientist for some top-secret lab, so he didn't seem to have a limit.

Lex clicked on her radio and paused to listen to the news report.

….recent incidents in parts of Boston

and Worcester have forced the V.A.S. to institute a new eight p.m. curfew on

weekends for all minors, until further notice.

Lex pushed the knob in, turning the radio off. "You don't think they'd change our curfew to eight p.m., right? I mean ten o'clock is already so early. We barely have anytime to do anything outside of school before we have to be home."

"Why should they? We haven't had any attacks lately," Lilly said.

"Yeah but Harbor Cove isn't that far from Boston. I wish the Vampire Assassination Squad would just hurry and wipe all the vamps out. How hard can it be to find a bunch of monsters that can't go out in sunlight?" Lex asked, as if it were the easiest thing in the world.

"Yeah," Lilly laughed uneasily.

Then Lex laughed. "You know what I mean. Not you obviously."

Lex pulled up and parked her car next to a dark blue Mustang. It wasn't hard to guess whose car it was. Lex and Kyle were the only high school students with vehicles. Kyle was still inside, drumming his hands on his steering wheel to the beat of some rock song Lilly had never heard of. When Kyle saw Lilly pull up he turned off the ignition and got out of his car.

Just keep walking, Lilly thought to herself.

"Hey Lilly," Kyle said, ignoring Lex completely.

Lilly smiled and slung her bag over her shoulder. She pushed past him and opened the door to the school.

He hurried after her, either oblivious to the fact that she wanted nothing to do with him, or just ignoring it completely.

"Hey, a bunch of us are going to go to Eddie's tonight. He's throwing a party while his parents are gone on business. What time can I pick you up?" He asked.

"How is he planning on getting everyone up to his apartment without anyone reporting it?" Lilly asked. It wasn't that she cared, she just figured if he didn't have an answer she could use it as an excuse not to go.

Eddie lived in the general population apartments. Each stood five stories tall and each unit was about eight hundred square feet, with fifty units per building. There were hundreds of them in Harbor Cove.

Lilly was lucky, as she actually lived in her own house. There were only about sixty houses in Harbor Cove. The rest of the population lived in government apartment buildings.

Apparently before everything went nuclear in California, in more ways than one, living in houses was a norm.

But after California, small cities were abandoned. Larger cities were walled up. Subdivisions were demolished to make room for the new norm. Millions of apartment buildings sprang up. All identical, it didn't matter if you had one or ten kids, everyone got the same size unit.

Only the very important got their own houses. And only the super elite got cars.

Lilly's dad had been some high-ranking military sergeant and so they had been given a house. They still had to walk or take public transportation though.

Lex on the other hand, had a house and two cars. Her dad was some super vital doctor that did experiments.

Lilly had no idea what Kyle's dad did but they had two cars also so she figured he must be someone important too.

Lilly turned her attention back to Kyle. He had been rattling off about how they had bribed one of the security officers to look the other way.

"Cool." She nodded, feigning interest. "But I can't, too much homework," she said, as she continued walking. It sounded lame, but she didn't care . Kyle was captain of the rugby team. He had blonde wavy hair, blue eyes, and he modeled on the weekends. All the girls were crazy about him, but Lilly couldn't understand it. He was conceited and rude.

"Come on Lilly. I'll hook you up. I'll just tell Rita to do your homework too tonight. She won't mind." Kyle put his arm around her shoulders.

Lilly skillfully slid out from under his grasp. "I prefer to do my own, thanks." Lilly glanced around for an escape route, but couldn't think of anything. She and Lex had arrived at school early and Lilly knew that even if she went to class, Kyle would just follow her.

"Then I'll just come over to your house and we can study together. I could use some work on my French." He brushed a hand through his hair and gave her what he may have thought was a charming smile, but she only found it creepy. He reached to put his arm around her again.

"She can't," came a reply from behind. Lex pushed between them and turned to face Lilly. "We have plans, remember? Movies, girls' night." She winked at her, then shouldered hard against Kyle, making him back up more.

He started to open his mouth, but Lex, sensing what was coming, continued. "And *you* are definitely not invited."

Lex gripped Lilly's arm and dragged her down the hallway towards their first class. "Thanks," she murmured as they sat down in AP English.

"No problem. But I really do want to go out tonight; I've been wanting to see that new movie," Lex said.

"Which one now? You know we've seen them all. I wish Hollywood was still there and they were still making movies, then maybe we could see something decent." Lilly pulled out her copy of Wuthering Heights and opened it to the chapter they were discussing in class that day.

"This one is new. Nobody's seen it. It was just discovered. It was set to come out in 1992, and somehow one copy survived the blast. It's called *The Cutting Edge*. The eye candy alone is supposed to be worth more than the price of admission. Plus it's the only way we get to see what life was like before the world became all crazy."

"I do really need to get some homework done," Lilly insisted.

Lex stared at her in disbelief. "You remember who you are talking to?" she asked. "I'm not Kyle. I have known you forever. And if you fish your binder out of that black hole you call a bag, I am sure we will find all of your homework neatly sorted by subject and that you are ahead in every class." Then she whispered, "I mean it's not like you forget *anything*."

Lilly laughed, while glancing down at her bag. She knew she was busted and had nothing to say.

"Pleeaassse?" Lex begged. "It's supposed to have something to do with ice skating. I wonder if they skate on a lake. Can you imagine people being stupid enough to skate on a lake? I mean vampires could be hiding underneath the surface and they'd never know till it was too late. I mean the cold doesn't affect you and you never have to breathe, right?"

"If I say yes, can we change the subject?"

"I knew you wouldn't let me down," Lex said.

*   *   *   *   *   *   *   *   *   *

Lilly walked down the sidewalk, enjoying the cool breeze against her skin; at least, she imagined it was cool. It was fall and people were walking along in long sleeves and jackets. Temperature didn't really affect Lilly, though she knew what fire would do to her.

20

She had been close to fire and felt nothing, but she didn't have a death wish so she had never stuck her hand in it or anything to see how that would feel. Snow didn't affect her either, but she always wondered about liquid nitrogen, that liquid that would shoot out of pipes in movies and freeze people in a matter of seconds.

She had on a pair of jeans, a long sleeved shirt, and her favorite college sweatshirt, the University of New Hampshire. It was her favorite not because she had some desperate desire to attend there, but because it had been her father's. She figured walking around in shorts and a tee shirt might draw some attention, so she attempted to blend in whenever possible.

It was getting darker sooner. It was just after seven, but the sun was already down and the street lights had lit up, illuminating the streets—not that she needed the extra help. Lilly was running a little late; her mom had a million questions for her before she headed out. It was actually funny when she thought about it. She could have run here from her house and made it with time to spare; unfortunately, humans weren't used to seeing people zoom down the street at amazing speeds, except in the movies. Or maybe some had, but for those few she doubted she'd be greeted with smiles and well wishes when she stopped, more like flame throwers and tranquilizer guns.

Lex had wanted to meet Lilly at this new place called The Broken Coffee Pot before the movie, but Lilly had to convince her against it. It was on the outskirts of town, on the coast and close to trouble. Everything else had been abandoned there. It was past the wall and too close to the beach for most people.

Lilly wondered what it would have been like to live in the pre-blast era. Although New Hampshire was one of the safest towns in what was left of the United States, the coast was still dangerous. Huge electric fences now surrounded Harbor Cove. Anyone leaving or entering had to have their blood scanned. There was a ten p.m. curfew. The buildings seemed nothing like the ones in the movies. Everything appeared run down. Many of the buildings were old and abandoned, falling apart.

Vampires didn't need to breathe, so they could ambush people fairly easily on the beach. This new coffee shop was just about a quarter of a mile from the coast. No one else had been crazy enough to build anything past the fence that surrounded the edge of the city, but now someone had.

She thought back to the movie she saw last year, *Back to the Future*. She wondered if vampires hadn't revealed themselves, thereby causing a war, would they really have flying cars, or more than two radio stations or two television channels? Or would they go on road trips and travel the country? Now no one used the highways. Everything was flown in on massive cargo planes. It was safer that way.

In history, she had been taught that after the nuke had gone off in California, the vampires had retaliated by setting off EMPs all over the world and targeting technology firms. These electromagnetic pulses had wreaked havoc on communications and technology throughout the world, sending everyone back to the dark ages for a time.

Since then, at least in the U.S., all their resources went towards developing weapons or scientific devices to detect or stop vampires. There were only a few factories and labs left. They had been refortified and flooded with marines armed to the teeth.

Lilly glanced around out front of the theater but Lex was nowhere in sight. The movie didn't start for fifteen more minutes but they had said they'd meet up at seven. Lex usually waited out front. Lilly noticed Ian, a skinny, little sophomore from her school, was manning the ticket booth.

She walked up and waited for the couple in front of her to purchase their tickets.

"Hey Ian," she said.

"Hi Lilly, you here to see *Rambo* or *The Cutting Edge*?" Ian asked.

She glanced around again; making sure Lex wasn't coming down the road. "Actually I'm trying to find Lex, She was supposed to meet me here. Have you seen her?"

He shook his head no. "If you want to go in and get seats, I'll let her know you're here when she arrives."

"Thanks, but I'll wait out here for her."

Ian gestured toward the *Cutting Edge* theater. "If you're going to that one, it's almost sold out, so you might want to go ahead."

The little theater only had two screens. Normally if there was anything even half-way decent playing, the seven-fifteen showing was sold out.

"I think I'm gonna wait," Lilly said as she turned and peered down the street. "Thanks though," she added before she walked off.

Just then, her phone dinged. It was a text from Lex.

Knew u'd never come with me, and btw this place is ttly awesome. Super hottie flirting with me. Met him at movies and came here. Not gonna make the movie. I'd tell u to come but know u won't.

Normally Lilly would never think of going there. She knew her mom would never let her out again if she found out, but there was no way she was going to leave Lex alone in a place like that.

She shoved her phone into her back pocket and started jogging slowly toward the beach. She wasn't exactly sure where this new hang-out was but thought she knew the general area based on a few conversations she'd overheard from people at school.

Finding it wasn't actually that hard. Getting past the wall was the difficult part. There were two entrances to the beach. Each manned by two guards and contained a special scanner designed to prick a finger and test the blood. Lilly had to wait until the power was switched off in a section of the fence and then speed through the door when it was opened, all without being seen. Lilly had never tried to get through before. She didn't foresee a problem in making it through the gate in time, the problem lie in the fact that few people were crazy enough to venture out on the beach, so she had to wait. It was past eight when she finally arrived at the place.

It reminded her of a bigger version of a beach shack she'd seen before in a movie. It was made up of white wooden planks with a wide deck and steps leading up to a big red door. The roof was made out of straw. She didn't think it would withstand an East Coast storm. It looked more like it belonged in Tahiti or Jamaica or some other tropical location. There was a big wooden sign that someone had painted "The Broken Coffee Pot" on. It was painted in black and whoever had painted it must have done it in a hurry. Big black drips hung dried at the end of each letter. Next to it, someone had actually driven in a nail, and hung a broken coffee pot. All in all, she bet this place could have been built in a day and could fall over any minute. Lilly didn't understand the appeal. She started up the steps two at a time when she heard some giggling around the back. Lilly slowed and headed toward the back of the building.

She heard a male voice whispering, "No it's completely safe, we'll just have a little more privacy back here."

A giggle came from behind the building. It was definitely Lex, though how she knew that, Lilly had no idea. She would never have even been able to imagine Lex giggling. Lilly approached quietly and saw a man with his arm wrapped around Lex, kissing her as he pushed her up against the back wall of The Broken Coffee Pot. Then, in a flash, he had her neck at an angle. He pushed her hair off her neck and had his hand around her mouth.

"It'll be so quick you'll barely notice anything," the man said. Then he winked at her and his eyeteeth extended into long fangs.

Lilly would never forget the look of terror in her friend's eyes. Without even realizing what she was doing, she lunged at the man and sent him flying.

The man stood up inhumanly fast, and dusted some sand from his shirt. He seemed amused.

"Listen doll, I don't know you, but generally speaking, when someone has their dinner ready and is about to eat, you go find your own. You don't try and steal theirs."

Lilly turned to Lex. "Run!" she yelled.

Lex stared hesitantly at Lilly for a brief moment and then took off in a mad dash, tripping on the sand as she tried to get away.

Lilly spun to block his pursuit. Her fangs slid out and a growl ripped through her teeth. She was taken aback at first, realizing the sound came from her and not the vampire in front of her.

The man stared at her, confused. Then he took a few slow steps forward with a look of awe on his face. "You're a sunwalker," he said with a hint of amusement.

"Yeah, and I'm stronger than the scum like you who are bitten into existence. So stay away from my friend," Lilly spat with all the spite she could muster.

Before she realized what was happening, the vampire had her now pinned to the wall.

"You listen to me, little girl. You are nothing but an infant," he scoffed. "You *will* watch how you talk to me," he ordered as he squeezed her wrist tighter. "I have been around a long time. I'm smarter than you, faster than you, and stronger than you. Sunwalkers might be rare. But don't ever assume you're the only one." He shoved her one more time hard against the wall, gripping her hand with one arm and using the other to hold her across the chest. Then, he released her.

"Ow!" Lilly said, rubbing her wrist. "That hurt." She looked at him, dumbfounded. He was not just another vampire, but a sunwalker.

"That was the point," he said, shaking his head, still trying to figure something out.

She rubbed her wrist. "It's just, I've never been hurt before. I didn't think we could get hurt."

His jaw dropped. He opened it to speak, then shut it again. He shook his head.

"You do that a lot?" Lilly asked.

"Do what?"

"Walk around and shake your head."

"I just don't understand you..." He started to shake his head and stopped himself. Stifling a laugh, he asked, "Where are you from? What hospital were you born at? I don't understand how we missed you. You must not have been born around here."

"Hold on, as much as I'd love to stay and chat," Lilly replied sarcastically, "you just tried to murder my friend." She turned and started walking back around the building. She heard him muttering "friend" as she stalked off.

"Wait!" the stranger called.

Lilly didn't bother turning around. "Yeah, I don't think so," she called, and then almost walked smack dab into him as he appeared in front of her.

"That was me asking politely, as a courtesy because you are my kind, and I fancy myself as a gentleman—" he began, but stopped as Lilly rubbed her wrist. "Well normally I am a gentleman. Someone stealing my dinner and then letting it run free seems to have put me in a foul mood. Nevertheless, as you've seen, I can make you stay." He stepped back, holding his hands up non-threateningly and then added, "Just answer a few questions and then I'll let you leave."

Lilly wasn't thrilled with this. She knew Lex must be going out of her mind right now. But after feeling his strength, she knew she really didn't have a choice. *Some kind of gentleman, threatening but polite,* she thought.

"Fine," she huffed. "Ask away. It's not like I really have a choice."

He gestured to a couple of crates and then sat down. Lilly hadn't really had time to process all that had happened. But sitting across from this man, she realized for the first time that Lex had been right about one thing, he really was a hottie. He had long dark eyelashes and deep blue eyes. His hair hung in black waves and was a little longer than the guys' at school, who kept their hair very short. It wasn't like medieval times long, just grown out a little. He brushed his hand through his hair, pushing a lock out of his face. He was about six feet tall. And he was pale like she was. He seemed to be about the same age as her. This surprised her most; something about him had made her think he was much older. He was dressed nicely too. He had on khaki pants and a long sleeved button-down

26

black dress shirt. Everything was neatly pressed with prominent straight creases. She didn't see a wrinkle on his outfit. He seemed like he had just stepped off the pages of a GQ magazine.

"Ok, so—" he began.

"How did you know I was a sunwalker?" she interrupted.

"Because I can smell the sun on your skin," he answered, appearing annoyed. "That and I can hear your heart beating. Now may I ask my questions?"

Lilly nodded. This was the first vampire she had ever met and a million questions flooded through her mind. But he did just try to kill Lex. She promised herself no matter how badly she wanted answers to her questions, she would just answer his and then go find her friend.

"Alright. Thank you," he added. "Oh, I forgot my manners. I'm Tread." He waited, then when he saw she wasn't going to reciprocate, he prodded. "And you are?" he asked with an exaggerated but dazzling smile. "Remember you promised to answer my questions," he reminded.

"Lilly," she said, trying to be as defiant as she could, although admittedly it was getting harder.

"Lilly," he repeated. Seemingly content, he continued. "Where are you from?"

Lilly gestured around her, "You're looking at it. Good ole' Harbor Cove, New Hampshire."

He leaned closer. "Here's the part that confuses me. What hospital were you born at? And you're how old?"

"Seventeen. And I wasn't born in a hospital."

"Seventeen! You really are just a baby. Hmmmm." Tread nodded to himself as if this confirmed his suspicions, whatever they were.

"What is 'hmmmm' supposed to mean? And how did you get past the fence anyway?" Lilly demanded after the realization struck that this vampire had been inside her city. Lex had said she met him at the movies, which meant he had gotten past the wall.

Tread laughed hard. "My questions, remember." He stood up. "Last question. Am I the first vampire you've ever met?" He regarded her intently.

"Yes. Can I go now?" Lilly asked as she stood up, following Tread's suit.

"Sure, unless you want to meet up with me again. Learn about our species. About what you are," he said with a note of pity in his voice. "Because you really don't seem to know much."

"You want me to meet up with you after you just tried to murder my friend, then threatened me into answering your questions?" she asked in disbelief.

Tread stepped towards Lilly, closer than a human would, and she glanced at him nervously. "Why do you hang out with these happy meals?"

Confusion on her face, she asked, "Happy meals?"

"Humans. Sorry, I forget you don't know the vampire jargon. Humans like fast food. And although they are not what I would call fast, that's what we call them. They are FOOD, you know." Then he grinned. "And they do make me so very, very happy."

Lilly stepped back. "You're disgusting. You know I sit here and look at you. Talk to you. You seem so human. But you're not. You're a monster."

"We're the same species, hon." Tread replied as she walked off.

Lilly rushed around the corner and then checked to see if Tread was following her. When she saw he wasn't, she pulled her phone out. There were twenty texts from Lex. She had been so engrossed in the scuffle and inquisition from Tread that the beeping hadn't even registered with her. Not bothering to read them, she texted back quickly:

Where r u? Omw.

As she headed back into town, she received a text back from Lex.

Ur house. Sorry☹

Great, Lilly thought, running as quickly as she could without drawing suspicion to herself. She arrived at her house shortly and paused to brace herself, knowing what she had to face would be far worse than the vampire she had just encountered...her mother.

Chapter 3
Stalker

Lilly lingered on the front porch. She tried to imagine if there was any way to avoid the confrontation that she was about to have. *Why did Lex have to come here? Couldn't she have just run home?* She knew her mom was going to blow a gasket. After a couple of minutes, standing there, racking her brain, she decided there wasn't any way around it and tentatively opened the front door. She stepped inside and was immediately pounced upon by her mother. Lilly thought that if she'd been human this hug would have felt more like strangulation.

"Are you OK?" her mother asked, still not releasing her.

Lilly saw a worried Adam sitting on the couch alongside Lex who peeked at her sheepishly and then down to the floor.

"I'm fine. Everything's fine," Lilly said as she gently pried her mother off. "Are you OK, Lex?" She asked as she sat down next to her friend on the couch.

"I think so," Lex said as she hugged Lilly. "You saved my life. I was so worried, I thought that other vampire might have gotten you."

"What happened to the other vampire?" Adam asked. "Did you kill it?"

Lilly stood up in shock. She had never killed so much as a fly. "No, I didn't kill *him*," Lilly amended.

Adam stood up waving his arms. "Why not? How did he get away? Did you just let him go?"

"Actually, he let *me* go," Lilly answered quietly.

Adam paused and stared at Lilly. "What do you mean he let you go? You're the N.V. Aren't naturally born vampires supposed to be the strongest?"

"He was a sunwalker," she paused after seeing Adam's confused expression. "He's an N.V. too. And apparently the longer you're a vampire the stronger you are. And he must have been a lot older, because he was definitely stronger than me."

Lex glared at Lilly. "How do you know that? What? Did you have a conversation with the monster that tried to kill me?" she spat angrily.

Lilly sat there silently. Unsure of what to say, she had already given away more information than she had intended to.

"No. Listen, he just mentioned something when I was leaving. Anyway he's gone. I'm home. We'll stay away from the *beach*," Lilly said talking mostly to Lex, "and we'll go back to normal."

Her mom had been sitting on the couch quietly watching all this unfold. "Back to normal?" she balked. "Lilly, there is another N.V. out there who can walk around in daylight. How do we know he won't come back? He could be out there every day walking around our city and we wouldn't even know it!" she shouted, then, realizing she was shouting, she lowered her voice. "That's it. For at least the time being it's school, then home and that's it."

"What?" Lilly protested. "That's not fair!"

Her mother stood up and put her hands up in front of her, letting Lilly know she wasn't going to argue.

"I don't care what's fair. You just told me that there is a vampire stronger than you milling around. We'll revisit this discussion in a few months."

Lilly opened her mouth to argue but her mother cut her off.

"Until then I will read the newspapers and search for signs of people disappearing. If in a few months we don't see any, then we can assume he really did take off."

"I agree with your mom," Adam interjected. "We need to be sure the threat is gone. We don't need anything bringing attention to you. It would be dangerous for all of us. Besides," he said as he walked over to Lilly and placed a gentle hand on her shoulder, "I'm going to be gone for a few weeks. It will make me feel a lot better if you are home where it's safe." He kissed her gently on the forehead and stepped back. "After all, what's a few weeks when you have eternity?" he laughed half-heartedly.

Lilly looked at her uncle and then back to her mother. She saw the resolute stare they both held. She couldn't believe Adam was taking her mom's side. He was always her champion whenever Elaine would overreact. Furious, she spun around and stormed off to her room, slamming the door. *Tread had let her go. If he had wanted to do something he would have already done it. Right?*

Then another thought crossed her mind. *What if he really did leave?* This might have been the only chance she had to find out more about her kind. *Why had she opened her mouth and informed them that Tread could walk around in the daytime like she could?* She felt so stupid and angry. *And why had Lex come and told her mom about what had happened anyway?*

She heard Adam offer to drive Lex home. Her mom stayed up cleaning the kitchen and then headed off to bed.

Lilly tossed and turned throughout the night, grieving for the loss of information she didn't know if she could have even gotten. She was angry at Tread and Lex for causing her to get grounded. She was also mad at herself for actually wanting to have taken him up on his offer, to learn more about their kind, despite the fact he had tried to eat her BFF. *What kind of person did that make her?* she wondered as she finally drifted off to sleep.

The weekend dragged by incredibly slowly. Lilly talked to Lex some, but Lex was too scared to leave the house, and Elaine wouldn't let Lilly leave, even to walk Lex over. So Lilly spent most of the weekend stuck in her room, avoiding her mom, with whom she was still upset. She read some and listened to music, and tried not to think about Tread, although that had been harder than she thought.

By the time Monday morning rolled around, she was jumping at the chance to get out of the house and go to school. She hadn't been this excited about school since she was five and had convinced her mom to let her go.

She pulled her hair back into a ponytail because they were going to be playing dodgeball today at school. Then she picked up her bag and practically ran through the door when Lex honked.

"Remember, straight home after school." Elaine called from her office.

Lilly rolled her eyes. She had always loved that her mom worked from home. She managed payroll for several companies in Harbor Cove, and could do it all from her computer. Today though, she wished her mom had a job away from home, so that she didn't have to rush right home after school.

Lilly jumped in the car. "Hurry up, let's go before she changes her mind about school. I've been going out of my mind stuck inside all weekend. There is no way I am going to last for a few months."

Lilly scanned the area as Lex sped off down the street.

"What are you staring at?" Lex asked.

"I guess nothing," Lilly shrugged and turned back around. "I just got the feeling that someone was watching me."

Lex laughed. "Probably your mom. You'd think she'd give you a little breathing room, seeing as how you are virtually indestructible."

"Not as much as I thought," Lilly said.

Lex turned, confused. "What do you mean?"

"Just that the vampire from the other night, he gripped my wrist really hard. It actually hurt. I never really understood pain." Lilly contemplated. "As much as my mom has tried to describe the word, I really didn't understand it until I experienced it for myself."

"So he hurt you, and then just let you go?" Lex asked. "Why didn't he kill you?"

33

"Who knows? I guess he doesn't kill his own kind. He was kind of a psycho. He referred to you and the rest of humanity as 'happy meals,' his own personal buffet." Lilly shook her head in disgust.

Lex crouched down in the driver's seat and pushed her sunglasses up. "Do you think he'll come back for me?" She asked, an edge of terror in her voice. "I keep having nightmares," she whispered.

"No, I think we will be fine if we stay away from the beach area. I mean we've never had any trouble before, right?" Lilly insisted.

Lex shuddered. "I hope you're right." Then she glanced over at Lilly. "Oh, and I'm sorry about getting you grounded. I was just so worried." She paused as she veered left into the school parking lot. "I couldn't go to my house and tell my parents. And I thought maybe Adam or Elaine could do something. I'm not sure what. Now that I'm not so shaken up and it's daytime, I really see how pointless it was to tell them anything. So, sorry again, not that it helps any."

"Thanks. I was pretty mad this weekend. But I knew you didn't do it out of spite or anything. I was more mad at the situation really, than at you. I didn't handle it very well."

Lex pulled into a parking space. There were so many to choose from. Lilly often wondered why they didn't bulldoze the parking lot and use the space for something worthwhile. With so few people driving nowadays, there was a lot of wasted space. Lex grabbed her backpack out of the backseat. "I'll see you at lunch. I've got to go straight to Mrs. McMillan's for math tutoring."

Lilly slung her bag over her shoulder. "OK. See you then."

Lex ran ahead into the building. Lilly glanced up at the sky. It was dark and overcast, so she pulled the top onto the convertible, in case it rained, then turned and walked into the school. She found her locker and began to pull her books out for the next few classes. She jumped back as she shut her locker closed. Tread had been standing at the end of the hallway. She only saw him for a second, but she knew it was him. *Was he following her? Had he come back for Lex?*

Hurrying as fast as possible, while still appearing human, she ran to the end of the hallway, peering to her right and left, but there was no sign of him. Just as she'd assumed.

School passed by slowly. Around every corner Lilly expected to see him again. But he didn't make another appearance.

After school, she walked to the car. Lex was already there waiting.

She turned and gestured to the passenger seat. "There was no note. But I'm assuming those are for you. Probably some lame attempt by Kyle to get you to go out with him."

Lilly shook her head.

"I mean how original, lilies for Lilly." Lex continued, "Seems like just the kind of thing he'd try. But I am surprised that there's not a note. You'd think he'd want to make sure he got credit. Unless of course the note blew away."

She glanced around Lex and saw a beautiful bouquet of lilies, tied with a red satin bow.

Lilly walked around and got in the car. She picked up the flowers and examined them. There was no card, as Lex had mentioned. But they were stunning. Each one seemed perfect, none were limp, or had brown beginning to form on the edges. They smelled wonderful. As if each one had been individually inspected.

She glanced around the rooftops and alleyways as Lex drove her home but saw no one, although she couldn't shake the feeling that she was being watched.

The next couple of days passed by uneventfully. Lilly no longer felt like someone was following her. She felt slightly disappointed when she thought Tread was gone for good, which in turn annoyed her. *Why should she care if she saw him again?* He had been a jerk. He tried to eat her friend. He had been rude and demanding with her.

He was a vampire. The first one she had ever met. And she had blown it. She had always had so many questions and so few answers. Since she was little, Lilly had dreamed about meeting another one. A vampire who was living among humans, secretly hiding their real identity from the world. Just like she was.

She walked into school lost in thought, went to her locker and opened it without really paying attention. She grabbed her pre-cal book and shut the locker.

Tread was standing mere inches away from her.

"What are you doing here?" Lilly hissed as she glanced around the hallway frantically, afraid somehow someone would sense what he was or that Lex would spot them together.

He casually pulled the book out of her hand and thumbed through the pages. "I just wanted to see what the fascination was about."

Lilly pulled him into an empty classroom. "What are you talking about? The fascination with what?"

She gave him a once-over. He was incredibly handsome. Standing there in his black fitted tee shirt and jeans, she almost forgot why she had to hate him.

He gestured around the room. "You. This. Why you choose to live with these happy meals? Why you spend your days in this higher learning place, as they call it, when you could read all these books in less than an hour? Do you have any idea the things we could be doing right now? Why stay?"

He stepped forward and gazed into her eyes. His eyes were a stunning blue. She could look into them and forget anything. He brushed a strand of hair out of her face, and his hand felt soft and warm.

She shook her head and stepped back, remembering Lex.

He turned and surveyed the classroom, as if he hadn't noticed her rejection. "So tell me...why?"

"I don't have to tell you anything," Lilly hissed. "You need to leave before Lex sees you."

He turned, confused. "Lex?...Oh, right, that's what you called my dinner after you let it run away." Tread nodded his head as he put the name to the face. "She's all the way across the school. Can't you hear her? What do you see in her anyway? She can't even grasp the concept of geometry!"

"Ha Ha. It's Pre Cal actually." Then she stopped abruptly. "Have you been following me this past week?" Lilly asked.

"Yes," he said unabashed. "Well part of it anyway. There are other things that occupy my time. At least you have *some* instincts," he said, seeming shocked. "I wasn't sure you had noticed at all. You are…surprising. And not much surprises me anymore."

Lilly checked the clock. Students would begin coming in soon. "Just go away. Leave me alone."

Tread shook his head. "No. Not yet."

Students began coming into the classroom and taking their seats.

Tread walked out of the classroom. "See you around." He winked wickedly.

Lilly followed him out of the classroom, but by the time she stepped into the hallway, he was nowhere to be seen.

Relief flooded through her. She didn't know what she would have done if Lex had seen him. And her mom…well she'd probably never have let Lilly out of the house again.

For the rest of the school day Lilly felt on edge, nervous about Tread showing up again, but also anxious in an excited way she kept trying to deny.

When the day finally ended, Lilly headed to meet Lex at her car. As she was about to push open the back door to the school she heard Lex call out behind her.

Lilly turned and walked to meet her as she came running down the hallway.

"Hey, I got another detention." Lex rolled her eyes. "I think it's a game to them. Let's see how many times Lex can get detention. You wanna wait for me?"

She shook her head. Lex got a detention at least once a week. Usually because she had no clue how to hold her tongue. "No, I'll walk. My mom is on edge, and I don't want to give her any excuse to extend this whole house arrest thing." Lilly put her other arm through the backpack strap so that it set squarely on the center of her back.

"K. Call ya later," Lex said.

"By the way. What did you do this time?"

"Coach Mack was just being a chauvinistic pig." Lex explained. "He was subbing in Home Ec. He had all the guys sit down and he told the girls they were to cook something and feed their men. That soon enough that would be their role in life so they'd better start practicing. So I whipped up some spaghetti, cause you know that's the only thing that I know how to make, and I dumped it in his lap." Lex smirked. "Oh and I may have called him a sexist pig, or something along those lines."

Lilly laughed loudly. "I would have loved to see that. Coach is always making inappropriate remarks."

"Well I better get going or I'll be in detention all week." Lex laughed as she hurried down the hallway.

Lilly stepped outside. It was a gorgeous, sunny day. She dreaded going home and being stuck inside all week. It reminded her of when she was little and her mother had been terrified to ever let her leave the house.

She walked slowly, taking her time, in no rush to begin her incarceration. She turned down Riverside Drive and stopped. This time, she could smell him. A mixture of sunshine and...smoke.

"I know you're there. Stop following me," Lilly growled.

Tread stepped out from behind a giant black spruce tree.

"You're getting better." He smiled. "Maybe you have some actual instincts after all. I wasn't sure, what with the bizarre way you were raised."

Lilly brushed past him, but he just spun around joining her stride for stride.

"So, Lilly, can I ask you something?"

Lilly glared at him. "Didn't you ask me enough questions the other day?" When he didn't respond, she added hopefully, "Will you leave me alone if I answer?"

"Maybe." He shrugged. "By the way, can you drop this whole hostile vibe? It's getting old."

"You tried to kill my best friend," Lilly reminded him, slightly annoyed.

"Seriously, how can you hold that against me? In my wildest dreams I never imagined a vampire living like a human, and actually fraternizing with them." He paused. "And I apologized. You did get my flowers right? I mean you had to know they were from me and not from that buffoon Kyle like your friend suggested."

"Fine. " She let out a long exaggerated sigh. "What? What is your question? I mean I have to answer it anyway or you'll just force me to stay."

Tread stopped dead in his tacks.

Lilly stopped and examined at him. He looked so serious.

"What?" Lilly asked, concerned.

"I will never do that again." His faced seemed to soften as he talked. "My behavior that night was deplorable. I should have never treated you that way. I truly am sorry. I'm not sure what came over me. You are just so...different." His face hardened again. "Regardless, there is no excuse. You intrigue me. But if you say the word, I am gone."

Lilly paused. She should tell him to leave and then run the other direction. He seemed like two different people; so concerned and sincere and then two seconds later so flippant, carefree and cocky at the same time. "I should send you away." She shook her head slightly. "Fine, just ask your question."

He raised an eyebrow and smiled widely.

And the cockiness returns, Lilly thought to herself.

He ran a hand through his beautiful dark hair. "So I don't get you. You act all indignant when I feed, and about how I view our food in general. But how do you distinguish between which humans you can eat and which ones are off limits like your friend, Lex? Do you just eat the dirt bags, the thieves and murderers? Or are the poor ones okay to eat, but not the rich ones? Or maybe it's okay to eat the ugly ones but not the pretty ones? I don't get it. Explain to me how you choose which ones are okay to kill and which ones aren't."

Lilly halted abruptly. "That's horrible. I'm not like that at all. I don't have some sick twisted parameters by which I go by. I don't distinguish. I don't feed on *any* humans. It's wrong." She looked directly at him and then enunciated slowly, "E V E R Y T I M E."

Tread eyed her with a confused expression. "So how do you survive if you don't feed on blood?"

"I feed on blood. I just don't murder people to get it." Lilly walked past him.

Tread stood there for a moment and then jogged to catch back up with her.

"So your friends let you feed off them? Or… oh wait, disgusting. Tell me you don't drink animal blood. Not that I've heard of a vampire who could survive on it." Tread said, seeming like he might hurl. "I tried it one time, on a dare, and it was disgusting, and I felt sick afterwards. Or at least what I imagine it feels like to be sick."

"I've already answered one question and you're still here. "

Tread stepped in front of her, blocking her path. "Fine. Answer this one and then I'll leave if you promise to meet me tomorrow. "

Lilly thought for a moment. Why should she meet him? Besides the fact that he was the most gorgeous guy she'd ever seen. And could answer all the questions she'd ever had. She didn't want him following her home. That was for sure. She couldn't put her mom or Adam at risk. Even if she didn't think he'd do anything to them.

"Fine," she answered, exasperated. "Blood bags," she said and then strolled past him.

"Gross," she heard Tread say quietly.

"Four p.m. at Hidden Hills Park," he called after her.

Lilly didn't answer. She just kept walking, relieved that he didn't follow.

Chapter 4
Rendezvous

The next day passed by slowly. Lilly tried to think of some excuse to get her mom to let her out of the house, but failed. Lex drove her home and Lilly reluctantly headed inside. She sulked around in her room the rest of the afternoon, hoping that her mother might feel sorry for her and change her mind.

 As four p.m. came and went, she imagined her meeting with Tread. She wondered if he was genuinely disappointed, or if he had even really expected her to show up in the first place. She pictured him cracking up at the idea of her being grounded by a human.

Lex called later that evening, apologizing again for getting her in trouble. She tried to cheer Lilly up by telling her all the things they'd do when she had her freedom back. Lilly knew Lex was just trying to help, but it just seemed to make her feel worse for all she was missing out on. Eventually she found an excuse to get off the phone and went back to sulking.

Later that night, Lilly came out of her room just long enough to down a blood bag and then told her mom she was going to bed.

She hadn't slept much the night before and was tired, plus she figured sleep was her one escape from boredom.

She hadn't been asleep long when she heard a tapping sound. Sitting up quickly, she listened again, thinking at first it was her mother still up, but as Lilly listened she could hear her mom's quiet breathing from the room down the hall.

"Open the window," hissed a voice.

Lilly walked over to the window and peeked through the blinds. She was stunned to see Tread there.

"Come on, let's go," he whispered.

Lilly opened the window. "What are you doing here?"

"Well, you didn't show, so I knew something must be wrong. I mean no one stands me up," he said, as cocky as ever.

"Yeah well, I kind of let it slip that you're a Sunwalker so I've been banned from everything but school and home for a few months," Lilly sighed. "Longer if you keep feeding on people in Harbor Cove," she added.

"Well as the saying goes, while the mommy's asleep, the mice will play." He gestured outside.

Lilly looked around the room one last time, then climbed effortlessly out the window. She glanced at Tread. He was more than handsome. His face was chiseled and hard when he wasn't watching her, but somehow seemed to lighten when he talked to her. Maybe she was just imagining it. He wore a black button-up long sleeve shirt, a pair of faded blue jeans, and some black leather dress shoes. She wasn't sure she should be going anywhere with him, but from what she had seen of him so far it didn't seem likely he'd just leave. It would be better to just go. Lilly couldn't even imagine how her mother would react if she found another vampire here. If her mom knew she was going out with him, she'd probably lock her up and throw away the key.

"Ok, fine," Lilly replied. "But we have to be back by like four. I don't want to take any chances of my mom waking up." Then she paused and turned to face him, narrowing her eyes. "How did you know where I lived anyway?"

Tread smiled slyly. "No problem, that gives us hours. And I just followed your scent. Pretty hard to hide from a vampire. That or I could have just followed you home from school the other day. Take your pick on which option sounds less creepy."

Lilly followed Tread through deserted streets and alleys as they headed downtown. She was enjoying really getting to run. Having never been able to let go like this with her mom around, she felt she as if her body was awakening to its true potential. She pushed herself faster, running toe to toe with him.

When they got to downtown, Tread scaled a large apartment complex, swinging from the fire escapes till he reached the roof. It was an exhilarating feeling, flying through the air. Once at the top, they leaped across several buildings until finally landing on one of the taller ones, where Tread stopped.

He gazed out across the city. "I love being up here. You can see the whole city and beyond. Someday we'll have a city like this full of vampires out in the open."

Lilly rolled her eyes. He was crazy.

"It will happen, you'll see. We are better than the humans. Someday we will run the world. We'll replace the cattle farms with human farms and take our rightful place at the top of the food chain. It's rumored some cities like that already exist."

Lilly looked abashed. "How can you say that? Humans are just like us. We came from humans. Not all vampires, but you had human parents."

Tread laughed darkly. "Human parents who tried to kill me." He picked up a small rock and tossed it. "I have no love for their species." He gazed deep into Lilly's eyes. "Don't you get it? We are their children, but because we are different, they murder us. You can get all high and mighty about the humans I kill for food to survive. But they just murder us for no reason at all, when we're infants, defenseless. Don't you see they're the monsters?"

Lilly sat there silently, unsure of how to respond. She did believe him partially. It was wrong what the humans were doing, especially to the baby vampires that were born into this world.

43

"Maybe," Lilly finally relented. "But, not all humans are like that. My mother went through a lot to keep me. How do you know there aren't more humans willing to do the same thing? Why can't we live together in peace instead of one species trying to take control of everything?"

Tread stood up and looked across the city, his hands in his pockets. "That will never work. We have to feed. We don't have another option. I've tried animal blood, remember? It just comes right back up."

Lilly shook her head dismissively. "Feeding is one thing, murdering is another. I feed off of human blood bags. You could too. It's another option. Maybe there are more. If scientists spent as much time trying to make a synthetic blood as they do weapons to kill us with, maybe there would be more options."

"That's a lot of maybes," Tread said, shaking his head. "And cold blood...I wouldn't call that an option...ugh." Tread made a gagging sound.

Lilly rolled her eyes. "For someone who's supposedly a lot older than me, you sure don't act like it." Lilly looked at him questioningly. "How old are you anyway?"

"Maybe some other time. You're so...human. It might freak you out. Humans get so weird when age comes up." He sat down on the ledge, letting his feet drape down over the side. "So I thought you had a million questions?"

Lilly sat down on the ledge next to him, only to be made aware of how silly she must appear to him. She hadn't realized till that moment, that while he looked like a model, she had rolled out of bed in her pajamas. She had been too excited when he knocked on her window that she hadn't even put on shoes. So here she was sitting next to him in her bare feet, a t-shirt, and flannel pants that her mom had given her last Valentine's Day that said "I heart you."

If she could have blushed, she would have. She decided there was nothing to do but try to distract him with her questions. After peppering him with endless questions for two hours, the realization hit that she knew nothing about her kind. Tread made them sound so incredible. She had never known that she'd stop aging when she turned nineteen, that her heart would cease beating for some unknown reason, and then she wouldn't get any older. She knew eventually her heart would stop beating, but she hadn't known when. That was about the only pertinent information that she ever found online. Now having an exact time made it slightly more frightening. In under two years her heart would stop beating. Would it hurt? Would she miss it?

She had never imagined there were secret communities of vampires all over the country, and probably even throughout the world. It seemed so weird to think that once she was nineteen her body wouldn't sleep anymore either. Probably the most shocking piece of information she learned was that there were vampires hidden in plain sight working in some of the larger hospitals, hoping to be there to rescue a baby vampire if they came across one.

It amazed her that they cared so much. Spending hours upon hours waiting for a possibility that was so rare, it probably wouldn't happen. But still, they waited just in case.

Lilly stood up on the ledge of the building and peered down. She imagined they were at least twenty stories up.

"So could I jump off this and be fine?"

Tread laughed easily. "You really don't know anything about being a vampire?" He shook his head in awe and stood up beside her. "Today was your first time to really run, wasn't it?" He smiled at her knowingly.

She glimpsed down, slightly embarrassed, and nodded.

"Yes, you could jump, but I wouldn't recommend it."

"Why, would it hurt?" Lilly asked.

"No, not really, but jumping from this high might make an impression in the cement below. We normally try to minimalize the evidence of our being in a town."

"But what about Lex?" Lilly asked, confused. "People would notice when she went missing. You didn't try and hide that."

Tread smiled. "You're right, but that's different. Lex was in a place people believe to be dangerous. If something happened when she was there, it's to be expected. But if our presence in the cities, where people believe that they are safe, became obvious, then things would change. Tighter security, more Vampire Assassination Squad units patrolling, who knows what added measures would be taken."

"So what can hurt me?" Lilly asked. She almost added "besides you," but remembering the hurt expression on his face when she had brought it up before made her think twice.

"Not much, and a lot, depending on how you view it."

Lilly looked at him, dumbfounded.

He grinned widely and then explained. "I have no doubt that if you jump from high enough, it could hurt you. We heal very quickly but I imagine if I jumped out of a plane, it might hurt. I've never been crazy enough to try it. And vampires of course could hurt you."

Lilly saw him glance quickly to her wrists and for a moment, she thought she saw a flash of sadness, or maybe regret.

"Dragon steel, but fortunately there isn't too much of that, and electricity if the voltage is high enough. But getting stabbed, getting hit by a car, shot with bullets, all the things humans worry about, just kinda bounce off of us."

"What's dragon steel?"

"That is the ninety-third naturally occurring element on the Periodic table."

"No, there are only ninety-two that occur naturally," Lilly corrected.

Tread rolled his eyes. "That's what they want you to think. A few years after vampires became reality instead of myth, a scientist discovered two chunks of rock in the bottom of a dormant volcano. They were red. The shiniest, deepest red he'd ever seen. He took it back to his lab and ran tests on it.

"Now all this is pieced together from various sources. So some of this may not be entirely accurate. But the bottom line is he discovered a new element. They kept it quiet. It was stronger than anything else anyone had ever come across. It was named dragon steel." He swatted a mosquito that kept flying near his face, and then continued. "Supposedly because the scientist always hoped he'd find evidence that dragons really existed and the red color made him think of dragon fire."

"So why don't they arm the VAS with weapons made out of dragon steel?" she wondered.

"Well they do, sort of. To my knowledge they have never found anymore than the original two pieces. Apparently the only thing strong enough to cut it is more of itself. So since they don't have that much of it they have to use it sparingly. Somehow, they discovered that this new element would penetrate our skin. After some vampire experimentations, scientists discovered that if a tranquilizer went into our bodies, it would affect us the same way it does humans."

Lilly listened intently. She had never heard any of this before. She was amazed the government could keep so much a secret.

"So they ended up making needle points out of the dragon steel. I'm not really sure how they pulled that off, but it uses very little steel and so as far as I know all the VAS are armed with these special tranquilizers." He stared away, off into the distance. "I've seen them used before and believe me, they work. Once a vampire is unconscious, it's easy to murder them. Just toss the body in a nice hot fire," he said sadly.

Lilly put her hand on his shoulder and rubbed it gently. "I'm sorry."

"Well that's life," Tread said, matter of fact. "That's why we tend to stay hidden and live together."

"So there are really hidden communities near here?" Lilly asked in wonder.

"I could take you to one sometime," Tread said nonchalantly.

"Really?" Lilly asked.

"Sure," he shrugged. "You could meet other vampires. Like my best friend, Koyt.

Lilly arched her eyebrows in disbelief. "You have friends?" She said it a little harsher than she meant to.

"Ouch." He grabbed at his chest where his heart was, mimicking someone who had just been shot.

"I didn't mean—" She stopped. "Sorry." She frowned. "I just meant you seem like such a loner it surprised me. How long have you been friends?" she asked, trying to make up for her rudeness.

"Koyt and me. Years. He's great, you'd really like him. Loyal to a fault." He looked away. "He's actually a little upset with me. I have been neglecting our friendship. I haven't spent much time with him these last couple of weeks." He turned back and smiled at her.

Lilly looked away, embarrassed at the attention. "So...how far away is the closest one?" she asked.

"Closer than you might think." Tread winked at her.

"Could we go and come back in the same night?" she asked eagerly.

"Sure," he shrugged, "but why would you want to? Don't you want to be around your own kind? We could leave tonight and I could show you our world." He reached and gently gripped her shoulders and turned her towards him, then added, "The vampire world. A place you'd fit in and could be yourself. No one would ground you or tell you what you could or couldn't do."

Lilly was amazed at how much he seemed to care. She was nothing to him, yet he was willing to answer endless questions and show her things she never thought were possible. A part of her wanted to just run off with him. No more hiding who she was or what she could do. But then she thought of her mom, Lex, and Adam. She could never just leave them.

"I'm sorry. I just can't leave them. This is all so new to me. I know I get mad at them sometimes, but they love me. My mom does what she does because she cares for me."

"How long do you expect to keep this little charade up?" Tread motioned to her pajamas. "Acting human." He shook his head. "You know when you stop aging and everyone around you gets older," Tread raised his eyebrows in a knowing expression, "people are going to notice. They're slow but most aren't that dumb."

Lilly was speechless. She hadn't thought of that. Until tonight, she hadn't even realized she would stop aging in less than two years. It was so soon. She hadn't had time to think about it.

"I guess we'll just move," Lilly said lamely.

"And it's just that easy to get in and out of the cities for you? And what happens when one of those humans slips up and says something?"

"They'd never say anything," Lilly insisted.

"What about your friend Lex? You plan on seeing her throughout her life?"

"Of course. She's my best friend."

"And what if she introduces you as her old high school friend? Or reminisces about high school with you in front of her husband or kids? That's the kind of things humans do. She may not remember every second to be on guard especially if she is around people she is comfortable with or once she gets older and her memory starts to fade or goes completely."

Lilly started to say something but Tread cut her off.

"Or do you ever think about the risk you are putting on these humans that you care about? The danger they are in by associating with you...just one slip up...anyone finds out, you might be able to get away but they would be executed."

Lilly sat there in silence, her head swirling with thoughts. She had never really thought of the consequences for her family and friends. She had never really thought it was possible to get caught, but then again she hadn't thought about things like Tread had. *Should she leave when she turned twenty-one or twenty-two? How would they explain her not aging? And even if they moved wouldn't that just put more risk on Adam, forging more papers and finding ways to cheat on the blood tests?* Maybe she should visit the vampire world. *Would it be safer for her family if she just left?*

"You're right. OK," Lilly said defensively. "I haven't thought about any of this. I don't know any of this stuff. Of course I don't want to put my family at risk. I don't—"

"I'm sorry," Tread interrupted. "I shouldn't have just hammered on you like that. Obviously this is all new to you. I should give you time to process without throwing my opinions out there. I'm sorry."

Lilly took a deep breath and didn't say anything for a moment. "I'd still like to visit, if you'd take me," she said, resting her hand on Tread's arm.

Tread looked disappointed, or maybe she was just hoping he was. He turned away from her, his eyes wandering across the skyline. "Yeah sure. Sometime I'll take you."

He seemed distant the rest of the night, his face blank, expressionless. As four o'clock approached, he walked her back home, not that she needed an escort.

Lilly paused by her window. She pushed the window up and then hesitated. Tread stood a few feet away kicking at the ground with his shoe.

"Thanks for tonight, Tread. And for putting up with all my incessant questions. It was nice to not have to hide for one night, to be myself. You gave me a lot to think about."

Tread locked eyes with Lilly. She wondered what he was thinking. He looked so amazing standing in the moonlight. He was so intense it made her nervous.

"Tread," Lilly hesitated. "I want to trust you."

He caressed her face softly. "You can," he insisted.

"Can you just promise me one thing?"

He stood there waiting.

"Can you just not feed on anybody I know?" she asked timidly. "Or even anyone in the city would be better, since you don't actually know everybody I know."

He stared at her for a long minute.

"Alright," he finally said. "I won't feed in the city." He laughed lightly. "I never thought I'd hear that from another vampire."

He stepped forward and leaned close to her, speaking so softly that no human would have been able to pick it up. "I like that you can be yourself with me. That's how it's supposed to be." He reached down and pushed a lock of hair out of her face, then ran his finger down her jaw line and paused on her chin. He stood silent for a long moment and then took a step back. "See you tomorrow night," he added as he winked at her and disappeared.

Lilly leapt quietly through her window and climbed into bed. She was exhausted. She could hear the sounds of her mother's even breathing from down the hall. She closed her eyes, wishing that it could already be tomorrow night.

Her mother came in at seven-thirty and woke her. "Lilly, are you alright?" her mother called from the doorway.

Lilly yawned. "I'm fine."

"It's seven-thirty." Her mom sounded alarmed. "You've never slept past dawn a day in your life. And Lex will be here in about five minutes to pick you up for school."

Lilly rolled back over in her bed. She was still tired from the previous night's excursion, or technically speaking, the early morning excursion. She wondered if she'd miss being tired and feeling fatigued.

Lilly didn't tire easily. Last night her limits had been tested and pushed past their breaking points. Tread told her she'd never tire once she stopped sleeping. That she only tired now because her body still needed sleep, as it was still changing and growing. "Yeah, I'll get up in a minute. It will only take me two seconds to get ready. I've been put on house arrest. I'm bored. So I decided to try sleeping in. That's what normal teenagers do, right?"

Elaine walked to the bed and placed her hand on Lilly's forehead. "You're sure you feel OK?" she asked.

Lilly scrunched up her face and then rolled over. "Are you really trying to see if I have a fever? I'm fine. I've never been sick a day in my life."

Elaine eyed her suspiciously. "Alright, if you say so," she responded as she left the room and closed the door behind her.

Lilly rolled over and peered up at the ceiling. She tried to imagine what it would be like in a vampire community. *Did everyone just magically get along because they were all vampires? Were there hundreds of vampires, thousands? Or just a few?*

Lilly kicked her sheets off and walked over to her closet. She searched through her clothes, trying to decide what she would wear

51

tonight. Definitely something a little more flattering than pajamas. She moved through her closet like a whirlwind, trying on various clothing, then throwing them back on the hangers and moving on to the next outfit. She finally decided on a dark denim pair of jeans. They were faded slightly and had three silver flowers embroidered on the back of each pocket with a scattering of sequins surrounding them. She pulled out a white fitted t-shirt and a black pullover hoodie that had Harbor Cove written across the front of it in hot pink.

She wanted to look good, but casual. She didn't want him to think she was trying too hard. It would be better than the pajamas, and she always seemed to turn quite a few heads at school when she wore this ensemble, although those had always been unsolicited.

Lilly threw the clothes on the bed and stripped down, tossing her clothes back on a shelf in the closet, to put away later. She wrapped herself up in her pink robe and went into the bathroom.

She turned the water on hot. She wasn't sure why, but she always felt cleaner when the bathroom got all steamy, even though she could have showered just as comfortably in freezing cold water. Maybe it was the movies; people always liked steamy showers. Maybe it helped her feel more human.

Lilly sped through her shower. She had plenty of time before Tread would drop by. Like maybe only fourteen hours if she was lucky. She hoped school would be a distraction.

She had thought of even more questions to ask him. *How many vampires existed in the world? Did he know them all? What did he do all day long? Did he ever get bored? Wish he could fall asleep?*

She thought back on the previous night. She still couldn't believe she had spent several hours with another vampire. He seemed so...human, at times. Other times he appeared anything but.

She wondered what Lex would think. She still seemed shaken up by the whole experience when they had talked on the phone. She had never seen a vulnerable side to Lex before. She was always so cool and confident at school. Lilly had always been the shy, quiet one. The one whom people assumed would need protecting...little did they know.

The school day seemed like the longest one ever. Lilly couldn't stop thinking of Tread. She just wanted to go home so she wouldn't miss him, even though it was still several hours before he'd show up.

He came every night for the next week, taking her on new adventures. Each day was incredible. She had never imagined her body was capable of so much. She could run for hours before she got tired. She could leap across rooftops and jump several stories high in a single leap. She was so much stronger than she could have dreamed. It was exhilarating to test her limits. Her body seemed to yearn for it.

Each night made it a little more difficult to come back home. Her body resented having to restrain such freedom at home and at school. The hours seemed to get longer and longer between visits as her anticipation heightened.

Lilly sprawled out on her bed with her iPod. It was a little beat up and had a crack on the screen, but she was loved it. It had been a Christmas present from her mom, a rare find.

She cranked the music up, finding one of her favorite songs. She was attempting to distract herself until Tread came over. The day had dragged on forever, and she couldn't quit thinking of him. She was ready to run. And she felt certain she was getting closer to beating him. He was definitely faster, but she thought if she could time her jumps right and run on the inside, that she might be able to beat him. They had been having nightly races. Tread knew all the back alleys and empty buildings they could run through and had set up quite a course.

Lilly wasn't quite sure when he would show up. They hadn't specified a time. *Would he come over the same time he had last night?* She hoped. Every night was different, but last night had been the earliest. If that were the case, she had another agonizing hour of waiting.

Her mom had drifted off to sleep about a half hour ago. Lilly reached a few feet in front of her and pulled her desk, which had been against the wall, closer to the bed. She flipped up her laptop and began responding to an e-mail Lex had sent earlier, when she felt a jolt on her bed. Tread lay there on his back beside her. He was half hanging off the end of the bed, flipping nonchalantly through a book.

"The ending sucks in this one," he said, tossing her copy of *Tuck Everlasting* on the floor. "They don't end up together."

"Oh my gosh!" Lilly whispered harshly. "Can vampires have heart attacks?"

Tread sat up casually on the bed. He smelled amazing, like sunshine and a slight hint of smoke. And he didn't look half bad in his jeans and white v-neck t-shirt that clung to his body. He gestured behind her.

"Might be a good idea to lock that window." He smiled mischievously. Then he reached across and tugged on one of her earphones, his hand brushing softly against her cheek. "And why don't you try lowering the music," he chided. "I could have thrown a brick through that window and I doubt you would have heard it. Ouch!" he said as he brought the ear bud up to his ear. "You do know we have superb hearing. How can you even stand that? Do you have those things plugged into an amplifier I'm not seeing?"

Lilly couldn't tell if he was teasing or if he was serious. Maybe a little of both. Even Lex thought she liked listening to her music too loud.

"Don't you ever crank the volume up on a song you really like?" Lilly asked.

"Sure, but I like to hear. Of course I'm sure you have proven that vampires can't go deaf, with that volume." He shoved her playfully on the arm. "Seriously, I could hear that song two blocks away, and don't even get me started on your taste in music." Tread rolled his eyes.

Lilly shoved him back, not so playfully, nearly knocking him off the bed. "So did you just come here to insult me and try to scare me to death?"

Tread jumped up. "That's not the only reason." He winked. "Have you ever been in the ocean?"

"Of course not. It's dangerous," she began. "Well dangerous for the humans I associate with. What's the big deal about the ocean, anyway? It's just a bunch of water, right?"

Tread grabbed her by her hands and pulled her up. "It's a lot more than just a bunch of water. Come on, I want to show you." He walked to the window and nodded outside. "Oh and make sure you keep up, we're going in a different direction tonight," he said. And with that, he was gone.

Lilly jumped through the window and raced after him. He was fast. She started to rethink the possibility of beating him anytime soon. Lilly followed him though the streets of Harbor Cove. Her muscles seemed to yearn for her to push them harder and faster. No matter how much she pushed herself she never came close to catching up to him. She wondered if she'd get faster with age, or if he'd just always be faster.

In movies when people were fast, everything rushed by in a blur. But that wasn't the case now. Even as Lilly ran down the street, taking corners at incredible speeds, she could see everything in detail. She could still see the tiny cracks in the cement. The dandelion that Tread had crushed, not bothering to step around. She deftly avoided the gum that someone had spit in the middle of the road. She loved having heightened reflexes. She felt bad for Lex. She was missing out.

Tread slowed down once they hit sand.

Lilly picked up a handful and let it slip through her fingers. "I've always wanted to build sandcastles or be buried in the sand just like they do in the movies."

"You would totally have loved to see the three-story castle I made then."

Tread kicked off his shoes and tossed his t-shirt on the sand.

Lilly watched in awe. The moonlight shimmered off his chiseled torso. He was a work of art. She turned away, embarrassed, hoping he hadn't noticed her staring.

"Now I'm officially jealous. What else have you done that's against the rules?" Lilly asked.

Tread laughed. "What rules?" he scoffed. "There are no rules for us, Lilly. That is what you need to understand."

He grabbed her by the hand and pulled her toward the water.

"Come on." He smiled.

Lilly slid her shoes off as he pulled her toward the ocean. The sand felt so different. Her feet sunk into it as they ran.

They stopped at the edge of the water. The waves rushed over her feet, getting the edges of her jeans wet.

"Are you ready?" Tread asked, squeezing her hand lightly.

She turned and glared at him skeptically. "Ready for what?"

"To go in the ocean," Tread said as if it were obvious.

"No way!" Lilly said shaking her head and stepping back. "I've seen Jaws I, II, III and IV."

"I really think you forget that you are a vampire sometimes." He pulled Lilly closer. "Sharks can't hurt you. You are stronger than anything in the sea. Not to mention," he added, "in nature, most living things can sense predators. Sharks tend to keep their distance."

Lilly took a deep breath, trying to summon her courage. She knew she didn't need to breathe but she had never had the opportunity to test the theory.

As a kid, when she and Lex would go to the pool, she had always wanted to try staying under for as long as possible. But with so many other kids around watching, she dared not try.

"OK. Let's go." She took a few tentative steps and then Tread yanked her under.

It was amazing.

Once Tread had pulled her down far enough, she could see little fish swimming below. She saw shells scattered along the ocean floor. There was also quite a bit of trash, which Lilly didn't appreciate. The floor was littered with cans and old tires. They even swam past a couple of broken fishing boats. Humans were so messy.

It felt odd not breathing. She had always just inhaled and exhaled because she had to blend in. It had become second nature.

Tread released her hand and motioned for her to follow. She followed him out deeper and deeper into the ocean.

Once they had gone deeper, there was less trash, and more amazing sea life to admire. Lilly was amazed at the different colors of fish and the variety she saw. Tread made her keep her distance from the fish.

This infuriated her. He had brought her out here to see all this and now she wasn't supposed to get close. She ignored him and swam closer. As she approached the sea life, it scattered.

She soon realized why he had kept her back. The fish sensed she was a predator.

Tread took her to different areas of the ocean. She saw dolphins and a huge gray whale. She was amazed by the color and the variety the ocean had to offer.

He led her to a small underwater cave. He surfaced inside the cavern and pulled himself up onto a wide, rocky ledge.

Lilly followed him. As she climbed out, water poured off of her clothing. Her shirt clung to her and she tried to wring out her jeans a little.

"Next time you could warn me and I could wear a swimsuit," Lilly teased.

"It's not like you get cold," Tread said seriously.

Lilly sat down next to him and let her feet dangle in the water. "No, but my mom might be suspicious of a soaking wet pair of jeans and t-shirt in the laundry."

Tread shook his head. "I still can't get used to that. You letting a human tell you what to do. You know you can take her, right?" he teased.

Lilly rolled her eyes. "It's not about strength. It's about respect. She's my mom." Lilly glanced around the cave. "So, let me guess, you take all the girls here."

"No. I've never brought anyone here before," he said seriously.

She had meant it as a joke. She sat there quietly, unsure of what to say next.

"I come here to think," Tread continued. "I need one place that's just mine. That I can go to and know no one will find me, no one will bother me."

"It's really peaceful here," Lilly commented.

He looked so vulnerable sitting there, seeming younger than he ever had before. A lock of his hair fell down in front of his eye. Lilly reached and started to brush it out of his face.

Tread reached up and intertwined his fingers in hers. He pulled her hand down and reached up to her face with his other hand. He brushed his finger gently down the side of her face and leaned forward.

Lilly's stomach tensed; she had never kissed anyone before.

"Beep beep."

Tread dropped his hand and looked down at his watch. "Time to get you home."

Lilly wished that stupid watch of his was broken. So much for her first kiss. Then again, maybe she had just imagined it. Maybe he had no intention of kissing her. If he had, wouldn't he still have kissed her after the watch had beeped?

Tread stood up and stretched. "Ready?" he asked.

Before she could answer, he dove back into the water. Lilly followed him back to the shore. She was glad he knew where the beach was. She had been too overwhelmed with all the beauty that lay hidden below the water to have paid too much attention to directions.

Tread didn't talk on the way home as they ran back. Lilly felt the mood had changed somehow. There was no longer any excitement. Maybe he had grown bored with her. He probably had some hot vampire girlfriend wherever he was from. She had never thought to ask.

They slowed down as they got to Lilly's street. They walked slowly. It was so quiet. The only sound Lilly could hear was the blades of grass bending as they walked across the lawn towards the back of the house.

"Let's go tomorrow night," he said a little too loudly.

Confused and startled at the sudden conversation, Lilly asked, "Where?"

"To my home, of course. The vampire settlement I was telling you about," Tread replied as if it was so obvious.

He opened the window and followed Lilly into her room.

"Tomorrow?" Lilly asked again, not sure if she had really heard him correctly.

The door to Lilly's bedroom slammed open, and Adam jumped into the room, gun raised toward the window. He had on his favorite black baseball cap that covered half his face.

Lilly was surprised, to say the least. What was her uncle, Adam, doing here at this hour? *Wasn't he supposed to be out of town for another week?* Before she could say anything Tread had thrown the gun across the room and flung Adam crashing into the headboard on the bed. The headboard cracked in half, and Adam lay there unmoving. His cap had flown off and he was face down on the bed.

Lilly rushed to Adam's side. "What did you do?" she cried. As she began to check for vitals, she was relieved to hear him moan.

Tread was flabbergasted. "He had a gun pointed at you!" he began, and then spun around as a woman came to the doorway armed with two guns.

Before Tread could react, Lilly yelled, "Stop! That's my mom!"

Tread staggered back but kept his eyes on the guns.

"Mom put down the guns!" Lilly demanded. "Since when do we have guns? Where did you even get those?"

Her mom looked at Lilly like she was insane. "No way. What are you doing in my daughter's room?" she demanded, and before Tread could answer, she continued. "Where did you take my daughter and what did you do to Adam?"

Lilly rushed in front of Tread before her mother could do anything. Tread kept glancing back at Adam.

"Mom, calm down," Lilly said soothingly. "I just went for a swim," then glimpsing at Adam, she said "and Adam was an accident."

Elaine tried to maneuver around Lilly to have a clear shot. "Swimming is dangerous," Elaine stated. "Is this the vampire who tried to kill Lex?" her mom asked, taken aback.

Lilly motioned to the window with her head. "Tread, just leave," she ordered.

"He's not going anywhere!" Elaine yelled irately, but before she could finish, he was gone.

Adam moaned loudly. "What happened?" he mumbled.

Elaine walked to the window, peered around and then slammed the window shut and locked it. As if locking the window would stop Tread if he wanted to get in.

"Bring him to the couch," Elaine spat angrily. "Then *we* are going to have a talk."

Lilly carried Adam to the couch and propped him up. He was coherent but in pain. Lilly made him an ice pack and looked at him apologetically. She turned to her mother who pointed to the couch.

Lilly took a seat, wishing she could be anywhere but here.

Her mother took a deep breath. " I don't even know where to start." She shook her head in exasperation. "What could you possibly be thinking? Sneaking out, lying, hiding things from me." She looked sternly at her daughter. "Lilly what were you thinking? He's a murderer. He tried to kill Lex. Lilly, he's a monster. He's the reason people hate vampires."

"He's like me!" Lilly shouted as she jumped to her feet. "You don't understand. He can teach me and show me things you can't."

Elaine pointed at Adam. "He almost killed Adam! What could you possibly want to learn from him?" she asked, raising her voice.

Lilly sighed and lowered her voice. "He was protecting me. He didn't know who Adam was, he just saw a gun pointed towards us," Lilly tried to explain.

"He's evil, Lilly. You are not to see him again, understand?" her mom said. She turned to leave the room, thinking the conversation was over.

"That's really not up to you," Lilly challenged.

Elaine turned around, "Excuse me?" she asked as she turned around, her mouth gaping open in surprise.

Lilly stood eye to eye with her mother. She was not backing down on this, no matter how mad her mom got. "You can't stop me mom. I'm sorry. I know you don't like him. But you don't know him."

"Does Lex know about this? How does she feel about you hanging out with the vampire that tried to *KILL HER*?" her mom shot back, enunciating the last two words, knowing full well that even if Lilly had confided in Lex there was no way she'd be okay with this.

Lilly started to respond but her mother continued.

"And I can make you stay away from him, Lilly. I don't want to but I will if it's the only way to keep you safe."

Lilly couldn't move. She just looked at her mother, dumbfounded. What could she possible mean?

"Try it!" Lilly yelled. "I can get to the door in a matter of seconds. Don't push me on this. I don't want to fight with you but—"

Lilly watched as her mom made a gesture behind her; as she turned to see what her mom was motioning about, she felt a sharp prick.

She reached behind her and pulled a dart from her left shoulder. "Dragon steel," she mumbled as she fell to the ground.

Adam stood up hesitantly, clearly in pain, holding the ice pack to his head. "I can't believe you made me do that to her," he said disgustedly.

Elaine walked over to her daughter, turned her over and caressed her face. "She gave us no choice." Elaine answered, her back towards him. "I have to keep her safe, even if she hates me for it."

She turned and regarded Adam, "I can't believe how far you've come. Not too long ago, you would have thought the best thing for me to do would be to lock her up."

Adam limped over, cringing with each awkward step. "That was when my hatred blinded me. I love Lilly, and I don't even think of her as a vampire most of the time now." He glanced down at the gun he held in his hands. "Where did you even get this? Dragon steel is so rare, most people don't even know about it."

"It was Dylan's. Each Sergeant was issued two guns. He always left one at home. He never thought he'd have to use it. He always assured me only the members of the VAS were in real danger. Regular military wasn't really targeted." Elaine stood up and put her hand gently on Adam's arm. "That vampire had her fooled. He must have done something to her. If this can just buy us some time to get her to listen to us, maybe she can see reason."

"Are you trying to convince me or yourself?" Adam huffed. "Somebody locks me up and the last thing I'm going to want to do is listen to them."

Elaine ripped her hand off of Adam angrily. "What would you have me do Adam, let her leave with that monster?"

Adam shook his head. "I don't know, Elaine. I just don't think this is the right answer." He put his finger up to her lips to hush her. "I don't know. But you are her mother so I will help you do what you think is right."

"OK then, I know you are in pain, but do you think you can help me get her down the stairs?"

"Yeah," Adam replied. "I've been through worse."

Adam and Elaine carried Lilly down the hallway to Elaine's room. She set Lilly's feet down, and pulled a book halfway off the bookshelf in her room, and a wall began to move. A dark staircase appeared. Elaine reached in and switched on the light, then knelt down and hoisted her daughter's feet back into the air.

"I never thought I'd have to use this on her. I didn't know much about vampires. Dylan thought they built this cell for some scientist to do experiments on vampires, and then somehow we got the house by mistake. I never even told Lilly about it. I never dreamed I'd be using it on her. The walls are steel, five feet thick, with electricity running through them when I flip the switch."

"Let's just get her in the room before she wakes up," Adam said. "Who knows how long this will knock her out for? You really did think this through," Adam said as he laid her in the tiny prison. He looked around, "You realize there is nothing in here, no bed, no pillow, no blanket. Is this how you intend to leave her?" Adam asked in dismay.

"I don't want to do this, but it's not like I had much time to plan this. We thought the possibility was small when I found her missing from her bed in the middle of the night. I didn't think I'd actually have to follow through. But now there's no time. I don't know how long the sedative will keep her knocked out for. I will have to keep her weak too, just in case. Spread out her feedings and give her smaller amounts. I think the steel is thick enough to contain her, but I really don't have a clue."

Adam stared at Elaine in disbelief. "Do you think that's really necessary?" he wondered.

"I don't know," Elaine sobbed. "I can't take any chances. I won't let that monster take her away."

Elaine stifled a sob, then turned to Adam. "Come on out. We don't know when Lilly will wake up."

Adam slowly stepped out of the cell. He was walking a little better, as if the movement had helped loosen him up.

Elaine shut the heavy steel door with a loud clang that seemed to echo for a long time. She locked the three huge latches and flipped a switch on the wall. Electricity crackled and hummed in the room.

"Let's go back up," Elaine motioned. "I'm gonna need to bring a few things down here if I am going to be spending a lot of time in this room."

Adam followed but glanced back one last time at the cell, a look of despair on his face.

Chapter 5
Treachery

Lilly woke up in a foggy haze. *Was she sick? Did vampires get sick?* She'd have to ask Tread...Tread. He had left...she had an argument with her mom...her mom had threatened her.

Lilly sat up and looked around. *Where was she? It looked like she was in some type of metal box. What was that crackling sound?* Lilly stood up and walked over to the door. She reached out to push on the handle and pain went shooting up her arm.

Had something happened to Adam and her Mom? Someone must had mysteriously kidnapped them. What was going on?

"Mom?" Lilly called frantically. "Uncle Adam? Are you OK?"

"I'm here, Lilly. Adam and I are fine," her mom said from the other side of the wall.

Why did her mom sound so calm? "What happened?" Lilly asked.

"I tried to warn you, Lilly. I hope you'll understand in time. This is for your safety," her mom explained in a pacifying tone.

Lilly looked around her surroundings, remembering their conversation from last night, remembering the prick. Adam had shot her! With...a tranquilizer of some type. Her mom had dragon steel. But how and why? *Her mom had locked her in a cell, basically just electrocuted her, and Adam had helped*. She panicked as the realization of the situation began to dawn on her.

"What are you doing?" Lilly called. "Let me out! How can you do this to your daughter? Do you have any idea how much it hurt to touch the door?" she yelled.

"Good. I'm sorry it hurt you, but I'm glad it will keep you safe," her mom answered.

"Let me out now!" Lilly screamed.

"Lilly try to calm down. This is for your own good. But I won't stay down here if you're just going to scream. And you can scream all you want because the basement is soundproofed. Not like you'd want anyone else to find you."

"Why are you doing this? So I won't spend time with Tread? Are you insane? Normal people talk things through, they don't lock their daughters in cells that electrocute them!"

"Lilly, he's dangerous. And as you pointed out last night, you don't have to do what I say. Maybe in a few weeks he will go away. I don't understand what he did to you. I mean, he tried to murder your friend. There is no way that you'd really want to hang out with him. He must have done some vampire brainwashing on you that we don't know about."

Lilly laughed slightly hysterically. "Mom, listen to yourself. You sound crazy. Let me out, and I promise we will sit and talk about this. I won't run off. I promise."

"I'm sorry but this is for your own good."

Lilly threw herself against the door as hard as she could. "Ahhhhh!" she screamed. The pain was excruciating and she had left barely a dent in the steel.

"Please, Mom," Lilly wept. "Let me out of here."
She heard a door close and footsteps echoing. She could tell by the heartbeat and breathing it was her mother. She had locked her in a cell and left. Lilly couldn't believe it. The betrayal stung worse than any pain the cell could cause. And Adam had helped. *How could the two people she loved most in the world do this to her?*

There was no clock or window in the cell, only blank steel walls, with a slit that looked wide enough for a tray to be slid through. The time seemed to drag on forever. She had no idea what time it was. Only when dawn came did her body seem to know the time, no matter where she was. Her mom had left her down there for three days, without so much as a word.

Lilly was starting to get hungry. *What was her mom thinking?* Elaine knew her feeding schedule as well as Lilly did. It should have been two days ago.

Lilly had tried calling to her mom...yelling...screaming, but to no avail. She had tried throwing herself against the door a few more times, but the pain didn't seem worth the small amount of damage she had done, and now that she was getting weaker she wasn't healing as quickly as before.

Where was Lex? Had she even noticed Lilly was nowhere to be seen? Had Tread come looking for her, like he had the first time she hadn't shown? And where was Adam? How could two people go insane at the same time? Had they just thrown her down here so they could forget about her?

Questions and accusations filled Lilly's mind. She kept imagining at any moment Tread or Lex would come and rescue her. But as the hours and days began to pass that hope quickly diminished.

After five more agonizing days, Adam came down. She could tell by the heavier set of his walk. He sounded like he was limping. His breathing was slightly labored. Tread must have really done a number on him when he threw him against her headboard.

Lilly lifted her head up from the floor of the cell. "Adam," she called out weakly.

She saw the metal slot in the door open as a blood bag dropped in. Lilly rushed to it, not sure where the strength had come from. She was famished. She lifted the bag and her face dropped.

"This isn't enough!" she cried as she looked at the bag that was only a quarter full.

She heard Adam linger.

Lilly stepped as close to the door as she dared. "Please Uncle Adam. Let me out. Please," she cried. "I love you Uncle Adam. Why are you doing this to me?"

She heard Adam sob and then hurry back up the stairwell.

At least it seemed Adam wasn't totally onboard with this. Lilly sank her teeth into the blood bag and drained it far too quickly. It was almost worse than not eating. The small amount of blood just seemed to fan the flame. The hunger seemed to roar to life inside of her.

By the end of two weeks, Lilly was desperate to escape. Though she was very weak, she began throwing herself at the cell door with all her strength, knowing soon she wouldn't even be able to stand. The pain was agonizing. She could smell her flesh burning as it hit the wall. After three excruciating throws, she paused to rest, waiting till her body healed. First it took several minutes, then what seemed like hours, and then she'd go again. She continued the pattern until one day, when she waited and waited and waited, but nothing happened. She laid there in pain but the healing never came. She realized, letting out a bitter laugh, that her body was too weak to heal.

Lilly was hungry, dirty, smelly, and in pain. Her mom had brought her clean clothes and tried to pass a shallow tin of water and a bar of soap to her, but she had knocked it away, refusing anything from her, hoping eventually her mother would feel some sort of sympathy and release her.

Her mom had attempted a conversation a few times, about what Tread had done to her, how he had changed her, confused her, taken advantage of her. Each time Lilly refused to engage. The only thing she ever accepted was the quarter blood bag she was given every week.

Laying on the floor feeling so exhausted, her mind so foggy, she realized she had lost track of the amount of days it had been since being incarcerated. Her last count had been forty-five days, but that could have been yesterday or a week ago for all she knew. She had heard Adam and her mom arguing on the stairwell. Adam had been angry, demanding her mom stop, and then Lilly thought he left.

What a coward. He had always been that way. Why hadn't he let her out? Forced her mother to unlock the cell? He always walked away when things got too tough. Lilly was beginning to realize how justified Tread's feelings towards humans really were. If her own mother could do something like this, there was no hope for the vampire community to ever live side-by-side with the humans.

She drifted in and out of consciousness until awakened by a loud ripping sound. Lilly tried to open her eyes but she just couldn't muster enough force.

"Lilly!" she heard the alarm in his voice.

"Tread." She couldn't be sure if she had said it aloud or not. She was so tired.

He swept her up; she could feel his strong arms carrying her gingerly. "Where do they keep the blood?" Tread yelled, out of patience.

"Up here in the kitchen," another voice said.

A girl. Lex? Lilly must be dreaming. There was no way Lex and Tread would be together. Lilly heard some noises and then felt something pushed towards her lips.

"Drink," came the quiet command.

Lilly tried but she couldn't seem to make her lips obey.

"What have they done to you?" Tread said angrily.

"I can't believe her mom did this," the girl, the imaginary Lex, said.

"Don't call her that," Tread spat. "She doesn't deserve that title. She's lucky to be alive. I would have ripped her to shreds if it weren't for Lilly."

She felt a hand tilt her head back and open her mouth. Then something glorious happened. What a wonderful dream. Blood began to slowly trickle down her throat. The dream was so lifelike she could actually taste it; it was like manna from heaven.

After a few moments, Lilly forced her eyes open. Tread and Lex were there, standing in her kitchen. Lex was opening bags of blood and passing them to Tread as he slowly fed her.

"Straw," Lilly managed after another moment. She felt a little stronger. The hunger in her seemed unquenchable. But slurping seemed faster than the rate at which Tread was pouring.

Lex poured the next bag in a glass and handed it to Tread. He picked up a straw from the counter and dropped it in the glass. Then he helped prop Lilly up and held the cup up to her lips.

Lilly sucked continuously until the cup was dry.

"More," Tread demanded.

Lex ravaged through the fridge. "This is the last one," she said handing it to Tread.

He poured it in the cup, as Lilly drank greedily.

"She seems to be looking better," Lex noted.

"Yes, but it will still take some time till she's back to normal." Tread turned back to Lilly, concern painted all across his face. "Do you think you can walk?" he asked.

"I thought I was dreaming." Lilly clung desperately to Tread's arm. "You're real though?" she asked frantically. "I'm not gonna wake up and find myself in that cell again?" she sobbed.

Tread pulled her into a hug, pressing her body against his. "I promise you will never see that cell again."

"I'm so sorry Lilly. I had no idea," Lex said, holding back the tears.

"Let's get you out of here," Tread said as he helped Lilly to the door.

Lilly looked around, panicked. "Where is she?"

Tread put his arm around her and squeezed her lightly. "I tied her up. I used thick ropes but I left a knife in there so she could eventually cut herself free."

Lilly looked back toward the hallway in a daze.

"I wasn't sure what you'd want me to do, but I can go end this now if you want," Tread said, gesturing to the hallway.

Lilly didn't answer at first. "No," she finally answered. "Just get me out of here."

Tread turned back to Lex. "Can you get home OK?"

"Yeah I'll be fine." Lex stepped around them and opened the door. It was dark outside. "When will I see you again?" she asked.

Lilly felt her feet slip from underneath her.

Tread scooped her up in his arms.

"Thanks," Lilly said. "Sorry, I thought I could manage on my own."

Tread caressed her face with his hand softly. "You have nothing to apologize for." He turned back to Lex. "I'm not sure. You have my number, we'll keep in touch."

"OK. See you soon." Lex said, slipping out into the night.

Lilly closed her eyes. She was still so tired. The blood had helped; her pain was lessening. Leaning her head against Tread's chest, as he rushed her to wherever they were going, she listened for a second, half expecting to hear a heartbeat. She always felt out of place when she'd lie on her mother, or Adam, and their heart would be pumping, knowing one day hers would cease beating. Now thanks to Tread she knew it would stop in barely over a year when she had her nineteenth birthday. It was just another thing that had made her feel different; not exactly an outsider but not exactly fitting in either. She had always envisioned herself like a square peg trying to fit into a round hole. But Tread was the same. He was like her, or how she'd soon be at any rate.

She had dreamt he might save her, but then reality didn't quite live up to the dream. In her dream when Tread was saving her, he wasn't making plans to meet up with Lex and call her on the phone. No, it wasn't the perfect dream come true. But she was out of the cell and never going back, and for now that was enough.

*   *   *   *   *   *   *   *   *   *

Lilly woke up ravenous. She looked around the room, remembering what had happened. It wasn't a dream. This was clearly not the cell. The room she was in was small but cozy. She sat up on a twin bed that was against the back wall. Next to the bed was a little white fridge with a note taped to it.

Lilly-
Drink up. Be back soon.
Tread

Disappointed that he wasn't there when she woke, she stared at the note again. He had surprisingly beautiful handwriting. Most guys she knew wrote in chicken scratch that one could hardly make sense of.

She opened the fridge and pulled out a blood bag. She downed three before finally feeling content, then sat back down on the bed and looked around the room. It was neat. Everything had a place. There was a shelf that ran along the top of the room, filled with books: *Les Miserables*, *The Brothers Karamazov*, *The Complete Works of William Shakespeare*, *A Tale of Two Cities*, and *Forget Me Not* were just a few.

A door stood directly across the room from the bed. To the side of the door against the wall was a large flat screen TV with huge speakers, and a bunch of black electronic-looking boxes underneath the table that held the television. On another wall was a glass mirror sliding door that Lilly assumed led to a closet. She walked over to the mirror, cringing as she prepared to take her first glance.

She knew her appearance must look horrific after not bathing in such a long time. As she opened her eyes, she was at first pleasantly surprised at the clean girl in the mirror, dressed in a clean t-shirt and sweatpants that were a little big. But immediately after, she was completely horrified. *How did she get this way? She had no memory of it.*

Lilly went back and sat on the bed. After awhile she walked to the door and slowly opened it. She stepped into a long, deserted hallway and tentatively started walking down the southern side. A door was open a few doors down and Lilly could hear voices. She peered her head inside and saw two vampires sitting on a couch with a person between them. They each had an arm and were feeding. Lilly was so horrified she let out a scream.

A tall, blond male looked up. "We can share?" He held the arm out to her.

Lilly turned and rushed back into her room, slamming the door behind her. *Where had Tread taken her?*

A few minutes later, there was a timid knock on the door.

"Go away," Lilly called as she pressed herself up against the wall, unsure of what had come calling.

The door opened slowly. A red-headed freckled boy stuck his head in.

"I'm Red. A friend of Tread's. I heard a scream and thought I'd come check on you." He stepped in cautiously.

Lilly looked at the boy. He was young, maybe only thirteen or fourteen.

"So were you really raised by humans?" Red asked unabashed.

Lilly nodded.

"Wow," Red said, amazed. "That must have been really weird." Red sat down on the floor in front of the bed and crossed his legs. "So is this really the first vampire community you've been to?"

Lilly nodded again, not sure of what to make of this freckled kid who seemed to know a lot about her.

"Well, I've only been a vampire for a few years now, but I don't know what I'd do if my mom locked me in a cell for three months."

"Three months?" Lilly asked, horrified. Had it really been that long?

The door swung open and Tread stepped in. He looked at Lilly, then back to Red. "Out," he growled at Red.

Red jumped up and vanished.

Tread set a big, brown bag he was carrying down on the ground. He was wearing khakis and a red polo shirt. Lilly was reminded again of how he always looked so handsome, and how he always seemed to catch her in pajamas.

Tread knelt down in front of her. "How are you feeling?" he asked as he gently stroked her knee. He glanced over to the trash-can with the blood bags sticking out. "Glad you found something to eat." He smiled reassuringly.

Lilly rubbed her hands against her face and sighed. "I'm not sure. I mean physically, I am feeling better." She shook her head trying to find the right words. "Where are we? What kind of place have you brought me to…Was I really trapped in there for three months? And what took you so long to come and get me?" Lilly cried as the questions seemed to pour out of her mouth. There was so much she wanted to know. So much she didn't understand.

Tread sat down on the bed next to her. He tenderly turned her face towards him. "Oh, Lilly. I have been looking for you every day for the past ninety-seven days. I looked around your house, but your scent was all over it. I had no idea you were still there. I was so stupid." He stood up and punched the wall angrily, making a hole into the next room. He paced in front of the bed, pausing every so often to look at Lilly as he talked.

"I know how you feel about your human family. So at first I just watched from a distance trying to listen for some clue as to where you were. When I didn't see you for two weeks, I went looking for Lex. She came over to your house, trying to track you down, and I followed her and cornered her a few streets down. She was a little freaked out at first, to say the least." Tread chuckled softly at the memory. "I apologized, promised I wasn't going to hurt her, and explained what had happened after I had made the mistake of trying to make a meal out of her. She actually took it all fairly well. She told me that your mom said she'd sent you to some relative you guys had, a distant cousin or something. That he had just moved into some of the government housing and you went to help settle him in. That you had said you needed time to think and that you'd be back in a few weeks." Tread looked at her remorsefully. "I still tried to look for you, but Lex had no idea which housing unit it was and there are so many. Your mom wouldn't tell her. She said you wanted space from everything. But I still looked. I wanted to make sure you were OK. But I couldn't pick up your scent anywhere. If I hadn't seen how protective you were of them, I would have scared them and threatened them into telling me."

Tread sat back down on the bed next to Lilly. His leg was pressed up against hers and he took her hand in his. "We started to get really worried after a few weeks had gone by and you didn't come back. I kept telling Lex something was wrong but she insisted Elaine wouldn't lie to her. That there had been no secrets since she had found out you were a vampire. Your mom kept making flimsy excuses. Finally, Lex had the idea to approach Adam. Who is he to you anyway?" Tread asked.

"He's my uncle, my dad's brother," Lilly explained.

A strange looked flashed on Tread's face before he continued.

"So Lex went and talked to him. She said Adam was acting really weird and begged me not to do anything to him. She went over every couple of days for a week until he finally broke down and told her what had happened. He wouldn't tell her where you were. She called your mom and demanded answers, but your mom just swore this was for your own good. That was day ninety-six. Lex called me the next day and filled me in. I stormed into Adam's house and scared the living daylights out of him till he finally told me where you were. I had to wait till the evening because he was working all day hosting a conference for a group of doctors and was never alone." A look of hatred passed over Tread's face. "He's lucky I didn't kill him. I'll be honest, I was so close."

"I felt like I was dying," Lilly said. "Is that even possible? Is that what would have eventually happened if I didn't feed enough?"

"No, you weren't dying," Tread reassured her. "It's kind of like how humans go into a coma. They are still alive on the inside but pretty much dead to the world." Tread reached up and brushed back Lilly's hair. "The longer you go without food, the harder it is and the longer it takes to come back. I can only imagine how painful it was for you."

Lilly leaned her head against Tread's shoulder. He moved his arm around her shoulder. "Seeing you like that...that was the hardest thing I've ever had to go through." Tread's face hardened. "If I had seen you before I tied that woman up, I would never have left her alive. What did she do to you?" He ran his fingers over what now looked like several-day-old bruises. Tread shook his head trying to erase the memory.

"Those were actually self-inflicted," Lilly said.

Tread looked at her, confused.

74

"You must have shut the electricity off before you ripped the door off. I tried to ram my way through the door. I got a little desperate, a little hysterical. It was agonizing, but I didn't know what else to do," Lilly explained.

"I'm so sorry," Tread whispered.

"It's not your fault. I'd still be there if it weren't for you," Lilly said. He looked so vulnerable, so broken, that she started to lean forward, but a ringing sound stopped her.

Tread stood up and reached into his pocket. He pulled out his phone. "Hey....no, yeah everything's fine...probably not for a couple of days at least...OK Friday for sure...yeah, thanks Lex."

Lilly turned away. Lex was calling him. It had slipped her mind with all that had occurred in the past twenty-four hours that Tread had made plans with Lex. That they talked on the phone.

Tread slid the phone back in his back pocket. He nodded at Lilly. "Lex says hey and she's glad you are finally awake."

Finally awake. "How long was I asleep for?" Lilly asked.

"Three days," Tread said. "It's normal when you are severely injured or um...dehydrated," he tried to suppress a smile, "for lack of a better word. Your body needs time to heal."

He offered his hand to her, "So are you ready to go exploring?" he asked.

Lilly thought back to her first experience in the hallway and cringed.

"Yeah, I'm sorry about that. Koyt told me what happened. I had wanted to try and prepare you a little," Tread explained, as if sensing Lilly's discomfort.

"So one of those was Koyt, your friend. That's not the way I imagined meeting him."

"Well, technically you didn't meet him." He half smiled. "Not officially anyway."

Lilly rolled her eyes, then shook her head. "It's just all so different. It's shocking. I mean they killed that girl...didn't they?" Lilly asked.

"Yes. But you have to try to understand. These aren't bad vampires. They would do anything for me." Tread scratched his head and sighed. "Try thinking of it this way. Do you hate an eagle because it catches mice to eat? No. It's nature. It's the natural food chain. Nature made vampires who need blood to survive. Human blood. You don't call all humans who eat beef murderers, right?"

Lilly shook her head. "I understand the logic. It just still seems wrong to me, especially when there are other options...like blood bags." Lilly gestured to the bin.

"I know. But not all humans are vegetarians, and that's an option, right?" Tread sighed. "Besides it's not that easy to get blood bags. Especially enough to feed a group this size," Tread tried to explain. "After spending some time with Lex, I get that not all humans are evil. But some are." Tread looked off into the distance, obviously thinking of some memory. "And it might take vampires a long time to even be open to the possibility. So just try not to hate the vampire because he or she is following the natural progression, okay?" Tread asked earnestly.

Lilly rolled her eyes. "I'll try."

"Oh and just so you know, you've already made some headway with at least one vampire." He smiled.

"Who?" Lilly asked.

Tread pointed to the fridge. "That's been here a lot longer than you have. I'm getting used to it. I still crave the warm blood straight from the vein, but I think in time that will fade."

"Why are you doing this? I thought humans were just Happy Meals to you."

Tread laughed. "I'm trying to evolve. I started for you. And I've been keeping it up in part for Lex. People like her don't deserve to be someone's meal."

Tread spun around and picked up the big brown bag he had brought in. "Oh, I almost forgot. I got you some clothes. I thought you might want something more than my old t-shirt and Vanessa's sweatpants. Vanessa, a friend of mind, cleaned you up. In case you were wondering." Tread winked. "You were still pretty bloodied up after you healed and she was sure you'd rather wake up clean."

"You'll have to tell her thank you for me."

"You can do it in about five minutes. I'll wait in the hallway. Hopefully something will fit. Vanessa helped me guess at sizes," Tread added before he vanished into the hallway, closing the door without a sound.

Chapter 6
Awakening

Lilly fished through the bag and pulled out a cute pair of jeans and a navy blue fitted polo and threw them on. She found a pair of black and gray tennis shoes at the bottom of the bag and also discovered a small zipped bag, filled with deodorant and other essentials. She finished getting ready and then pulled on her shoes, guessing those were about a half a size too big, but everything else seemed to fit great. She slipped her shoes off, slid on an extra pair of socks, and stepped into the hallway.

Tread smiled warmly as she came out of the room. He offered her his arm and started to walk down the hallway. Lilly hesitated. "Can we go the other way first?" Lilly asked.

She was sure she wasn't ready for a repeat of earlier. She wondered what they did with the bodies when they finished. *Did they leave the bodies somewhere so at least the families could have closure?* She wasn't sure she could live in a community with such a wanton disregard for human life.

Tread nodded. "Sure, we can go see Vanessa first."

As they turned back the other direction, she noticed some of the doors were open. She was hesitant to look in any of them, afraid of a repeat from her earlier excursion or something worse, but her curiosity eventually won out. Relief flooded through her as she looked in and the rooms were empty. She noticed none of the rooms had any windows.

"Why aren't there any windows?"

"Two reasons. First reason, most of the vampires down here are not Sunwalkers. Well actually none of them are, excluding us of course. And the second reason is we built all of this underground. We're really about thirty feet under the city," Tread explained. "It took us awhile to build all of this, but then again we don't have many options. If the humans discover us they send in the VAS," Tread said bitterly. "So the rooms are pretty small, but so far we've kept this place a secret."

Tread stopped in front of the last door that stood directly at the end of the hallway. All the other doors were painted a beige-y white color like the hallway except this one. This door was bright yellow with different colored flowers painted all over it. He raised his hand and gave three quick knocks.

A woman came to the door who looked to be in her late forties or early fifties. She had wrinkles around her mouth and crow's feet around her eyes. She was short and a little heavy-set, redheaded, and didn't appear to have any gray hair. She would have looked younger had it not been for the wrinkles. Her smile lit up when she saw Tread and she pulled him in for a warm embrace, kissing him on the cheek in the process.

"Lilly, meet Vanessa." Tread waved toward the red-haired woman.

"But you're old!" Lilly blurted out.

"Well she's not the shy one you portrayed to me." Vanessa laughed.

Lilly looked down at the ground, embarrassed. "I'm sorry, it's just that Tread told me we stop aging at nineteen, and it's not that you look *old*," Lilly tried to explain, "just older than nineteen. I'm sorry," she apologized again.

"Don't worry. You really are like a newborn vampire," Vanessa said curiously. "You won't age past nineteen. But I didn't become a vampire until I was forty-nine. Of all the benefits I have received from vampirism, turning back the clock just never happened." She winked and smiled at Lilly; it reminded her of Tread.

"Tread," a voice called from down the hallway.

"Will you ladies excuse me for a moment?" Tread gave a little bow and then disappeared.

Vanessa stepped away from the door and invited Lilly inside. Her room was at least twice as big as Tread's. Probably even three times the size. There was a queen bed in one corner, with a floral comforter and brightly colored pillows. Twice as many books as Tread had were stacked on high bookshelves, almost to the point of overflowing. There were two other doors; Lilly thought one might be a closet and the other a bathroom. Vanessa motioned to a small sitting area with a couple of chairs and a loveseat, and a round coffee table in-between.

Lilly sat down in one of the chairs, as Vanessa made herself comfortable on the loveseat.

Lilly tried to think of something to say and finally came up with, "So how long have you known Tread?"

Vanessa smiled. "Tread is one of the few I have known for almost his whole existence."

Why didn't vampires ever use numbers when they talked? Vanessa had known him his whole life and Lilly still couldn't figure out how old he was.

"So do you know how he got the name Tread? I've never heard it before."

Vanessa laughed. "I should. I gave it to him." She sat quietly for a moment, caught up in a memory. "There's a lot you don't know about our species and our history, from what Tread has told me, but I think even you know what happens when a baby is born a vampire?" she asked.

Lilly nodded sadly. It was one of the few things she hated about the humans. "Well, testing for the vampire gene in 'would-be' parents only became standard practice about thirty years ago. Before that, people didn't know a lot about vampires. They knew something existed but we were more commonly grouped with

80

demons. Many parents would just leave their baby in a field somewhere or in a dump to die, or even throw them in the ocean or in a fire. They were scared because their children were different. Plus, because vampires hadn't been identified, some people tried to hide the fact that they had a baby. They were ashamed of what they had given birth to. Some thought it was a curse, that God was punishing them for some misdeed.

"And you were right," Vanessa chuckled, "I am old. I just celebrated my three hundred and ninety-seventh birthday last week. And in all my time I've only come across about a half a dozen Sunwalkers and that's including you." She smiled. "I found Tread in a garbage dump. He had been tossed away like a piece of trash. I was about a mile away, hunting, when I heard a cry. Normally when a baby cries, you'll hear a parent pick it up after a few minutes and try to soothe it, but it never happened. I went closer to investigate. I found him crying and hungry, half-buried in a pile of old tire tread." Vanessa shook her head. "I've never been very creative, as you can tell by the name."

"How heartbreaking. How could someone do that to their child?" Lilly asked quietly, more to herself than to Vanessa. She thought back to what her mom had done and what she had risked to keep her, and found it hard to believe that every mother wouldn't do the same thing for their child.

"So how old is Tread anyway?" Lilly asked.

Vanessa shook her head. "That's something you'd have to ask him. Although most of our kind get along, there are a few who'd like to take control of our species...make themselves a king. Age is power to a vampire. Most vampires won't attack another vampire unless they know they are older and therefore stronger. Most don't normally throw out ages like I do. I'm well known, so it's no big surprise. Sunwalkers are always the most powerful. So if a Sunwalker wanted to rule our species there wouldn't be too many others to pick off. So Tread, along with the others, keeps his age a secret; it helps keep a target off their backs. I only know his age because I found him. I don't think he's ever told another soul."

Lilly thought about what Vanessa had said. *Would vampires try to kill her if they found out about her?*

She stood up to leave. "Thank you for your help," she said, motioning to her new clothes. "I think I'm going to go look for Tread."

Vanessa stood and put a hand on Lilly's shoulder. "It's probably better if you wait. You don't know where to start looking."

"That's OK, Tread was going to show me around. I'll just explore a little on my own."

"Sorry hon, but you actually do have to wait for Tread," she explained, placing a hand on her shoulder. "There are areas you're not allowed in."

Lilly looked stunned. "There are places in the vampire city that not all vampires can go to?"

Vanessa returned to her loveseat. "Not normally, no. It's just *you* that can't go there."

Lilly looked at her confused. "I don't understand. I'm a vampire. Why am I the only one to be kept in the dark?"

Vanessa leaned forward. "We have certain codes as vampires. Unwritten laws. Knowledge that we keep secret from humans and other...things. The thing is, hon, we are not sure where your loyalties lie. You're a unique case. A vampire raised by humans, living among them, loving them. If the wrong human found out certain things, it could put our whole city at risk. We don't know if we can trust you yet. I'm sorry if it seems harsh or unfair," she apologized.

Lilly stared at her, dumbfounded. So now she wasn't accepted with the vampires or with the humans. *Would she ever fit in anywhere?* "Am I allowed to go back to my room?" Lilly asked indignantly.

Vanessa stood. "Sure. I'll escort you back."

Lilly was about to tell her she knew how to get back, but then realized she probably didn't have a choice.

As they walked back though the hallway they found Tread. He was arguing heatedly with another vampire, though their voices were too quiet for even her to understand.

He stopped as he heard them approach and came to meet them.

A silent expression passed between Vanessa and Tread.

Lilly pushed past him angrily and went back into her room.

Tread came in right behind her and closed the door.

"What's wrong? Did something happen?" Tread asked as he strode over to where Lilly stood, her back to him.

She turned around, her face a mixture of sadness and disappointment. "You told me things would be different here. That it would be great, that I'd be one of you," she murmured. "But it's just the same," she said more loudly, "secrets and a lack of acceptance." She turned so her back was facing him, arms crossed.

Tread turned her around and pulled her closer, cradling her face in his hand. "It's not like that here. I just haven't had time to explain everything to you, and there is a *lot* I need to tell you."

There seemed to be a sense of pleading in his voice.

His phone beeped. He growled under his breath and pulled it out of his jacket. He texted something and slid it back in his pocket. "Sorry, that was Lex," he explained.

Lilly stepped away from him. She turned, facing the mirrored doors. "And you're so confusing, one minute you're being so nice to me and I think..." she trailed off. "And then the next, you're talking on the phone to Lex. Making plans to meet up with Lex. Texting Lex. And I feel so stupid for feeling anything."

Tread laughed quietly.

Lilly spun, infuriated by his laughter.

"You are so funny, Lilly." Tread shook his head exaggeratedly. "Lex...as if."

He gripped Lilly gently around the waist and pulled her close. He leaned down and pressed his lips against hers, softly at first and then more desperately. She reached up pulling him closer, not able to get enough of him. He smelled like a fresh, new day. He had been right, she could smell the sunlight on him, only she hadn't known the difference until being around other vampires like Red and Vanessa. She had never had anything to compare his smell to.

She felt so safe and accepted in his arms and happier than she'd ever felt before.

Nothing in her life had been as sweet, or made her feel so alive as she did right now, kissing him. Her heart seemed to swell. She knew it was fast, but holding him, kissing him, now, she knew she loved him.

She had been hesitant to admit it to herself before, but now with Tread and Lex beginning to accept one another, any guilt she had felt that made her doubt her true feelings had been pushed aside.

Tread started laughing and pulled away. "I still can't believe you thought I had a thing for Lex. She has been calling and texting to check up on you. She has been asking when she'll get to see *you* next." Tread leaned down and gave Lilly another long, lingering kiss followed by a short kiss. He caressed her face gently with his strong hands. "I told her maybe a couple of days; I wanted to give you some time to adjust." He stared at her for a moment. "You are so beautiful, Lilly." He ran his hand through her hair, playing with the ends.

"Now let me see...I think before you flung yourself on me," Tread winked, "you had just finished a long rant of questions...no actually, it was more like a ramble of statements, so give me the chance to clarify a few things." He took Lilly's hand and led her to the bed. "Sorry I don't have any other actual furniture. I don't have many guests over."

Lilly sat on the bed leaning back against the pillow, crossing her legs. "OK, I'm listening."

Tread shoved Lilly's feet off the bed playfully and then sat down, facing her. He rubbed his face with his hand.

"Where to begin...hmmm. OK, well first of all, you are a one-of-kind vampire, at least I don't know any others raised by humans. So not everyone is exactly at ease that I brought you here."

Lilly nodded, she had gotten that much from Vanessa.

"But I don't care about that," he continued. "I trust you completely, so if you tell me that whatever I show or tell you stays between us, then I'll believe it."

Lilly sat up and put her hand on his knee. He lifted it and intertwined his fingers with hers.

"If you tell me or show me something you want kept private, I won't tell anyone," Lilly vowed.

Tread cocked one eyebrow up. "Even Lex?" he asked.

"Even Lex," she promised.

Tread nodded his head. "Good enough. So what did Vanessa say that put you on edge?"

"How old are you?" Lilly asked, ignoring his first question.

"Fifty-seven." Tread answered immediately.

Lilly gasped. "Really?"

"Yes, I know I look awesome for my age right....And now I've freaked you out."

Lilly lifted her hands up, placing them on both sides of his face. She turned him from side to side in a mock examination. He really was gorgeous.

"I guess you'll do," Lilly said, stifling a laugh.
Tread pushed her away playfully. "Ha. Ha. Ha."

"Is your age really some safely guarded secret? Because you answered that question quickly and easily."

"Yes. It really is, but I trust you. You and Vanessa are the only people on this planet who know," Tread said. "And you should never tell anyone how old you are."

"Doesn't everyone know already?" Lilly asked.

Tread shook his head. "The vampires here...well, yes. Or if not, they'll figure it out pretty quickly." He pointed to her chest. "The heartbeat thing is a dead giveaway. I know I had offered to bring you here sooner, but the more I thought about it the more I thought better of it."

"I don't get it," Lilly said, confused.

"Let me explain. I want as few vampires as possible to know that you are a Sunwalker. But given what happened, I didn't really have any other options, and I was in a hurry to get you somewhere safe. So I brought you here because that was my only choice. Now anyone who comes in the vicinity of you will hear your heartbeat and know that you are a Sunwalker. I don't think anyone will say anything. We are a pretty loyal group, but it's still a risk no matter how small."

"So should we leave?" Lilly asked.

"Because you won't stop aging until you're nineteen, it's actually better for us to stay here till then. Since everyone here is already going to know, we should really just stay put and then move on once your heart stops beating. Then we can blend in anywhere." He stood up and sighed. "I'm sorry, I should have figured something else out."

Lilly was stunned. So even in the vampire world she couldn't really make a home till she was nineteen.

"Lilly, I want you to know everything about me." He paused. "But not all of it is...well I'm not proud of everything in my past." He looked away and seemed so far off.

"It's OK. It's in the past," she reassured him. She walked up behind him and wrapped her arms around him. "It's OK," she whispered. "You don't have to tell me anything you don't want to. I know you've made changes...for me."

Tread shook his head and turned around to look at Lilly.

"But I didn't do it for you. Maybe at first. But now I want to live a certain way because I feel it's right...I'm not sure where to start, so I guess I'll start at the beginning."

"OK, so I grew up as normal as a vampire can, not that you'd have any idea what that was like," he said, arching an eyebrow. "But when I was forty, that's when I really started hating, despising... I don't really think there is a word that can define how much I detested humans."

"So what happened?" she asked curiously.

"Did Vanessa tell you how she found me?"

Lilly nodded yes.

Tread was quiet for a moment. A look of anguish covered his face. "Well, I'm sure Vanessa didn't tell you that she didn't find me alone."

"No, she didn't mention anyone else," Lilly answered.

Tread shook his head. "She never does. Anything too personal she leaves to the individual to share." Tread sat down on the bed. "I'm sorry." He placed his head in his hands, now avoiding her gaze. After a moment he looked back up at her. "It's just hard for me to talk about."

Lilly sat alongside him, and took his hand in hers.

Tread gave her a faint smile and continued. "Well, you know Sunwalkers are a pretty rare bunch. Takes a rare gene, and then the odds are still small, but I was even more of a rarity. I was a twin."

Lilly's eyes widened. *Was.* She thought. *No wonder he's so damaged.*

"Vanessa found me and my sister in a dump. We had been thrown out like trash," Tread spat bitterly. "She found me in a pile of old tread, the kind those big eighteen wheelers lose when they're driving down a road; hence the name. Then she found my sister. She had been left wrapped up nicely in a pink blanket alongside a patch of wildflowers. Apparently it was harder to treat a girl like trash. Vanessa named her Sage after one of the flowers."

"What was your sister like?" Lilly asked.

"Amazing. She was absolutely amazing," Tread said, smiling.

Lilly noticed his eyes seemed to light up when he talked about her.

"She was courageous. She tried everything and never held back. She was funny and was faster than anyone. It was hard for me at first. I tried so hard to beat her. Then I was just proud of her. She was my sister, my family, my best friend. We did everything together."

He paused. "Anyway where was I...so Vanessa took us to a very small close-knit colony in Texas. She trusted them. There were only five other vampires. We lived in a system of caves located in San Antonio. It had been a tourist attraction years before. Then when vampires became fact instead of fiction, people ceased visiting dark places.

"Vanessa had good friends there. She kept us in the dark, never letting us go out in daylight. She was afraid someone might spot us. We stayed there till we were nineteen, when we stopped aging." Tread was silent for a moment, thinking back.

"We traveled around a lot; Europe, China, South America. Sage wanted to see it all. We walked the Great Wall of China, climbed the pyramids in Egypt, ran with bulls in Spain, watched fireworks from the Eiffel Tower, rode in a gondola in Venice. We saw everything, but eventually found ourselves back in the United States. We ended up in Boston, and we loved it there. There was a huge population of homeless people, so when someone went missing no one noticed." He smiled guiltily.

"One night we were heading to one of our frequented alleys to feed when I realized I had forgotten my book." He motioned around his room. "These are only the beginning. My most cherished. I have an entire library hidden away here. Anyway, normally after we fed, we'd find a tall building where we could overlook the city and I would read to my sister. So I told her we needed to go back, but she just laughed, told me I better hurry if I wanted there to be anything left for me when I got back."

Tread looked down at the ground, his voice full of sorrow, his face full of shame. "I will regret going back for that book everyday for the rest of my existence.

"I could hear her screaming for me from miles away. I ran faster than I think I ever have or ever will in my life. I was a few blocks away when I could see her. She was terrified trying to scramble up the side of a building, but there was some type of steel netting over the top. Below her were VAS officers, dressed like the homeless. They were all armed with flamethrowers. One of them stepped forward and burned my sister to ashes." He shook his head and didn't speak for a minute.

"I stopped," he went on, "horrified, unable to do anything. I should have gone then and ripped their hearts out but I just stood there."

"I'm so sorry. I'm sure there was nothing you could have done," Lilly tried reassuringly. "No wonder you hated humans so much. They took everything from you. I can't even imagine."

"That's not the end of it," Tread whispered. "I followed him...the VAS leader...I waited till he was alone and then I abducted him. I didn't kill him, I tortured him...for years." Tread wept.

Lilly was unsure of what to say. It was quite shocking. *But what would she do if someone killed Lex in front of her?* She knew the rage she had felt when Tread had tried. She didn't even think, she just reacted.

"Well, there is nothing you can do about what's already been done." She took his hand and squeezed it lightly. "Maybe you could try and make amends to his family. Do you think you could find them?" Lilly asked.

"I already found them. I stumbled upon them a few months ago," Tread answered, looking intently at Lilly.

"Well, then maybe you could do things to help the family. Try to make up as much as you can for their loss. You can't bring him back to life, but you can try to make sure his family is looked after, and you can live a better life," Lilly suggested as she hugged him, attempting to offer some comfort.

"I never said he was dead. He's still alive," Tread said cautiously.

"Then why don't you just let him go?"

He looked at Lilly, the pain in his eyes so evident. "I think the years of torture may have made him crazy. Do you think his family could ever forgive me?" Tread asked desperately.

Lilly wanted to console him, to tell him "of course, who wouldn't love you and want to forgive you if they knew the real you?" But she couldn't. "I'm not sure," Lilly admitted honestly. "Maybe they could understand, considering what he did to your sister, but only if you in fact let him go and return him to his family. But it doesn't matter to me if they forgive you or not." She stroked his face. "I know you've changed. You are trying to be better for yourself, and that's all that matters to me."

"Oh Lilly, you don't understand how desperately I want to believe that." He kissed her again. "I love you. I want you to know that. Promise me you'll always remember that."

"Of course. I love you too, Tread." She kissed him back longer and softer, less desperate than his kisses had been.

"Lilly, there's something else I have to tell you about the man…"

Chapter 7
Resurrected

"...The man's name is Dylan." Tread watched for her reaction.

"My dad's name was Dylan," Lilly commented.

He laid a hand gently on each of her shoulders and looked her in the eyes. "Lilly...It is your father."

Lilly stepped away from him. "No, he just has the same name. It's a coincidence." She shook her head. "My dad is dead. He died in a car wreck. He wasn't on the VAS," Lilly explained, more for herself than for Tread, while sitting down on the bed in a daze.

Tread stared at her desperately. He knelt down on a knee in front of the bed, and took her hand in his. "You have no idea what I'd give for that to be true. But it's not. It's your father."

Lilly pushed Tread away. "Stop saying that. My father's dead. You don't even know what he looked like—"

"He's a twin," Tread interrupted. "Adam is his twin brother."

"You've known all this time and never told me?" she gasped.

He reached out towards her, wanting to comfort her, but she moved away. "No, Lilly. It wasn't like that. I didn't know till the night I hit Adam and saw him. Then I was going to talk to you the next day, but you were gone," he explained.

"I didn't know until today...for sure," he said, trying to convince her. "Before that all I knew for sure was that I had Adam's brother. I didn't know who Adam was to you, friend, relative...." He trailed off. "I'm so, so sorry."

He reached for her, but she recoiled.

She saw the hurt in his eyes but couldn't do anything. "I just need some time. I need to process this." Then turning toward the door she added, "I need to see him. Show me where he is."

Tread stood and set his hand on the doorknob. "Lilly, maybe you should wait a second. This is a lot to take in."

"You've held my father prisoner for seventeen years," she barked, wrenching the door open. "I'm not waiting any longer."

Tread followed her out into the hallway and then took the lead. He glanced over at Lilly who tried to avoid eye contact with him. "I only mean, you should prepare yourself. He doesn't know you exist. I mean, he knows his wife was pregnant but he doesn't know what you are."

Lilly stopped. "I'm his daughter."

Tread sighed, slumping his shoulders. "I know, but you have to remember he hates vampires. He hated them enough to kill my sister. He hates them even more after seventeen years."

Lilly pushed Tread against the wall. She gripped the front of his shirt in her fists, tears streaming down her face. "Of course he hates you. You tortured him and kept him captive for seventeen years! You kept him from his wife and daughter. I hate you!" Lilly cried.

"I know," Tread whispered. He glanced down at the floor, unable to look her in the eyes.

Lilly stepped back and sobbed into her hands. "I'm sorry. I don't...I can't even think right now."

He waited till she had finished crying. "He's this way," Tread said, gesturing down a long, dark stairwell.

Lilly walked tentatively down the dimly lit stairwell, following him into the darkness. It curved around and around, going deeper, just like she had seen in the movies whenever people visited the dungeons. At the end of the stairwell was a big, metal door. Another vampire stood outside it.

He nodded to Tread as they approached and opened the door.

Lilly didn't know what to expect. A dirty cell with her father in rags, some moldy bread, dirty water. Seventeen years...seventeen years. Her father had been tortured in a cell for seventeen years. Would there even be anything left of him?

She walked through the door cautiously and was surprised that it didn't squeak when it opened. She stepped into a smaller room that was dark, with one wall covered in glass windows. The rest of the room was bare, just a tile floor and a light switch to the right of the door when she walked in.

Lilly steadied herself before looking through the glass wall. Taking a deep breath, she closed her eyes and tried to imagine the worst possible scenario. Then she slowly opened them and looked into the room. Through the windows she saw a man sitting in a chair staring at the wall, obscuring his face.

Lilly reached gently toward the glass, placing her hand over the space where her father sat.

"It's a two-way mirror," Tread explained, touching the glass, then waving his hand in front of it. "He can't see in here but you can see him."

Lilly was surprised. The room was neat and clean. There was a twin bed in the corner, with a fluffy pillow and dark green bedding that looked brand new. In the center of the room was a small wooden table and a second gray folding chair. On the middle of the table sat a bottle of water and a ceramic bowl filled with fresh oranges, bananas, apples, and peaches. There were a couple of books stacked in one of the corners of the room. The man in the chair had on a clean pair of gray sweatpants and a white t-shirt.

"It's not what I was expecting," Lilly began. "You treated him better than I was imagining."

"Look Lilly," Tread began. He ran a hand through his hair and shook his head lightly. "I don't want to lie to you or try to fool or deceive you. If you had seen him and this room a few months ago..." he paused as he pointed around Dylan's room. "Well, it wouldn't have looked like this."

"What?" Lilly asked, confused.

"When I saw Adam, saw you protect him, that's when I realized he was probably someone important to you. That's when I changed his...um...treatment." Tread looked away, ashamed.

Lilly nodded, understanding dawning on her.

The man on the chair stood up and turned toward the window. To say he was skinny would have been a gross understatement. His face was hollow, dark circles were prominent under his eyes from a lack of sleep. He was covered in bruises in various degrees of healing, some black and blue, others a faint greenish yellow. He had two noticeable scars. The smaller of the two had been a cut across his right eyebrow. The second larger one ran from somewhere underneath his t-shirt sleeve down to his wrist. He had a long scraggly beard and long hair.

He looked almost nothing like Adam in his current state. That fact probably made this hardest for Lilly to bear. To know what Dylan's twin looked like, what he should have looked like in a normal, healthy state, and then to see him as this pathetic, crumpled shell of what he should have been.

Lilly let out a quiet sob and covered her mouth, turning away from her father and Tread. She cried quietly.

"I'm so sorry," Tread repeated.

Lilly dried her eyes and turned back around. Then walked to the glass and placed her hand softly on the glass. "I want to see him," she demanded.

Tread nodded. He went to a door she hadn't noticed and turned a bolt. There was a loud click.

Lilly watched as her father cowered in the corner as the door opened.

Tread stepped in the room first.

"Dylan. I'm not here to hurt you," he announced as he entered the room.

Dylan's eyes darted around the room frantically. "Just k-k-k-ill me already....Pleeeease," he pleaded. "Why are you being n-n-

93

nice to me now? What sick g-game have you planned for meee now?" Dylan asked as he sat huddled in the corner.

Tread put his hands up in a calming motion. "Someone wants to see you. No one is going to hurt you."

"P-p-please don't send *him* in again," Dylan cried. "I'm sorry! Haven't I s-s-suffered enough? Kill me. Please," Dylan begged. "J-j-just kill m-m-me."

Lilly stepped through the door.

Dylan looked at her and then sobbed into his hands.

"Please don't h-h-hurt me," he cried as he cowered in the corner.

Lilly's eyes welled up with tears. She tried to keep them at bay.

"I'm not going to hurt you. I promise. No one is ever going to hurt you again," Lilly said. "I'm here to take you home."

Dylan picked up a book and hurled it at Lilly. "Stop l-lying to to me!" he screamed.

The book hit Lilly in the face. She could have easily dodged it, but was too stunned to move.

Tread appeared by her side. "Are you OK?" he asked.

Lilly pushed past him and approached Dylan. She walked slowly and crouched down in front of the whimpering form in front of her.

"I am here to take you home. Home to your wife Elaine and daughter Lilly," she explained.

Dylan looked up. "I have a d-daughter?" he asked quietly.

Lilly nodded.

"Please do-d-d-don't hurt them," he pleaded as he tugged on Lilly's shirt. "Please k-k-kill me. They don't even kn-kn-know I was on the VAS. They h-h-had nothing to do do with this. Please."

"What do you think you're doing?" a male vampire yelled as he stormed into the room. The vampire had on jeans and a ripped sleeveless t-shirt. He was bigger than Tread and would have had to work out a ton to maintain his form had he not been a vampire. He had short, spiky blond hair that was covered in too much gel. Lilly recognized him as one of the vampires she had seen feeding on the girl earlier. She wondered if this was Koyt.

Dylan cowered back farther into the corner. "Anyone but but but *him*!" he trembled.

Tread stepped in front of the other vampire, gripping his arm. "Go away Koyt," he said.

So she had been right. She wasn't impressed so far. They certainly didn't seem like BFFs.

He shook off Tread. "He is not leaving!" Koyt yelled as he pointed at Dylan.

Lilly stood in front of her father as a shield. "Yes, he is," she hissed, fangs extending.

He looked at Lilly as if she were garbage. "You have NO say in this!" Koyt shouted at her.

Tread took a step forward. "She has the only say in this," he said firmly.

Koyt looked stunned. "I don't care whose father he is. He doesn't get to walk away, not after what he did."

Tread positioned himself between Koyt and Lilly. "Lilly, take him upstairs. I'll be there in a second," Tread said.

Lilly turned around and reached to help Dylan up.

Dylan looked at her strangely. "F-f-father? L-l-Lilly?" he asked, dumbfounded. "It can't be. E-e-e-Elaine would have killed y-you. You can't b-b-be my daughter!" he shouted as he tried to wrench himself away from Lilly's grasp. "Life could-couldn't be that cr-cr-cruel."

Koyt grabbed Lilly by the arm while Tread was watching Dylan. "He is not going—" he began. Tread plowed into him, throwing him against the far wall.

"Don't EVER touch her again!" Tread threatened.

Koyt stood and brushed some of the dust and drywall off his clothes. "Sage would be ashamed of you. How dare you dishonor her like this." He glanced one more time at Lilly, threw his hands down to show he was done with them and then disappeared up the stairs.

Dylan was hysterical when Tread turned back around. He was trying to claw his way away from Lilly. He kept muttering, "it can't be," over and over again.

Tread pulled a syringe from his pocket and injected it into Dylan's arm.

"What the heck?" Lilly gasped. "Haven't you done enough to him?"

Tread held his hand up. "It's just a mild tranquilizer. It will put him to sleep for a couple of hours. Just enough time to get him out of here," he explained. "Besides, I can't let him know the location of this place anyway."

Dylan slowly slumped down into the corner of the room mumbling, "it's not real," over and over again until he was finally out.

Lilly sat on the bed, trembling. Her father hated her. *What should she have expected? Would he have hated her regardless, or did the hate emanate from his time held as a captive while he was tortured for almost the past two decades?*

Tread sat beside Lilly. He tried to comfort her, but she shrunk back at his touch. "What can I do?" he implored.

"Just help me get him back to my house." Lilly shook her head. "I'd do it myself but I don't think I can go back to that house on my own," she shivered.

Tread gently picked up Dylan and draped him over his shoulder.

"OK, let's go," he said.

They walked back up the long staircase in silence. She followed him through hallway after hallway, passing several doors. A couple were cracked open with heads peering out, watching them. Tread led her down a long corridor that brought them to an elevator.

Tread pulled a long black key out of his pocket and inserted it into the slot beside the elevator. "Helps keep any unwanted visitors from dropping in." He explained. A moment later the door dinged open and they stepped inside.

Lilly hit the up arrow and counted the seconds until the door dinged open. She was relieved they didn't have to wait long. It was too quiet.

They stepped inside the elevator and rode it up in silence. When the elevator door opened, Lilly stepped into a big, empty, dimly lit parking garage.

Lilly looked around. "Where are we?" she asked.

"In the parking garage of Harbor Cove National Bank."

She turned and began walking toward the exit to access the street.

"Where are you going?" Tread called out to her. "It's gonna look a little suspicious if I carry a body through the streets. We might want to take a car."

Lilly stopped. "You have a car?" she asked, surprised.

Tread laughed lightly. "Um... Yeah. Walking isn't always practical." He fished some keys out of his pocket and walked over to a silver Honda Civic. Lilly opened the front passenger side door, as Tread gently laid Dylan on the back seat.

They drove in silence. Lilly had a million things going through her mind. She was nervous and scared about going back to her house and had no desire to see her mother again. At least not this soon. *And what about her dad? Would she ever get to know him? Could he get past his hatred for vampires enough to accept her?* Then there was Tread. He had tortured her father. Kept him from his family. Denied her of all these years when maybe he wouldn't have hated her. But Tread had also saved her. She couldn't think about him right now.

Staring out the window, she numbly watched the buildings go by and dreamed of a time when the buildings weren't old and falling apart. When things were new and fresh like in the movies she watched. *Why couldn't they live in a world where cities weren't surrounded by walls, where people weren't scanned upon entrance to verify that they were in fact human?*

Why had she been born a vampire? The desire to be a human was nothing that Lilly had ever considered before. Her mother had loved her and raised her to believe that she was special, perfect, just as God had intended. But now she wondered if life wouldn't have been simpler, easier, happier even, had she been human.

Lilly's thoughts were broken by Tread's voice. "I know you hate me right now, Lilly. I can't even begin to imagine what you're feeling or thinking." He kept his eyes focused on the road ahead and didn't look at her. "But I just don't want you to get your hopes up...about your father I mean. I know Adam loves you, but it may take a long time for your father to come around or it may never happen. It's not instant for everyone like it was for your mom and Adam."

"Oh, it wasn't instant for my Uncle Adam either. It took him awhile to come around."

"Oh, I just assumed from the way he tried to protect you. I mean, it's obvious he cares about you."

"He came around eventually and never looked back. My dad will too, he just needs time."

Lilly thought back to twelve years before when she had first seen her Uncle Adam, at age five.

She had just woken up, and was staring at the ceiling. Never needing to look at the clock, she had known it was sunrise. She always woke up at sunrise.

Her room had been dark, dark for a human anyway. Her mom had put up blackout blinds and thick heavy, denim curtains, but they didn't help much. As a vampire, her eyesight was far superior to a human's and everyday when the sun began to rise her room was flooded with light.

She remembered lying there as a nervous excitement had swept over her. In just a week school would be starting. She was anxious to make a friend. Her mom had kept her pretty secluded since birth. She hadn't even been sure she'd be allowed to go to school. Her mother had been against it from the start. Finally Lilly had convinced her that it was time.

Her mother was still riddled with worries, but Lilly had persuaded her that she could handle it. As a vampire, Lilly had superior sight, hearing, speed, and strength. Those were just some of the reasons Elaine had concerns. But a vampire's brain also worked differently than a human's. She learned quickly and had total recall, never needing to hear or see anything for a second time, putting her well ahead of the average five year old. This had assured her mother that Lilly would be able to control herself and blend in at school.

She remembered jumping out of bed when she heard footsteps approaching. Someone was walking up towards the front door. It was so early. No one ever came here, other than the occasional delivery man, but it was too early for that.

She had listened. Her mother was still asleep; she could hear her quiet snores. So tiptoeing silently to the front door, she peered out the window between the slits in the blinds.

There was a man standing on the front porch. He wore dark leather loafers and black slacks. He had a pinstriped button-up shirt and his hair was dark, wavy, and a little ruffled. She couldn't see his face. He hadn't knocked, he was just standing there. He appeared to be staring at the door.

Lilly tried to crane her neck to get a better look, but was never able to get the right angle.

She watched him for a few minutes. Finally he turned to leave, and for the first time she was able to see his face. Impossible.

He was walking back to his black Jeep. She remembered flinging the door open, standing there in her pink princess nightgown and bare feet.

The man halted and turned around. He froze, his eyes locked on Lilly.

"Daddy!" Lilly had yelled, running down the sidewalk. She had her arms around the man before he had even realized she had moved.

"Daddy, you're alive!"

She heard her mother get up and rush to the front door. But Lilly didn't turn. Her father was alive. It was the happiest moment in the world.

"Adam," Elaine gasped.

Lilly remembered turning, confused that her mother had not called him Dylan. "Mama, it's Daddy. He's alive. He's come back to us."

"Lilly, come back inside. Now," her mother had demanded. "That is not your father. That is your uncle."

She had released him. She remembered the feeling of disappointment that it was not her father, but also excitement at having an uncle. She looked up at him again, and then walked slowly back to her mother, turning every few steps to look back at the man who had briefly made her the happiest girl in the world.

"What are you doing here, Adam?" her mother had demanded as she stepped outside, closing the door behind her.

Lilly remembered watching their confrontation as she peered out between the blinds.

He stood there. She remembered that he opened his mouth to speak but no words came out.

Her mother had glanced up and down the street, ever vigilant, making sure nothing that transpired was being watched by unwanted eyes.

She had sighed, probably relieved for the moment. "Well, are you coming in?" she asked, slightly annoyed. She reached back and opened the door.

Adam looked back at his car momentarily, then turned and walked briskly into the house.

Once the door was shut, her mother seemed to relax. She invited Adam to join her in the dining room. The dining room was fairly large and open. She led him to a large rectangular oak table surrounded by six matching chairs.

Elaine gestured for him to take a seat on the right, which faced into the living room, and sat across the table from him.

Lilly remembered peering in at them while standing in the foyer.

"It's been a long time, Adam. I was under the impression that I would never see you again," Elaine stopped, waiting for him to explain himself, but he said nothing. "What are you doing here, Adam?"

Adam gazed past her. Elaine looked over her shoulder and saw Lilly there.

"Can we talk alone?" Adam finally managed.

Elaine turned back around. "Adam, she could be next door and still hear every word we say, every sound we make."

He looked back at Elaine.

"I can't talk to you with...h-her...watching us," he seemed to struggle with the word.

She remembered Elaine turning to her. "Lilly, could you please go read in your room for a few minutes?"

Lilly remembered frowning, walking sullenly to her room and shutting the door. She went and sat on her bed and listened to what her mom and Adam were discussing.

"Adam. Why are you here?" she heard her mother ask again, this time a little impatiently.

There was a pause and she heard her mother speak again.

"Adam?" she said gently.

"I don't know," he had finally answered. "I should be at work now." There was another pause and then he continued. "I got in the car and next thing I knew I was here. I came up to the door but I didn't knock. I had decided to leave when the door opened and...the girl... came out."

"Her name is Lilly," her mother had stated.

"How could you? I didn't really think you were serious."

"It's what he wanted," her mother explained.

"For a REAL child," her uncle had said, his voice getting louder.

"So, what now, every five years you are going to come by and make an appearance?" she had asked flippantly, then yelled, "Adam you made her think her father was alive!"

"I shouldn't have come."

"A little late for that don't you think?" Lilly could tell her mom was angry. "You know, Adam, I wasn't upset with you when you left five years ago. You did all I needed you to do. I haven't felt any resentment for you not being here, not checking in on us. We were fine. But this…" she paused. "You can't just come back and turn our lives upside-down. What do you want?"

"To ease my guilt!" he shouted. "For five years I've tried to put you out of my head. I even put away any reminder I had of Dylan, my own brother, so as not to think of you. What kind of person does that make me?" Adam had asked. "I don't want to be here *but* I can't not be here."

"I can't look at myself anymore," he continued. "I don't want to pretend I never had a brother. He would be ashamed of me. I can't pretend you aren't here, whatever I think of the…g-girl. I have to be involved. It's the only way to honor Dylan's memory. He should be here, not me. I mean who dies in a car accident on a secret military mission? Not by friendly fire, or an enemy, but death by car. That stuff doesn't happen to people you know. That happens to strangers, people far away with no real identity. Dylan's life was stolen away from him. The least I can do is be there for his…dau…for the girl."

"Adam, I'm sorry you have all this guilt. You really shouldn't feel guilty, but if you want to be a part of *our* lives—" She said the "our" part very slow and clear, as if talking to a little child, "and to be honest, I'm not even sure that I want that, or trust you to do that, you will have to call her by her name."

There was a long pause, so long that Lilly had thought he had left and somehow she'd missed hearing the door open. "OK," he had finally said. "So what now?"

"I want you to think long and hard about this Adam. You are either in or out. This is Dylan's daughter. You will treat her as such. Lilly knows very little about vampires, and I want it to stay that way. If you really want to do this, then your coming over has to be a regular occurrence. Think hard. You are either all in or all out. You have no idea how hard this is for me to even offer you that. I'm only doing it for Dylan."

"OK. I'm in."

"No matter what?" Elaine had asked.

"No matter what. So what now?" he asked.

"Go to work. You can come back tomorrow after work. I know you've said you're all in, but I want you to have time to really think about this. If you don't come back tomorrow, I will understand. But if you don't come tomorrow, never come back. And I mean never. If you do come back then you should get to know your niece."

Lilly heard him get up and open the door. "See you tomorrow," he had said, and then the door had been shut.

Lilly remembered her mother had sat her down and explained that they would probably never see her Uncle Adam again. But she had faith.

The next day seemed to drag on slowly, but he finally arrived. Lilly remembered the first few days he had been standoffish, but by the end of the week he would sit next to her and watch a movie. By the end of the first month he was there every night, and would greet her with a hug and a peck on the cheek.

It had been hard for Adam to get past the stereotype of what she was. Five years to be exact. But once he finally gave her a chance, they became a real family in no time.

*　　*　　*　　*　　*　　*　　*　　*　　*

Tread pulled up in front of her house a little after nine p.m. There were still lights on, but it was already dark outside. Lilly slowly opened her door. Tread pushed open his door and started to get out.

"No," Lilly said. "I need to do this on my own." She stepped out of the car and then turned back to Tread. "Just don't leave...just in case."

She turned back and walked nervously up to the house. Scared any minute her Mom or Adam might jump out and try to tranq her again.

Lilly took a deep breath—not like she needed one, but it just made her feel calmer—and knocked three quick raps on the door.

Her mom peeked out and then threw open the door. "Lilly!" she shouted as she tried to throw her arms around her.

Lilly jumped back a few paces. "Don't touch me," she warned.

Her mom stopped. "Lilly, I've been so worried. I'm so sor—"

"Don't," she said cutting her off. "I can't even stand to look at you. Let alone listen to you trying to rationalize how you locked up your daughter and starved her."

Lilly could see the hurt in Elaine's eyes, but she didn't care.

"I didn't come here to see you," Lilly continued. "I came here because Dad's alive."

"What?" Elaine gasped. "That's not possible."

She gestured behind her. "He's in the car. He's been held prisoner for all these years. He hates vampires. He was a member of a VAS."

Elaine braced herself on the doorframe. "He's been a prisoner? Who had him?" she asked quietly.

"He's going to wake up soon. I'm going to bring him inside, and then I'm leaving," Lilly answered, ignoring her questions.

"No, wait Lilly," Elaine sobbed.

Lilly ignored her. "If you do anything to try and keep me here against my will, I can't make any promises about your safety or what will happen to you," she continued.

Elaine stood up and looked back at the car for the first time. Seeing Tread, she gasped. "That's who had your father, isn't it?" she demanded. "Lilly, he's a monster!"

"Yeah, keeping someone prisoner against their will does make someone a monster. I guess you two have something in common after all," Lilly replied angrily.

Her mom tried to say more, but Lilly walked back to the car and carefully picked up her father. She carried him in through the front door, avoiding eye contact with Elaine. She could hear her mother begin to sob when she saw him. Lilly wasn't sure if it was because she was overwhelmed at seeing him alive, or if it was because of the state he was in.

She laid him on the couch and left.

As she walked back down the sidewalk Tread got out of the car. Lilly looked at him and then turned and started walking down the street.

"Wait," Tread called as he jogged up to her.

Lilly could see the anguish in his eyes. "Don't, Tread. I know you're trying to change. I know what my father did to your sister. I know that I love you. But it's too much."

Tread reached up to wipe a tear rolling down her face.

"I can't," Lilly cried. "I need time to sort through all of this."

Tread stopped. "At least tell me where you're going?" He put his hands in his pockets and looked down at the ground. "I'm so, so sorry."

Lilly could hear the sadness in his voice. "I know. I'll be at Lex's," she added, and then she ran. She ran harder than she ever had, not caring who saw her. She just had to get out of there, away from everything before her head exploded.

*　　*　　*　　*　　*　　*　　*　　*　　*　　*

Lilly knocked on Lex's door. A few moments later, Lex pulled it open.

"Lil, what's wrong?" Lex asked as she wrapped her arms around Lilly and hugged her.

"Everything," Lilly whispered. "Can I stay here?"

"Of course," she replied while stepping aside and motioning for her friend to come in. "Come on in."

Lilly followed her to the back of the house to Lex's room. She sat down on the bed as Lex pulled a chair up and sat in front of her.

"What happened? Is it Tread?"

"I don't know where to start," Lilly cried. "My dad's alive. I love Tread. He tortured my dad. I left him at my mom's. She still claims she loves me," Lilly choked out between sobs.

Lex shook her head. "Wait hold on a sec, slow down. Go back. Did you just say your dad is alive?"

Lilly nodded. "Yeah, oh and he hates vampires and wants to kill me." She looked down, wringing her hands trying to clear her mind.

Lex reached out and put her hands over Lilly's, stilling them. "Everything is crazy right now, but we'll make everything right. Just start from the beginning and tell me the whole story, everything that happened after Tread left with you, up until now."

Lilly took a few deep breaths and tried to calm down. Even though she had never needed to breathe, something about inhaling and exhaling slowly a few times seemed to relax her. She told Lex everything that had happened. She had fallen in love with Tread. She had thought Tread liked Lex. Tread loved her too.

Then she told Lex about the torture and finding her dad. About how he flung a book at her and was terrified of her; hated her. About leaving him at her house and confronting her mother.

"Wow that is....man...I don't even know what to say," Lex said, throwing her hands up. She stood up and sat down on the bed next to Lilly. "So why didn't you just go back with Tread? You did say you both love each other, right?"

Lilly sighed. "I can't even look at him right now. All I see is the man who stole my father from me. Not only did he take him and torture him, but now my father despises me."

"I know Tread hasn't made the greatest choices in the past. I mean he tried to eat me." Lex laughed half-heartedly. "But I saw the way he looked at you when we found you. He was frantic. He loves you. And from what you've told me he has been trying to change. The blood bags, actually treating me like an equal and not a piece of meat. And he told you immediately about your father. He could have hidden that from you. How would you have ever known?" Lex looked into Lilly's eyes. "He had to know in doing so he might lose you and he still did it. I mean shouldn't that mean something?" She squeezed Lilly's hand gently.

"I know it makes sense. But I keep thinking... how can I hope to have a relationship with my father if I am with his torturer? I lost him for seventeen years. Is Tread worth losing him forever?"

Lilly flung herself back on the bed and sighed. "Or what if I let Tread go and my father still never comes around and hates me forever."

Lilly looked up at the ceiling. It was plastered with old movie posters. Tom Cruise, Shia LeBeof, Hugh Jackman, and Lex's favorite, Chris Evans. It seemed like a lifetime ago when they would lie on the bed arguing over who was cuter, Chris Evans or Hugh Jackman. Life seemed so much simpler then.

Lilly had always dreamed of having her father alive. To finally meet him, to see him interact with her mother, to be a real family, was all she had ever wanted. Her imagination had been nothing close to what reality had thrown at her. She couldn't have dreamed up her family in her craziest fantasy. Her father had been a vampire hunter, for lack of a better word. He wanted to kill her. *And her mother? Did she even deserve that title anymore?*

Lex reached out consolingly and brushed her fingers through Lilly's hair. "I don't even know what to tell you. This is some deep stuff Lil, and only you can decide what you should do." She sighed. "I just think you owe yourself some time. There is no rush to make any decisions. This is all so new and raw. Let's try sleeping on it. Maybe things will look different in the morning. "

"I know. It's just so overwhelming. I just want to get out of my head for awhile."

"How about we just sit here and watch all our favorite movies?" Lex suggested. "Maybe if you laugh hard enough, you just might forget for a moment or two."

Lilly shrugged. "Sure, I could use a good laugh. What do you have?"

Lex jumped off the bed and looked at her mischievously. "Well, I rented a new one that some guy in New York found in an old apartment and they just finished making copies of it. It's called *Mrs. Doubtfire*. The actor is kind of old, but it's supposed to be funny."

"An actual new movie. And a comedy? Since when have you rented anything besides those unrealistic action movies, or movies with super hot actors?" Lilly laughed.

Lex walked to her desk and picked up the movie. "I have many layers," she replied in mock disappointment. "They just repeat themselves."

Lilly raised one eyebrow questioningly.

"Alright, alright. There was a new guy working today and H-O-T doesn't even begin to describe him." Lex winked. "Anyway he suggested it, so I thought I'd give it a try. AND even if I hate it, well, at least it will give me something to talk to him about next time I'm in there."

Lilly knew she probably would have enjoyed the movie based on Lex's laughter, but being able to pay attention was out of the question. Too much was swimming around in her mind. She laughed when Lex did. But she couldn't get the memory of her father throwing the book at her, how he scrambled to get away from her, and how he was surprised Elaine hadn't killed her, out of her mind.

Lilly watched another movie with Lex before finally succumbing to sleep.

Chapter 8
Upside-down

Lilly awoke early the next morning to a pounding on the front door. It was still dark outside when the pounding started. She guessed it was probably about two or three in the morning.

"Who could that be?" Lex wondered.

Lilly sighed. "It's Tread. I can hear him. A few hours is not what I meant when I said I needed time."

Lex rolled out of bed. "I'll get rid of him." She walked to the bedroom door and then looked back at Lilly still in bed. "Good thing my parents sleep like the dead."

Lilly could hear Lex as she walked to the front door and opened it.

"Hey, where do you think you're going?" She heard Lex say. "Lilly wants space. Get out of my house."

A second later Tread barged through Lex's bedroom door.

"We have to leave now," Tread said urgently.

Lilly sat up. "GO. AWAY. TREAD." She laid back down and buried her head under a pillow.

Tread walked over and yanked her out of bed. "Lilly, I'm not kidding. We have to get out of here now. " He scanned around the room and then threw a pair of shoes and jeans to her.

"What the heck, Tread—" Lilly started to say.

"Lilly." Tread began raising his voice. "You are not safe here. Please trust me. Hurry. We need to get out of here. I'll explain everything as soon as we leave."

Reluctantly, Lilly stepped into the bathroom and threw on the jeans and shoes in mere seconds. "Tread, this better not just be some new way for you to get me to talk to you."

Tread glanced around nervously. "We have to go." He gripped her wrist and started pulling her toward the door.

"I'll be back soon," she said to Lex as she struggled to wrestle her wrist free of Tread's grasp.

Tread stopped. He looked at Lex. "No, she won't be back Lex. And you haven't seen her and have no idea where she is."

"What?" Lex and Lilly asked simultaneously.

"There is no time for this. It will make sense later. We have to go."

Lilly sighed and turned and followed Tread out of the house.

"Follow me and keep up," he said as he stared at her more intently than he ever had before. He waited until she acknowledged him with a nod, and then he turned and ran.

Lilly followed him down several alleys and up a few fire escapes. He was running harder and faster than she'd ever seen him before. Maybe something really was wrong. He seemed so driven, so determined.

He finally stopped on top of a building in the business sector of town.

"What's going on?" Lilly asked.

Tread shook his head and looked down at the ground. "I'm sorry. I know this is all my fault. I had no idea," he mumbled as he began pacing back and forth. He looked up at Lilly. "I'm sorry. I didn't know if you'd believe me if you didn't see it for yourself." He looked so devastated.

Lilly wished she could make him feel better. "Tread, I don't understand. Just tell me. What's going on?"

He walked forward and put his hands gently on her shoulders. Then he turned her around so that she was facing a giant billboard—the kind that flashes and changes every few seconds.

It took her a moment to realize what she was looking at. It was a wanted billboard. She had never paid them too much attention before. It flashed pictures of people wanted for crimes in the area with a description of what they had done underneath. After a moment, three familiar faces flashed on the screen one after another. WANTED Adam Marsh—TREASON, WANTED Elaine Marsh—TREASON, WANTED Lilly Marsh—VAMPIRE, REWARD $100,000 DEAD OR ALIVE.

Lilly staggered back; Tread wrapped his arms around her. "I'm sorry," he whispered.

She sat down on the cement roof, staring blankly at the billboard, her arms wrapped around her knees.

"How? What?" Lilly finally mumbled.

Tread knelt down in front of her and took her hand gently. "I'm sorry, Lilly. It was your dad."

She looked up at him with a confused expression on her face. "What are you talking about?"

He continued. "He turned in your mom and your uncle. It's considered treason to not report a vampire, and well, what your mom and uncle did went way beyond that." He paused. "Maybe it's his military training taking over," he added.

Lilly stood up and shook her head. "No, that can't be right. He wouldn't do that. He loved my mom. And Uncle Adam, well, he's his brother. This doesn't make sense. Why would he want them dead?" she asked, turning back towards him.

Tread shrugged. "It may not make a lot of sense. I don't know what Dylan was thinking. I'm sure he wasn't thinking straight. I just know what Adam told me."

Lilly leaned forward. "You've seen my uncle?" she asked, surprised.

He nodded. "I went to see him after you left. I wanted him to make sure you were OK. I also felt... Well, I know you care about him; I felt like I should apologize to him too for..." He let the sentence trail off.

Lilly nodded, understanding flashed across her face. "I get it. But then what happened? How did he know this was going to happen? Did he say why his brother would do something like this?"

Tread ran a hand through his hair. "While I was there, talking with him, I heard them coming. I looked out the window and could see the VAS driving down the street. I assumed they were coming for Adam." Tread shrugged. "I mean what are the odds, that there was someone else on the same street as he lived with a connection to vampires?" He was quiet for a moment looking back at the billboard. "Anyway, I told him we had to leave and I got him out of there quickly. We waited on a roof a few houses behind his. He was in denial too. Adam didn't think they were coming for him. After all, it's been seventeen years and there's been no trouble. But once they were inside tearing up his place, he was convinced. That's when I heard them mention that a former VAS agent had phoned in the tip—"

"But that doesn't mean it was my dad," Lilly interrupted. "That could have been anyone. Maybe someone saw me running. There were a few times that I wasn't as careful as I should have been. Or maybe I was caught on some surveillance camera," she said, trying more to convince herself than him.

He waited for her to finish. "The man said the tip had been phoned in by Adam's brother," Tread hesitantly added.

Lilly turned away and cradled her head in her hands. "Ahhh!" she screamed out in frustration. Then she took a deep breath and turned around. "Am I in some alternate universe? My life has turned inside-out and upside-down. Is life ever gonna be easy?"

He assumed it was a rhetorical question so he didn't bother responding.

"So where is my uncle now?"

Tread pointed towards the south. "He's waiting in an abandoned office building downtown. Don't worry. He's fine. He's safe."

112

"OK," Lilly breathed. "So where are my parents? I'm assuming they are with him, right? And away from any phones?"

Tread looked surprised. "Lilly, I have no idea." He looked down guiltily. "I mean, after I got Adam to a safe spot, I went to find you. I rushed straight over to Lex's, and you know the rest."

She waved towards the flashing billboard. "OK," she stated calmly. "It says wanted. Soooo that means they don't have them yet, right?"

"Right," he agreed.

"Well, we have to go find them. We can start with my house." Lilly turned to run but Tread caught her sleeve, stopping her.

"Lilly, that house has to be crawling with VAS officers by now. You can't just bust in there. That's the first place they would look. I am sure they are just combing through your stuff, trying to find anything that might lead them to you."

"I can't just let them execute my mom. I know things are totally screwed up with us right now. I don't know if I'll ever be able to get past what she did to me. But I know I can't let her die. For what? For not killing me when I was born?" She looked pleadingly at him. "I have to go."

"Of course," he agreed. "But I'm coming with you. I've dealt with the VAS before. We need to be smart about this. Stay back and check things out first."

Lilly walked forward and wrapped her arms around him. "Thank you," she whispered.

*   *   *   *   *   *   *   *   *   *

It didn't take long to get back to her old street. Tread had them stay back a couple of blocks and they perched themselves on some random person's roof.

The house was covered in yellow tape. There were several black SUVs out front of the house along with three military-looking Humvees.

113

Tread scouted ahead so they could have a better view into the house. Once he was sure the VAS was just focused on Elaine's house and street, he motioned Lilly over to the house kitty-corner behind her own.

She was surprised to see her mom sitting on the couch in their den. Dylan sat next to her, as Elaine just kept muttering over and over again, "What did you do?"

He put his arm around her and looked as if he was trying to comfort her, but it didn't seem like Elaine even noticed.

An officer sat in front of them in a chair he had pulled from the kitchen table. By the way he was ordering the other soldiers around, he seemed to be a high-ranking officer.

"L-l-l-look, my wife n-n-needs help right now. She doesn't n-n-need to be interrogated," Lilly could hear her father saying. He was still jittery and jumpy. He kept glancing around the room like someone was going to pounce on him at any moment.

"She h-h-has been brainwashed by the the vampire. She needs coun...seling or some type of of therapy. I don't u-u-under...stand what's with all the wan...ted signs. My wife wasn't run...ning. We just went to the store. I can't bel...ieve how you've treated us. Do you have any id...idea who I am?" her father demanded. "My wife didn't even kno...ow I called you. This has been hand...handled all wrong. "

"We are well aware of who you are, First Sergeant Marsh," the officer replied. "Your wife harbored a vampire for seventeen years. She has broken countless laws. She is a traitor, not only to her country, but also to the human race. She will continue to be interrogated until she gives the creature up."

Dylan stood. "This is ridiculous, I want to...to speak to Sergeant M-m-major Matt Taylor right n-n-now."

"Sergeant Major Taylor is retired," the officer responded, looking bored. "Look, we appreciate all you've done for your country, but right now I am going to need you to leave and give us some time alone with your wife."

"No! Abso...lutely not!" Dylan yelled. He turned and started pulling Elaine to her feet. "We are l-l-eaving, and I am going to take my wife to...to get the help she needs."

The officer stood and motioned to two other military men. They approached Dylan and each grabbed him by an arm.

"Let go-o-o of me," Dylan hollered as he struggled against the two men.

"Staff Sergeants Rice and Bell, please escort him out front. If he is still unruly cuff him and throw him into the back of an SUV."

"Yes sir, Master Gunnery Sergeant Hill," the men answered in unison.

They walked Dylan out front. He shook them off. "I'm fine. Just get...get off me." He began pacing up and down the sidewalk, still shaking. He kept looking over his shoulder in a panic.

One of the officers whispered to another, "This should be over soon. Once they get a location on the monster, we have orders to execute the wife onsite," the soldier said while pointing inside to Elaine, "and then we can drop this loon off in a psych ward."

Lilly gasped. She started to get up but Tread prevented it.

"Hang on a second," he hissed.

"For what, them to shoot my mom?"

"No, no, of course not. I won't let that happen," Tread reassured her. "But look, there are about two dozen soldiers down there. They are all armed to the teeth with tranqs that are specially made to penetrate our skin. Going in all gung ho is only going to get us all killed." He pulled a phone out of his pocket. "Let me make a call."

Tread punched a few keys and put the phone up to his ear. "Vanessa, I need to call in a favor." He quickly explained the situation, rattled off the address, then hung up the phone.

"Why would your friends help a human?" Lilly asked when he had finished.

"They wouldn't," he answered as he shoved his phone back into his pocket. "They could care less about humans. But they owe me." Tread shrugged. "Even if they didn't, we normally try and help each other out. We live a very long time. Sooner or later we all need help. And if they get to take down a few VAS soldiers at the same time they're helping me, well, it's just icing on the cake."

Lilly glanced nervously at the house and then back to Tread. "What if they don't get here in time? My parents could be dead soon and," she glanced up at the sky, "the sun will be up in another hour, making it impossible for any of your friends to help us."

Tread took her hand and squeezed it gently. "If they don't make it in time, we'll go in and hope for a miracle."

Lilly turned her attention back to her mother. The officer continued to pepper her with questions. All the while her mom stayed silent.

As the officer was asking Elaine where Lilly was for the tenth time, his phone began to ring.

"What did you find out?...Uh huh...Great!...OK, we'll pick her up after we are finished with the mother...Sure."

The officer slid his phone back in his pant pocket. "Look, Elaine," he said leaning forward, "I'm gonna ask you one more time and then I'm through here. Turns out the school says that your daughter has a best friend. And I'm willing to bet that if she's not at her house, then her friend most certainly knows where she is. And hey, I'm betting a seventeen-year-old girl will be a little easier to break." He grinned sadistically as he stood up. "So, last chance, tell me where your daughter is or I go torture it out of her friend. Hmmm, wonder how long she'll hold out after we water board her?"

"You're disgusting. Leave Lex alone. She doesn't know anything," Elaine pleaded, leaning forward desperately. "Please, even if I wanted to tell you, I don't know where Lilly is. We fought and she left. Lex doesn't even know that Lilly is a vampire," her mother lied.

The officer scoffed. "We'll see about that." He turned toward the door and motioned to a soldier. "We're done here. Terminate the prisoner."

Elaine gasped.

"But take her to the school. Make everyone watch. Show this town what happens to traitors who don't put their own species first."

The soldier came and started dragging Elaine out front. Elaine screamed. "Dylan!"

Dylan was out front and turned to see his wife being pulled out of the house.

He ran up to her and decked the man escorting her out. Once he was down Dylan continued to punch him over and over again.

Four soldiers came running up, pulling Dylan off the fallen soldier.

"Throw him in the back of the Humvee and bring him with us. He might still be useful," the officer ordered. "Take care of the wife and then meet us back at the base."

*   *   *   *   *   *   *   *   *   *

"We have to do something now," Lilly urged as her mom was being pulled from the house.

Tread glanced back at Lilly. "OK, you're right. Looks like we are out of time." Tread stood up. "Listen. I know you're panicked right now, but stealth and speed are still our best option. We need to pick off the soldiers that are on their own first. We should work from the outside perimeter in. There are only two of us, so we don't want someone sneaking up behind us."

"Pick them off? I can't kill anyone!" Lilly declared.

Tread grasped her shoulders and looked her in the eye. "Listen, I can't make any promises. It's us or them. But if you try and just hit them hard on the head, you might just knock them out. But like I said, I can't make any promises. We are a lot stronger than them. I am not sure how hard to hit someone to knock them out instead of killing them. It's never really been an issue for me."

Lilly nodded. "Alright," she whispered.

Tread motioned to his right. "You take the right and I'll take the left. We'll work around the sides of the house and then look for soldiers grouped together. You will have to work fast if you want to take out an entire group at once. No hesitation."

Lilly nodded, then began to sneak around the side of her house. There was a soldier smoking a cigarette with his back towards her, oblivious of her presence.

Lilly counted to three and sped up behind him, hitting him hard on the head with her right fist. She had never hit anyone before and it didn't feel natural. He crumpled to the ground and made a soft thud.

"Dylan!" she heard her mother scream. Lilly turned the corner and forgot all about being stealthy.

She stopped as she saw her father striking a man on the ground, over and over again. He looked so full of hatred as he continued to hit him again and again with his bloodied fists. Lilly turned back in time to see a terrified soldier pointing a shaky finger at her.

"There...there she is," he yelled as he fumbled around, attempting to pull a gun from his holster.

Lilly sped towards him and quickly hit him, hoping desperately he was only knocked out. She glanced around but didn't see Tread, worried that something could have happened to him.

"Stop!" a voice hollered. "You move again and I kill both your parents."

Lilly turned to see the Master Gunnery Sergeant who had been interrogating her mother, standing behind her parents, both of whom were kneeling, with a gun alternating between the back of her mother's and father's heads.

Lilly froze, terrified.

"Staff Sergeant Bell, please tranq the monster so we can all go home," he ordered with a sickening grin.

Lilly turned as another soldier, presumably Staff Sergeant Bell, slowly began to load his gun with a tranquilizer.

118

This couldn't be the end. Her parents weren't safe yet. She'd never get the chance to see if her father could ever come to accept her, love her. Even with super human strength and speed, she had still failed and now she would die. It wasn't worth the risk of him getting a shot off and killing one of them. She only hoped this would buy Tread enough time for his friends to come. Hopefully her sacrifice would mean their survival. Lilly thought of Tread and wished she could have seen him one last time.

The soldier carefully pointed the gun at her, his hand shaking, and then it was pure chaos.

His arm went sailing across the yard. Lilly gasped in horror as it landed a few feet in front of her, his hand still clutching the gun.

Lilly didn't even hear him scream, it was so fast. First the arm went flying and then his neck was snapped in such rapid succession that Staff Sergeant Bell had no time to react.

Behind his body stood Red, blood dripping off his face. He winked and turned towards another soldier.

Lilly turned and stood, her mouth gaping open, stunned at the scene before her. All around was madness; blood and body parts littered the ground. Vampires were swarming in on the VAS. A few she recognized from her visit to Tread's home. Koyt, the vampire who appeared to hate her father so much, seemed to relish in the violence. He was covered in blood, grinning from ear to ear.

Others she had never laid eyes on. Soldiers were dropping like flies. None of the vampires seemed the least bothered by the loss of life. The two soldiers Lilly had attempted to knock out were being drained of their blood by vampires she had not met. All Lilly could see was red everywhere she looked; her once tranquil home was now a graveyard dripping in blood.

When she finally turned back to her parents, she saw the officer who had been holding them at gunpoint was dead. His head had been mounted on a crude wooden stake in the front yard, his body scattered across the lawn.

Her thoughts returned to Dylan and Elaine. She scanned the yard frantically.

Her parents were gone.

Lilly turned in panic. Then she felt a tiny prick in her right thigh and fell into blackness.

Chapter 9
Trust

Lilly awoke in a darkened, dingy room. She heard shouting coming through the wall. It was Dylan and Adam.

Walking slowly out of the room, she saw her uncle and father in a heated conversation. Her mother was sitting on a windowsill with Lex sobbing quietly onto her shoulder. Relief washed over her. Everybody was safe.

She glanced around, looking for Tread, but he was nowhere to be found.

"You don't deserve them!" Adam was yelling irately. "How could you turn us in? We'd be dead by now if the vampires hadn't helped us." He stepped forward and shoved him hard. "Dead! Your own daughter saved you. She's the one responsible for you even coming home. And you repay that by trying to get her mother executed!"

Dylan regained his balance and cowed slightly. "I know. I'm s-s-sorry. I've already a-a-apologized. My judgment might have been a little cl-cl-clouded, what with having been held prisoner and t-t-tortured by the vampires you love so m-m-much! I only m-m-meant to turn h-h-her in," he said, getting louder towards the end but still shrinking slightly as if he were afraid of being hit. "I th-thought y-y-you and E-e-elaine would just get h-h-help."

Adam kicked a box across the room angrily. "Are you kidding me? Do you even hear yourself? So you were only trying to get your daughter killed." Adam walked towards Dylan, stopping when he was practically nose-to-nose with him. "You disgust me."

"Enough," Lilly said crossly. "This isn't helping anything." Lilly looked over at Adam. "Where is Tread anyway?"

"Who cares?" Dylan asked. "Did it e-e-even phase you? That b-b-b-bloodbath in front of o-o-our house? You're supposedly my...my daughter." He glanced at her up and down, a look of contempt in his eyes. "Are y-y-you ok with that? Or what a-a-about the fact that your boyfriend t-t-tortured me for seventeen years? Does that even m-m-matter?" He shifted from one foot to the other nervously, glancing wildly around the room, as if waiting for someone to pounce on him.

"It's complicated. Oh, and we are the ones that just saved you remember?" Lilly said as she turned back to Adam.

"He went out to get us clean clothes and some food," Adam explained.

Elaine walked over with Lex. Lex threw her arms around Lilly. Her eyes were red and puffy.

"Are you okay, Lex?" Lilly asked.

"Tread said we have to leave. I don't think I'll ever see my parents again," she sniffed, and rubbed her nose with the back of her sleeve.

"I'm sorry. This is all my fault," Lilly confessed.

Lex wiped her nose again. "This isn't your fault. It's no one's fault. It just sucks. Maybe someday I can come back."

"Lilly, I'm so glad you're OK. Thank you for coming back for us," her mother interjected. She reached forward to give her a hug.

Lilly stepped back. "Not wanting to see you dead, and forgiving you are two very different things."

"Please, Lilly. I made a mistake. Can't we get past this?" her mother pleaded.

"I need time. I don't know if we can get back what we lost. It will be a long, slow process, but I guess we're leaving here, so we will probably be spending a lot of time together."

"We're n-n-not going a-a-anywhere with you," Dylan said, taking a step back. "Things will d-d-die down here, and then I j-j-j-just need to find the r-r-right connection and explain everything."

Lilly was about to respond when Elaine said, "Shut up, Dylan."

Dylan stepped back. He looked like he'd been slapped.

"Dylan, I love you. Having you home has always been a dream of mine. But you almost got Adam and me killed. I know this hatred of vampires comes from being kept prisoner for all those years and things would have been different if you had been part of Lilly's life from the start, but so help me, we are leaving with them, and if you give us anymore trouble I'll tranq you myself."

Dylan huffed, then turned and walked over to the windowsill.

"He still would have hated me. He was on the Vampire Assassination Squad. Just another thing you lied to me about," Lilly said disapprovingly as she walked over and gave Adam a hug.

Elaine turned toward Dylan. "What? That's not true. He was in the Marines. I thought you mentioned something about that last night when you brought him home, but I was so overwhelmed with seeing your father alive again, I thought I must have heard you wrong. He trained the soldiers who protect the labs and the energy plants. Tell her, Dylan."

He turned and looked back at Elaine. "It was confidential. I couldn't t-t-ell anyone. I w-w-was protecting you."

"You lied to us for years," Adam said in disbelief.

"So how did you get taken by vampires if you were trained to kill them?" Elaine asked.

"He murdered Tread's sister so Tread kidnapped him as some sort of retribution."

"Wait, Tread, the vampire who brought us here?" Elaine clarified.

"What do you think we've been talking about?" Lilly asked.

"Somehow I missed that. So let me get this straight. Your new friend tried to eat Lex and kept your father in a cell for seventeen years and none of that bothers you." She shook her head. "What spell does he have you under? I mean, you can see how crazy that sounds, right?"

Lilly sighed. "It's not that simple. He saved me. He just saved you. People can change. Dad's not innocent in this either. He murdered someone. We need to end this cycle of hate and start new."

"He killed a vamp—" Elaine stopped herself before she finished her declaration.

Lilly stood there, stunned. "Come on, go ahead. Finish," she goaded. "I'm a vampire too. All along, my whole life..." she scoffed. "How did I not see it? You tried to, what, pretend?" Lilly shrugged her shoulders. "What, that I wasn't a monster? Not a vampire? Or did you always think I was less than a human? Not your equivalent. That's why you kept me hidden, tried to hide everything about vampires from me?"

Elaine threw down her hands. "Come on, that's not fair," her mother began.

"Did you build that cage for me? From the beginning?" Lilly demanded.

"No!" Elaine shouted, horrified. "Wait...you're right, Lilly," she continued calmly.

Lilly's face dropped.

"I've never seen you as a vampire. I don't know that I ever will. You're just my Lilly. My daughter." She shook her head and looked down at the ground. "I've always known you were extraordinary. Did I try and keep information about vampires from you? Yes. I view vampires as a lower class, as scum, even. But I never consider you in that group. I know technically you are a vampire. But I just see you as my daughter. I see you as the most amazing woman. I'm learning now," Elaine sighed, "that I may have been wrong about categorizing a whole species as evil. But for better or worse, I never grouped you with them. You've always been above them, above me, heck, above everyone. Nothing is more valuable to me than you."

"And the cage was just a coincidence? You have a vampire daughter and just happen to move into a house totally prepared to contain one?" Lilly asked sarcastically.

"Come on guys. We don't have time for this now. I know you two have a lot of issues to deal with, but for now," Lex intervened, "let's just agree that not all humans are good, not all vamps are good. That doesn't make them all bad. Look at Tread. Once he met Lilly he started thinking differently, going against his natural instincts. He started feeding on blood bags too. Once he could see past his predator instincts to view us all as food, he stopped feeding on humans."

Dylan scoffed.

Tread opened the door, carrying several bags. He looked around and saw Elaine and Lilly a few feet apart. Everyone was silent. Dylan scooted back farther into the corner.

"So what did I miss?" he asked cynically as he set the bags down on the floor in the center of the group. "Look, we may not all like each other," he continued. "Actually I think that's probably a huge understatement, but we are losing time and we need to get out of here. It won't take long before this whole city is swarming with VAS soldiers."

Lilly fished through a bag and pulled out a clean shirt and a pair of drawstring pants.

Dylan looked at Elaine and Adam. "OK. You're right. We have to...to...to leave. But we don't need to go with him...him," Dylan said while avoiding eye contact with Tread. "We can make it on our own. St-st-start new somewhere else."

Elaine looked to Lilly. "He's right. Come with us, we don't need him. We can be a family. We'll start over and you and your dad will have plenty of time to get to know each other."

Lilly ignored them and turned to Tread. "Can you get us out of the city? Past the gates?"

"Yeah. There is definitely some risk, but I don't think we really have any other options."

She turned back towards Lex, her parents, and Adam. "We are leaving in five minutes. If you plan on coming with us, I suggest you change and eat an energy bar. Otherwise, don't expect us to come save you again."

Lex walked to the bag, ripped open a box of Cliff bars, and took two out of the box. Then she opened a twenty-four pack of water and twisted the top off one. She walked over and stood by Tread as Lilly went into the other room to change.

Adam glanced at Dylan and Elaine. "You guys can do what you want, but I'm going with Lilly." Adam walked over to Tread and started asking him some questions about their plan to escape.

Elaine slowly walked over and dug into the bag, pulling out a clean set of clothes for herself. She tossed a pair of jeans and a t-shirt at her husband.

Lilly walked back out as her parents were entering another room to change.

Tread walked over to Lilly and spoke softly. "So what's the plan after we get out of the city? Your profiles will be sent all over the US. It will be impossible to start over."

"I'm not sure," she answered honestly. "But we can't stay here. I have to believe there is somewhere that humans and vampires can coexist peacefully. You mentioned vampire cities. Maybe we can head to one. Maybe they could accept four humans. It's not like they'd pose a threat to them."

126

"Those are just rumors," Tread reminded her. "I don't even know if they exist or what kinds of places they are. Maybe we just find an abandoned small town for now and stay holed up there for awhile until we can sort things out."

"What about Red, Vanessa, or Koyt?" Lilly began, noticing Tread cringe slightly when she mentioned Koyt. "Is it possible they know anything about any cities?"

Tread shook his head. "No, we've discussed it before and it's all just rumors. No one knows anything definite. And Koyt and I are done."

"What?" Lilly asked, surprised. "Why? I mean, he came and helped us when you called. I know I saw him before I was hit."

"Oh he was definitely there. But it wasn't for me. After the attack was over, and the VAS were taken care of, he went for your dad."

Lilly gasped.

"I stopped him. But he made it clear we were finished, and I made it clear if he came near your father again, I wouldn't just let him leave."

"I'm so sorry."

Tread shook his head. "It is what it is."

"What do you think about heading south?" Lilly asked, trying to change the subject.

"Any particular reason?" he said, glancing automatically to the south.

"It will be winter soon. It's warmer down there. I am assuming if we find an abandoned town, they won't have electricity. Cold can kill humans."

"Right, south it is," he said as he reached into his back pocket and pulled out two blood bags. "Time to fuel up. This won't be as easy to find out there."

Lilly hadn't given much thought to herself or how she'd feed. Luckily she could feed once a week and still be OK. She normally liked to feed twice a week.

She took the bag gratefully and sunk her fangs into the pouch, reveling in the sweet taste as the blood flowed down her throat. *This could be it for a while*, she thought.

Dylan walked back in with Elaine, just as Lilly was finishing her meal. He turned away, repulsed.

She slurped down the last few drops and then tossed the empty bag onto the ground.

Elaine walked over and looked at Tread. "So how are you going to get us out of the city?"

"Well that's the tricky part," he answered. "There are a few places in the wall where we have been able to cut off the electrical current."

"How were you able to do that?" Adam asked.

"We have some skilled engineers among our kind," Tread replied. "When repairs are done on the wall, or even routine maintenance, we've installed little devices that can disrupt the current for short distances. It's only for a width of about two and a half feet, but it runs all the way up and down the wall."

"But how does that help us?" Elaine asked. "Can you really jump fifty feet?"

"Umm, no." Tread laughed. "But we dug in tiny grooves every so often. They are not spaced together super close but it's fairly easy for us to get from one to another, and climb over."

"Ok, then where does the risk come into play?" Elaine questioned.

"If we are going to do this, it has to be done at night, when it's dark. However, there are still giant strobe lights that patrol the walls every so often. Which normally isn't a problem. Lilly and I could do this with our eyes closed. The problem is we have to do it carrying one of you at a time.

"Our senses are pretty awesome. We can sense the hum of the electricity. And Lilly will even be able to see our devices that divert the flow, once I point them out to her. So we can stay in the safe zone without a problem. But carrying one of you makes it risky for us. If you can't hold on tight enough, or stay still enough, and your hand, foot, arm, you name it, strays into the electric field, we both get fried. Granted, it is not going to kill Lilly or me. It will still be painful though, or so I've been told. I've never had that experience," he glared at Elaine, then looked sympathetically at Lilly. "Anyway we'd both more than likely fall. And I'm guessing whichever one of you we are carrying is going to be dead."

"So basically you w-w-want us to tr-tr-trust that you both can get us a-a-all over the wall," Dylan said. "It sounds like the h-h-humans are taking all the risk."

Tread started to speak when Elaine cut him off.

"So all we need to do is hold on?" Elaine asked, ignoring Dylan's previous comment. "That doesn't sound too hard."

Tread leered at Dylan, then turned to Lex. "Lex, climb up on Lilly's back."

Lilly turned her back facing Lex so she could climb on.

"No, Lilly," he corrected. "You can't hold her like you would for a piggy-back ride. You'll need both hands to climb."

Lilly pulled her arms out from underneath Lex's legs.

"Ok Lex, you need to hang on tight and be as still as possible. Lilly will be moving very fast to avoid the search lights. Lil, just do a small fast jump to start."

Lilly nodded. "You ready Lex?"

Lex squeezed her arms around Lilly as tight as she could, too tight for a human to handle. "Ready."

Lilly took a small jump. As she lifted she could feel her friend's arms slip from around her neck. Lex flew back, did a sloppy looking somersault, and would have crashed hard into the wall if Tread hadn't moved to intercept.

He set a shaky Lex down. "OK, I can see where this might be problematic," Lex said as she took a few wobbly steps.

"Can you get some rope?" Lilly asked, looking at Tread. "Maybe if we lash them down it will help them to stay on."

"Yeah, that might work. We'll need to tie them tight, though, to counter against the momentum of our jumps. Do you think they will be able to handle that?" he said, gesturing to her family.

Lex nodded. "I think I'll take a little pain over electrocution and falling to my death."

Adam looked a little uncomfortable. "How much pain are we talking about?"

Elaine put her arm around him. "You'll be fine. Did you see how fast she jumped? I wouldn't have even known she had moved if Lex hadn't flown across the room. It'll only be for a minute or so."

"Do you think we have time to go by my house? Leave a note or something for my parents?" Lex asked, hopeful.

Tread shook his head. "Sorry, Lex. I don't think we can risk going back. I am sure the VAS will be watching your house."

"I figured as much." Lex nodded. "At least I can text them from the road. Keep them updated every so often, so they'll know I'm at least alive."

Tread grimaced. "Lex," he sighed, "you can't text them once we are outside the wall."

"Oh, don't worry. I won't tell them which direction we are going in, just general info, like I'm alive and still here," she explained.

"No, Lex. You really can't—" he began.

"It'll be fine, Tread. Just let her text them," Lilly interrupted.

"Let me be clear," he said, sounding impatient. "It's not that I have a problem with her texting them. It's that it won't work. Cell phones don't work outside of city limits."

"Of course they do," Lex laughed. "My dad calls me all the time when he is out of town on government business."

"Well then he must have a satellite phone. But you don't." Tread held up his hand to stop them from interrupting. "I know in those movies you watch, cell phones could call anywhere. And that used to be true. But not anymore. I understand you not knowing, since you've never left the city. Vampires tore down cell towers all across the United States to cease communication. Now there are only a few cell towers left. Typically one or two per city. So your phones will only work here." He shrugged apologetically.

Lex looked at her phone and then threw it across the room. "Guess I don't need that anymore." She walked away, shoulders slumped and stood looking out of a window.

"Just give her some time," Lilly said.

He nodded. "I'll be back in a minute. There's a hardware store not far from here that should sell rope. Be ready to move when I get back. I'd load up on those energy bars if I were you."

After Tread left, Lilly brought the box of Cliff bars around the room. Adam and Elaine started on a bar each, and Lex took two more and stuffed them in her pocket.

Lilly offered Dylan one next.

"I'm fine," he said shortly.

"We don't know when we'll find food again."

"I said I'm f-f-fine. I'm a survivor. I'll f-f-find my own food."

Lilly pushed the box towards him again. "There may be nothing for you to scavenge. If you won't do it for yourself do it for Mom. She doesn't deserve to have to worry about you more than she already does."

Dylan begrudgingly took a bar, ripped it open with his teeth, and took a big bite. "Happy?"

Lilly smiled. "Ecstatic."

Her mother walked past her and tried to make eye contact but Lilly looked away.

Elaine took Dylan into another room. Lilly wasn't trying to eavesdrop, but she couldn't stop herself from overhearing.

"Enough," Elaine said.

"What?" he asked.

"I love you, Dylan. But every second I'm with you, you are tearing my heart out."

"I'm s-s-sorry. I just need some...some...time. I love you too, but we-we've both changed a lot. We just need to get to kn-kn-know each other again."

"No Dylan. I'm talking about Lilly. She's your daughter. You are going to try or I am leaving you here."

"She's a v-v-vampire, Elaine."

"I know what she is. She came from me and you. So if she's a monster then we're monsters too. We created her from our love. This is non-negotiable. I am not saying you have to start holding hands, hugging, telling her you love her. But you have to try. You have to have conversations, spend time with her. Try."

"Elaine. This is hard. You're a-a-asking me to just let go of the p-p-past seventeen years," Dylan explained. "All that hatred. Just l-l-let it go. It's not like I can just f-f-flip a switch."

"Well I guess that's your answer." Lilly could hear her mother walking back towards the main room. She saw her reach the doorway.

"OK. W-w-wait! I'll try," Dylan conceded.

Elaine turned back, and Lilly could see a big grin stretching across her face.

"I'll try. I can't pr-pr-promise it will make a difference. You can't i-i-imagine what I've been through the l-l-l-last seventeen years."

"Just try."

"I will," he promised.

Lilly could hear them kissing and, trying to distract herself, turned to see what Lex and Adam were doing.

"So," Adam said, turning toward Lilly, "assuming we all make it over the fence without falling, getting electrocuted, or dying, what's next?"

"We find a new home," Lilly said, as though it were just that simple. "So how is Dylan really doing?"

"Honestly?" Adam shrugged. "Extremely well for someone who went through what he did. To have his mental capacities still intact—that alone is a miracle. Just since last night when I checked him out, his stuttering has improved and he is less jumpy."

"Really?" Lilly asked in disbelief.

"Yeah, I could barely understand him last night. I'm sure it will take time, but he is progressing way faster than I would have thought possible. Just give him time, sweetheart. He will come to see how amazing you are." He reached forward and gave her a big hug and then kissed her lightly on her forehead. "I'm sure it won't take him five years like it did me," he added with a wink.

A few minutes later Tread came back with a neon yellow bundle of rope.

He shook his head. "I know. But it's all they had. As long as the light doesn't hit it we should still be OK." He handed the rope and a knife to Adam. "Start making some lashings. About eighteen inches should do the trick." He turned back to Lilly. "I figure we can tie their hands in front of our necks, tie them once or twice around their torso and three or four times around each leg."

"That seems like a lot," Lilly noted.

Tread scratched his forehead. "It may be, but better too many than not enough, right? We'll be going fast and with that much momentum...Well, we don't want to take any chances, right?"

Lilly grabbed Tread's hand and pulled him over to a corner. "Thank you. Really, for everything."

He opened his mouth to speak but she stopped him. "Look, I appreciate all you've done. But this isn't your problem. You have a home here. You don't have to leave," Lilly said. "After we are all over the wall you can go. You don't have to stay with us. I'll figure it out. Your friends, your books, your life...it's all here."

Tread slowly caressed Lilly's face. "You are my life now." He spoke slowly, looking deep into her green eyes. They were so alive, just like how she made him feel. "I know things are complicated between us. I'm not trying to put any pressure on you. But I am staying. I'll stay till you make a decision, no matter how long it takes. And even if you told me right now that nothing could ever happen between us, I'd still come. At least till I make sure you and Lex find a new home. Besides, I can't stay here anymore. I need to give Koyt space. I do understand why he's so angry. He loved my sister."

Elaine and Dylan finally came back into the main room. Dylan had his hand intertwined with Elaine's. It seemed odd to Lilly to see her mom seemingly happy, in love even. Odd but nice.

"It's getting dark out. We'd better get started," Tread called. He pulled two backpacks from the bottom of a bag he'd previously brought in and handed them to Lex and Adam. "Fill these with the rest of the water and granola bars and then we'll head out."

Chapter 10
Walking

Slow. That's the word that came to Tread's mind as he was traveling in alleys and dark streets with a pack of humans. Actually, lethargic or comatose might have been a more accurate description. It took them well over an hour to get to the deactivated spot in the wall—a place he could have reached in five minutes tops.

Between their sluggishness and having to wait for patrols to pass since it would have taken forever for the humans to scale buildings, Tread thought they were lucky to have reached the wall at all.

Once they were close enough, Tread pointed out the small devices that re-routed the electricity and showed Lilly the small gouges that could be used as hand holds. No one else could see anything.

"OK, I'll go first," Tread whispered. "That way you can watch me and see how it's done. Then I'll come back and you can go."

"Wouldn't it be faster if I just go right after you instead of waiting for you to come back?" Lilly asked.

Tread shook his head no. "Not by that much. Plus I think it's better to have one of us on this side with your family. If there is any trouble from the VAS, it will happen on this side. They don't care as much about outside the wall." He turned to the rest of the group. "So who's first?"

"I'll go," Adam volunteered.

Lilly fastened him on to Tread as tight as she dared. Each time she tied one of the ropes she could hear him gasp in pain.

"Sorry," she whispered.

Tread turned back to Lilly. "Just watch, it'll be a piece of cake," he said with a wink.

After the strobe light passed, Tread ran out to the fence. He was almost to the top when the light swept past again and he had to pause. A second later he was over the fence and after a few more seconds he was back with the group.

"Okay. Your turn," he said to Lilly.

He sensed her nervousness and added, "You'll do fine."

"Of course," she said, mocking his typical cocky tone. "As long as I don't fry my best friend," she added low enough that only Tread could hear.

He just rolled his eyes.

Lex climbed up on Lilly's back and Tread went to work securing her.

"Let's hope this goes smoother than last time," Lex joked.

Lilly waited till the light passed and then hurried across in the darkness. With Lex strapped down, it was easy for Lilly to stay in her lane and climb up quickly. She had to pause near the top like Tread did, but then it was just one quick jump and they were over.

Once they were over the wall, she tore the ropes off Lex, hoping, as an afterthought, that they wouldn't need them again. She looked around but didn't see Adam.

"Pssst. Over here," he called from behind an overturned bus.

Lilly and Lex walked over to the bus.

"I was told to wait here," he said in a hushed tone. "The lights pan this side of the wall too, but not as often."

"Good, stay out of sight. I'll be back soon," Lilly said.

When she got back on the other side, she could hear arguing.

"Come on, we don't have time for this," Lilly said in a bored tone.

"Mom. Just go with Tread and I'll take Dylan."

"I don't want y-y-you to go with him either!" Dylan exclaimed.

"Shhh. Someone might hear you," Elaine whispered. "It will be fine."

Elaine climbed up on Tread's back. "Hand me a rope and I'll do her hands while you work on the rest," Tread said.

Lilly picked up a rope and started to hand it to him. Dylan ripped it out of her hand. "I'll tie it. I d-d-don't trust you." He walked around and avoided looking at Tread, which was a little difficult considering how close they were standing to each other. His hands trembled as he tied the knots.

"Make sure it's tight," Tread added.

"I know how to t-t-tie knots, I'm a Marine."

Tread ignored him and waited for the light to pass by. Then he hurried across the field. He jumped up high to the first handrail and heard Elaine gasp. He paused.

Elaine's right hand flew off and almost hit the electric current. The rope flew against the wall, causing a few sparks to fly and a sizzling sound.

She pulled her arm back and clung as tight as she could to Tread.

"Hold on tight. I will try and go slower."

The searchlight halted and came soaring back in their direction.

"They must have seen the sparks," Tread hissed.

He climbed up the wall as quickly as he dared. The light swept back across, barely underneath them. Tread reached the top of the wall just as the light made another sweep, this time at the top.

Lilly shuddered at how close the light came to hitting them, a mere millimeter or two.

Tread was back a minute later, fuming.

"You idiot! I said tight. You almost got us killed," he hissed quietly as Dylan cowered. He looked back at the wall. "You're lucky that enough birds fly into the wall that they probably just assumed that's what made the noise and they didn't send anyone out to investigate."

"I've never had a knot come un-un-tied. I just didn't want to hurt Elaine. I guess the...the...the force of your jumps put more strain than I...I thought."

Tread was about to say more when Lilly interrupted. "We can argue about this later. The important thing is that everyone is OK, so far. So let's finish this." She laid her hand gently on Tread's shoulder and shook her head slightly. Dylan was half-standing, half-crumpled, arms in front of his face like he was about to fend off an attack.

Lilly wondered what they had done to her father over the past seventeen years, and then thought it was probably better she didn't know.

Tread tied Dylan up tight. It took all of his will power not to just keep pulling. But he knew Lilly would not be happy if he really injured him.

"OK. You and Dylan first. I'll follow right behind you."

After Tread and Elaine were almost spotted, Lilly was more nervous the second time. She had faith that Tread had fastened Dylan well, but she still felt a knot in the pit of her stomach.

It took her no time at all to climb up and over. She was glad it had been uneventful.

Tread untied Dylan and they walked over to the bus together.

Dylan ran over and hugged Elaine. "I'm sorry. I thought I tied it t-t-tight enough."

"I'm fine," Elaine said reassuringly.

"So what now?" Lex asked.

Lilly turned to Tread. "You don't happen to have another car stashed out here somewhere?" she asked, hopeful.

"No. Out here I've never needed one. There aren't a lot of people outside the walls. So no need for discretion when traveling."

Lilly looked at her small group. "Looks like we walk."

"Where are we walking to?" Adam asked as he shouldered one of the packs.

"Texas," Lilly said.

Tread glanced over and cocked an eyebrow up.

"It's warm, and has lots of open spaces, small towns, and rivers for water," she explained.

He shrugged. "OK, Texas."

"We're gonna walk all the way to Texas?" Lex asked. "That'll take weeks."

"More like months," Tread said, tapping her gently on the back. "Better get moving."

Lex picked up the other backpack.

"No, give it to me," Lilly insisted. "We've got a ways to go and the pack will just seem heavier the longer we go. It won't bother me at all."

Lilly put her arms through the bag and secured the straps.

Tread watched Lilly, then turned and took the other pack from Adam.

"Always the gentleman," Lilly noted.

"Not always." Tread laughed. "But I'm trying to change." He turned back to address everyone. "Make sure you stay close to Lilly or me," he warned. "Since these walls were built and the roads have pretty much ceased being used," he pointed around them into the trees, "it's gotten wilder out here. Animals that used to be controlled by hunting have been left free to populate. Bears, mountain lions, wolves, coyotes, all roam unchecked out here."

Lilly noticed her mother grip her father's hand. Adam glanced around nervously.

They started walking down the road. Lilly looked back and saw that Lex hadn't moved. She was looking back at Harbor Cove.

"Will my parents be alright?" she wondered aloud.

"Tread said your father's position is a very powerful one. They won't touch him. He's too important. And there is nothing they know."

Lex took one last look back and then headed out.

Lilly was amazed at all the stuff everywhere. There were broken down cars and the roads had weeds sprouting up every so often. There were abandoned gas stations and houses all over the place. She had never been outside the wall before but always wondered what was out here.

She envisioned the other side as more of a jungle, green lush plants so thick it obscured one's vision. This looked sadder. Remnants of a past life left to decay and rot.

After they had walked for a few hours, Lilly called for a break. Her family looked tired.

Elaine, Dylan, Adam and Lex all sat down gratefully on the road. Lex took a pack from Lilly so they could refuel and rehydrate.

"I'll be back in a few minutes," Tread snapped.

"Um, OK. What's your problem?" Lilly asked.

"I'm sorry. I didn't mean it to come out that way. Have you ever seen a movie where a family gets stuck behind a really slow car? It's so annoying and frustrating, and they just can't find a way around it?"

"Yeah," Lilly answered, although she was still confused.

"Well now I know how they feel. I'm surprised there wasn't more road rage portrayed in those movies." He gestured with his hands. "I am going crazy. These people move sooo slowly." He ran his hand through his hair. "I know it's not their fault. I guess you're used to this. Moving so slowly around humans. But I'm not."

Lilly looked at him. "You don't have to stay."

"No, that's not it. I'll stay. I want to stay. I just need to go run. Burn off some energy. Move."

Lilly laughed. "Have fun." She watched him run off into the darkness, jumping, weaving, letting it all go. She had always been forced to keep a human's pace, never giving it a second thought. It had never occurred to her how aggravating it might be for someone not used to the pace. Could Tread really handle months of this, if after a few hours he was ready to pull his hair out?

She looked back toward Harbor Cove. It wasn't visible anymore, but she felt like someone was out there. Like the VAS had somehow followed them and that they were going to jump out at any moment. After scanning the area for the hundredth time and not seeing or hearing anything aside from the noise from her own group, she pushed it aside. It must just be paranoia after all that had happened in the last few months.

After a quick rest, they continued on their way. Tread made it his mission to run ahead and push any debris out of their way. It helped them to move faster and it kept him occupied, a double win in Lilly's mind.

They took another break midday and Lilly was shocked to find Dylan attempting to walk beside her.

"Uhum," Dylan cleared his throat. "So Elaine said you heard our c-c-conversation back in that old building."

Lilly nodded. "I wasn't trying to eavesdrop, I just can't help from hearing things sometimes."

He gave a curt nod. "So, I want to try. Try to get to know you. I w-w-wish I could flip a switch and look at you as my daughter, the way your mom does. But I can't. I look at you and I don't s-s-see my daughter. I'm sorry. I don't think I'll ever see you that way."

Lilly felt like she had been stabbed through the heart. So that was it. This was trying.

"I don't know if it will e-e-ever change, but for now can I just try and get to know you? Start with being a-a-amicable with each other and see where it takes us?"

"Sure," Lilly answered, trying to disguise her disappointment.

"So what do you do for f-f-fun?" Dylan asked.

They talked for the next mile or two. There were some long awkward pauses, but it was a start. It was more conversation than they'd had since she had found out he was alive.

Dylan was stuttering less and wasn't nearly as shaky as before. *Maybe he was starting to feel more comfortable around her, or at least trusted that she wasn't about to sink her teeth into his neck,* Lilly thought.

She was thankful that Tread kept his distance. It was hard enough to have a conversation with her father on her own, but she didn't think he'd even attempt it if Tread were there.

After another few days of hiking, everyone was really beginning to get bored and tired. There wasn't much excitement on the road. Tread had scared off a couple of coyotes, but they'd been so far down the road that Lilly doubted anyone else had even seen them. Tempers were short. They were out of food and running low on water.

"Lilly. We need to stop. We're tired," Adam said.

"And hungry," Lex chimed in.

Lilly looked around her. They were on a huge open expanse of highway. There was nothing around for miles.

"We have to keep going," Lilly insisted.

Tread opened a pack and looked in. They were down to a bottle and a half of water.

"You guys stay here and rest. I'll go scout ahead," Tread volunteered.

"Why don't I come with you?" Lilly offered.

Tread shook his head. "I don't think we should leave them unprotected. It doesn't happen very often, but vampires do travel out here. Plus I don't think they'd do well against a bear or bobcat." Then he dropped his voice down low. "Plus I didn't want to bother you with everything else you had going on but I'm worried about Koyt."

"Why?" Lilly asked.

"When we parted ways at your house, he was beyond furious," Tread explained. "With that much rage, I wouldn't put it past him not to try something stupid."

Lilly nodded. "So you think he might come after us?" Lilly asked. "He really hated my dad."

"I don't know. I don't know anything for sure. This is all just purely speculation on my part. I just think we should take all the precautions we can. I mean, he knows he can't beat me in a fight. Hopefully he cools off and lets this go." Tread looked around. "I'm sure I'm just overreacting."

"Does he know you're a Sunwalker?"

"No, but he assumes I'm older than him since I have run with Vanessa for so long and she is old and well known."

"If he does come, it would be at night. Am I stronger than him?"

"He'd be a fool to try and attack one of us. Vanessa is stronger than you, but that's because she's very old. You really only have to worry about more Sunwalkers. I haven't come across too many vampires as old as Vanessa."

"That you know of," Lilly corrected. "Most don't go blabbing about how old they are right?"

"True," he conceded, "but older vampires seem to carry themselves a little differently. I may not know their exact age, but I can spot a youngster from an elder."

"Unless they've been around so long, they just know how to act like a new vampire. Maybe that's one reason they survive for so long," Lilly hypothesized.

Tread thought about what she had said for a moment. "You may be right." He looked up at the sun. "It'll be dark in another hour; keep your eyes open. I'll be back as soon as I can."

The temperature had been dropping at nights, so they had been making a fire to try to keep the group warm.

Elaine and Dylan dug a pit, and found rocks to encircle it. Lex, Adam, and Lilly scouted for wood. Lilly didn't really need their help, but it made them feel useful.

Once the fire was going, Lex and the others sat close to warm themselves up. Lilly kept her distance.

Lex leaned forward, holding her hands closer to the fire. "OK, so how about a story. Come on guys, we need some entertainment. Something, anything," she suggested.

"Go ahead," Adam invited. "We are all ears."

"Not me," Lex said, aghast at his suggestion. "Dylan, Elaine. I don't think I ever heard the story of how you two met?"

Lilly perked up at this. Her mother had always been so sad when the topic of her father had been broached. So she had tried to steer clear of any questions that might be too painful.

"Oh, there's not much of a story," Elaine said. "We met, fell in love, and got married."

"Pleeeaase," Lex whined.

"Go ahead," Dylan encouraged as he tugged up the collar of his jacket and blew into his hands for warmth. "You'll do a better job than I would."

Lilly noticed how relaxed her father had been since Tread left. He wasn't shaking and she hadn't heard him stutter all night.

"Fine," Elaine relented. She smiled at Dylan as he took her hand.

"Let's see, where to start," she mused. "It was a long time ago. Longer than I care to admit."

"We're not *that* old," Dylan chimed in.

"I was seventeen. I was working at the only grocery store in Newton, a small city just outside of Boston. Most smaller cities had been abandoned, but Newton had a military training center there. I think back before the blast they were called boot camps. The Navy, Army, Air Force, and Marines all used to have separate ones. Now, they all go to the military training center which basically just trains them how to march and answer their superiors." Then she added, "Oh, and make sure each soldier is in tip-top shape." She winked at Dylan.

"So there were always cute soldiers coming into the grocery store. I had gone out with a few, but there was never any spark." She smiled at Dylan and squeezed his hand. "Well, one day this extremely good looking soldier came in. We chatted and I hoped he was going to ask me out, but nothing happened and he left. He came back every day for the next two weeks and we talked whenever he came through my line. Finally after two more weeks, he asked if I wanted to meet him for dinner at a diner the next evening."

"I was so excited. The next day was Saturday and I just had to work a few hours in the morning. But as I was walking home to get ready, I saw him coming out of the theater with a beautiful blonde. She kissed him as they got into a car and drove off.

"I was so mad that I stayed home and never went to the diner. The next day was Sunday and I was off so I stayed home and stewed in my misery." Elaine poked at the fire with a long stick, thinking back.

"On Monday I went back to work and Dylan came back through my line, but this time he didn't buy anything." Elaine paused as a wolf howled in the distance. Lex scooted closed to Adam.

"He asked me what happened, and I told him what I saw, and that if he wanted to date a different girl for breakfast, lunch, and dinner then he could count me out.

"He asked me to meet him after work so he could explain. I refused. He promised if I would meet him for five minutes after work, he'd leave me alone for good." She chuckled. "So I finally relented, mostly to just get him out of the store. My line was getting long and my supervisor was giving me a dirty look.

"After work, I had intended to ditch him, but he was parked right outside the store, in the same car I had seen him get into with the blonde.

"He told me he just wanted to introduce me to his brother and then I could leave. So he opened the door and out stepped Dylan number two."

"The hero of the story," Adam added, raising his eyebrows up and pointing to himself.

"Or the villain. I almost missed out on being with the most amazing woman on earth because she saw you and one of your nurses," Dylan clarified.

"Well after that, we were inseparable. We spent every second together. We just meshed. And after four short weeks we were married before he was deployed for his specialized Marine training in Harbor Cove.

"We were apart for about six months while he had to stay on base with no leave and then, after flying through the ranks, he was assigned a house and I moved in. That's it. The rest is history, as they say."

Dylan leaned forward and kissed Elaine softly.

Lilly was glad to see her parents becoming closer again. She had wondered how'd they'd been with each other before he "died," and now every once in a while it seemed like she was catching glimpses.

Once the story was over, everybody started to wind down and one by one headed off to sleep.

Lilly stayed up, waiting for Tread. The longer he was gone the more nervous she became. What if something had happened to him? What if he found a city and the VAS were there waiting for him? What if he had ended up just like Sage?

The night seemed to drag on slowly. Sometime close to sunrise, Lilly was jolted awake by a rumbling in the distance. She stood up and looked in the direction of the sound, angry at herself for falling asleep.

A truck was coming in the distance. It was still several miles out. Lilly couldn't see much. Anything past a mile started to get a little fuzzy.

Lilly threw dirt on the fire to put it out. "Everybody wake up. Someone is coming this way."

Chaos ensued as everyone started getting up and bumping into each other in the dark.

"Quiet," Lilly hissed. "Try to find a tree or something to hide behind."

Lilly watched as they slowly fumbled around, mostly feeling their way to some type of cover. She wondered how long it would take for their eyes to adjust to the darkness.

Lilly hid behind a fallen Exxon sign and waited. She heard the vehicle slowing down as it approached. Then she heard the door open and close. As the footsteps got closer, Lilly tensed, preparing for an attack.

"Lilly," Tread whispered as he stepped past the sign.

She hit him hard in the arm and he stumbled forward a few steps.

"What the heck? I called out to—"

"You also scared the crap out of us. You said you'd be back soon. It's been hours."

Lex and the others emerged from the trees. They didn't seem as clumsy as before.

"I would have been back sooner, but I didn't think I'd find a truck. It took longer to drive back. I had to keep stopping and clearing out debris, fallen trees, broken down cars, that sort of thing."

"Sorry," Lilly apologized. "I was just worried about you. Do you know where we are?"

"We're about thirty minutes outside of Albany." He turned to the others. "I found a friend of a friend inside the city. I was able to get us more than I bargained for and I was gifted the truck."

Adam walked around and looked into the back of the truck. It was like Christmas. There were a couple of tents, sleeping bags, and some cases of water, along with several bags.

He opened one bag and found it full of shampoo, conditioner, deodorant, toothpaste, toothbrushes and other toiletries. Another bag held more clothes. And several other bags contained food; chips, bread, peanut butter, beef jerky, nuts, trail mix, canned soups, and cans of chili were just a few of the goods he had procured.

He grabbed a bag of chips, opened them and then passed them to Lex. She reached in and stuffed a huge handful in her mouth. More crumbs seemed to fall than actually get in her mouth. He opened another bag and passed it to Elaine and Dylan.

Lilly pulled Tread away from the others and walked behind the truck.

He looked at her, concerned. "What's wrong? You seem a little jumpy."

"I don't know. Probably nothing. It's just…" Lilly sighed. She glanced back behind her, scanning the area. "You remember when you were following me, you know just after we met."

Tread nodded.

"Well I just keep getting that same feeling. But I don't see anything, or hear anything. Do you think the VAS is following us?"

"No, they aren't that quiet," Tread assured her. "Especially out here in the middle of nowhere. I haven't sensed anything out of place. You're probably just still on edge after all that has happened. Let me know if you get that feeling again."

They walked back toward the others. Lilly smiled as she saw Lex dumping the remnants of a bag of chips into her mouth. Adam and Dylan were taking turns throwing grapes into each other's mouths. They were definitely enjoying pacifying their hunger pains.

Tread pulled out a small cooler from the back of the truck.

"This was not easy to come by," he said as he opened it up and revealed two glorious bags of blood.

"You are amazing," she said, reaching up to caress the side of his face.

He leaned forward to kiss her.

"I can't," Lilly said as she pulled back. "I want to. I really do. But we can't move forward until you and my father can make some kind of peace." She put her finger up to his mouth, hushing him. "You should have seen him earlier, when you were gone. He wasn't shaking or stuttering. He was the most relaxed I've seen him. Try to at least convince him that you are never going to hurt him again. I don't know how to be involved with you until there is some headway."

Tread sighed. "Right. So what you're really telling me is never." He looked over at Dylan, who always seemed to be glaring at him. "Seventeen years is too long. I've really tried to come to terms and forgive him for...for Sage," he spoke quietly. "I try to rationalize it away based on how we were both raised, our hatred for each other. But even though I keep telling myself that, I don't even know if I one hundred percent believe it."

She looked to her father who was so full of hatred and back to Tread who seemed to be full of pain. "I know," Lilly said. "I know how impossible it sounds, but if we want to have any hope of ever finding a new home, we have to start with our little group. If we can't make this work, then there really is no hope for this world," Lilly said sadly. "Just try for me."

He turned, facing the back of the truck, setting his hands on the tailgate. He looked out at the seemingly endless road that stretched before them. "I am," he answered. "I hope you know that. I let him go. You don't know how difficult that was. I helped rescue him, and asked *Koyt*, of all people, for help. I've destroyed my relationship with one of my best friends. I am trying," He turned back towards her, his eyes a desperate plea. "I just hope you know that."

Chapter 11
Road Trip

Between the food, supplies, and new mode of transportation, spirits were at an all time high since Tread's return. They were making much better progress with the truck, and for the first time since the wanted posters had appeared, Lilly felt things might actually work out for them. They had escaped, they had found food and a vehicle, now all they needed was a home.

Lex or Adam spent the majority of the time in the front of the cab with Lilly and Tread. Her mom had sat up there for about an hour, but things were still too strained between them for there to be anything but awkward conversation.

Adam seemed to be really warming up to Tread. Dylan, however, declined to ever take a turn in the front seat.

They drove most of the day before the gas ran out.

"So I guess it's back to walking," Lex sighed after climbing down from truck.

Dylan and Elaine climbed down and started digging through one of the grocery bags.

"The next city we'll hit is Nashville. But it's a good six hundred miles from here."

"Where exactly are we?" Adam asked as he opened a bottle of water and took a swig.

"I saw a sign a little ways back that said Winchester. So somewhere in Virginia," Tread answered.

Elaine looked up from the peanut butter sandwich she was making. "Can't you just run there, get us some gas, and come back?"

Tread laughed. "I may be wicked fast, but that trip would still take me a couple of days. Then to try and carry that much gas back..." he trailed off. "Well, it's not very feasible."

"Winchester. That's not too far from D.C., right?" Adam asked. "Can't you just get us some gas from there?"

"You want to send him into the capital of the United States? Where the headquarters of the VAS is stationed? Probably the most secure city in the United States?" Lilly asked, stunned.

Tread smiled. "I think it's a little too risky. I think the most logical decision would be to push the truck. I know it will take *forever*," he said, emphasizing the last word. "But I think it's our best option right now. At least then when we get to the next city we will still have a vehicle."

"So we'll stay here for the night, then pack up and head out at first light," Lilly said.

Dylan volunteered to look for firewood.

Lilly went with him, hoping for a little alone time with her dad.

"So..." Dylan began, struggling for something to say. "Um...Tell me what was it like growing up? Your mom said you went to school? Was it hard to act normal?" He stretched down and picked up a small stick.

"Normal?" Lilly scoffed. "What is your definition of normal?" she asked hotly.

"I didn't mean... I just meant to blend in. Was it hard for you to pretend to be...human? Normal was the wrong word," he apologized, shifting the wood he was collecting under his arm while reaching for another branch with his other.

"It was and it wasn't," she answered.

151

He looked confused, so she continued. "It wasn't physically hard. It was easy for me to slow down. School work was never hard. I was eager to be around kids, make friends. The hard part was more...emotional. Not ever getting to be myself. Lying to everyone around me. I had to dumb myself down. I learned I had to keep myself at the same pace as the other kids, so I didn't draw attention to myself. And I had to make intentional mistakes on my papers." She shook her head. "That was really hard. Intentionally not doing well on my schoolwork. Mom had taught me to do my best. I had to pretend all day long. Mom had to pack me a lunch. I had to pretend to eat, when actually I'd palm the food and slide it into an empty pocket in my bag." She kicked at a small rock on the ground and it went soaring across the sky. She glanced up at Dylan and paused. "Mom made me practice at the table. I had to be so quick that she didn't notice and that I looked normal. It helped that most people were too busy talking or eating their own lunches to really pay attention to what I was doing," Lilly looked back at camp. "But even though it was tough, and I had to make sacrifices, it was worth it. If I hadn't gone to school, I'd have never met Lex."

"So did you ever have any close calls at school? Did anyone find out about you?" he asked curiously.

"Not really. We had a few problems that came up. But we figured them out. Like when Mom's blood supplier went on a trip and got snowed in. So we didn't get our order on time." Lilly smiled remembering back. "Mom was getting pretty worried. She called Uncle Adam, wondering if he could get some from the hospital. He couldn't. It's all too secure."

"So what did you do?" Dylan asked anxiously.

"Uncle Adam came over. Calmed Mom down, and drew some of his and her blood. It was enough to last till Mom's supplier got back two weeks later."

He accidently dropped a few pieces of firewood. "You drank your mom's blood?" he asked, looking a little green, as he bent over struggling to hold his pile together.

She shrugged. "Yeah, it wasn't a big deal. She was fine. It's not like I sunk my fangs into her."

152

Dylan turned his head and started staring very intently at a rock by his feet.

"Lilly, do you want me to be a father to you?" he asked, catching her off guard.

"I'm not really sure how to answer that," she answered truthfully. "I mean growing up, I would have given anything to have you back. But now, I'm not a little kid anymore. I don't need a father in the same sense. I'm glad Mom's happy. I'd like to have a relationship with you. But I'm not stupid either. I know a lot has happened. I know nothing is simple."

"Send Tread away," he said. "Send him away and give us a real chance." He looked at her desperately.

Lilly glanced back towards camp, watching Tread attempt to show Lex and Adam how to put up the tents. "I can't do that." She stopped, trying to figure out the right words to say. "I know what he did to you was horrible." She glanced down at the ground avoiding eye contact. "But what you did to him was horrible too. You murdered his sister. If he were just some guy, I'd do it. I'd send him away. But he's not. I love him." She slowly looked back up until her eyes locked with her father's.

"How can you love someone capable of this?" Dylan yelled, pointing to the scars on his face and arm. Then he took his shirt off and Lilly turned away, horrified.

He was covered in scars and burn marks. His back was crisscrossed in what appeared to be lash marks.

"Seventeen years of this," Dylan sobbed. "And you want what? For me to forgive him?" Dylan scoffed. "That will never happen. He's the reason I didn't get to be a father to you. And you are choosing him over me?" He shook his head, frustrated.

"It's not that simple," she said, trying to look anywhere but directly at him. Tread had tried to tell her he'd been a monster, but actually seeing what he'd done, that was harder to rationalize away. "I have seen him change, he is trying to become a better person. We have to stop this. Don't you see it will never end? The hatred keeps building. He's trying to get past it. He did let you go."

Dylan just balked.

153

"I'm not trying to erase what you went through. But he is trying to find some way for, well, if not acceptance, then at least tolerance. I'm not so naive as to think you'll come to think of him as a son, or even a part of the family. But he came for you and Mom. If it weren't for him we'd all be dead."

"Did you see what they did?" Dylan gasped. "Did you see the pure savagery of what they are?"

"I'm not going to pretend I wasn't horrified. But that wasn't him. And they were trying to kill Mom, me, Adam, and probably you."

"I just don't see how there can be anything real between us with him here," he said, throwing his hands up in exasperation.

"He's at least making an effort. I know there isn't really anything he can do to make amends for what he did. But he saved me. He saved you. He is here trying to help. What you did to him was horrible too and I don't see you trying at all," Lilly sighed. "Maybe I am a fool. But I'm hoping that won't always be the case." She took the stack of firewood Dylan had collected and headed back towards camp.

Throughout the evening, Lilly noticed Tread keeping his distance. Everyone ate and sat around the fire talking, but Tread sat on the hood of the truck looking out across the horizon.

After Lilly said goodnight and the others turned in, she walked over to the truck.

"You've been quiet all evening," she noted. "Is something wrong?"

He looked at her, and Lilly could see the pain behind his eyes.

"I saw Dylan take off his shirt earlier," he stated, turning away from her. His legs hung down from the truck, swaying slightly as he picked away at a spot of chipped paint. "I figured I was the last person you'd want to be around after that." He stopped picking at the paint and looked up at her sadly. "And don't say you forgive me. How can anyone be forgiven after that?" he looked up at the stars and sighed.

"I'm not going to try and pretend that it wasn't horrendous. I know you tried to tell me, but seeing it... well, there aren't really words. But, to me at least, that's in the past."

Tread jumped down from the hood. "Lil, how can you say that? How can you say that doesn't change anything? I did that," he said, looking towards Elaine and Dylan's tent.

"Hatred did that and I'm sure Koyt helped," Lilly said. "Hatred that you are trying to let go of. There's the Tread of the past, and there's the Tread of the present. I fell in love with the Tread of the present. You've changed. And although it's hard for me to see some of the things you once did, to wrap my head around how you could ever have been that..."

"Monster," Tread supplied.

The wind gusted, whipping Lilly's hair in a hundred directions. "I know that's not who you are now," she said as she tried to straighten her hair. "If my mom had left me for dead, and I grew up with the entire human race trying to kill me, I probably would have turned out the same way."

Tread pushed a strand of hair she had missed out of her face gently with his hand.

"Never. You could never have been like that."

Lilly leaned forward and kissed him. She closed her eyes and pressed her lips softly to his. She had been holding back from too much her whole life. Suppressing who she was, what she could do. And she was tired of doing that with her feelings. She was making the decision to be happy. To follow her heart. Life was probably always going to be messy. She had to start being proactive and take the happy moments when she could get them.

She pulled gently on his bottom lip, and just let herself go. She pulled him more urgently. Her hand slipped behind his head pressing him closer. His lips were soft and tender, but she could feel his desire despite their gentleness.

Tread pulled back. "Are you sure?" he asked. "I haven't made peace with—"

"Yes." She yanked him closer. "Now shut up and kiss me."

155

He picked her up and sat her down on the hood of the truck. She wrapped her arms around him as he kissed her.

She wished she could feel like this all the time. Safe, ecstatic, feeling like nothing else mattered.

Tread halted abruptly.

"What's wrong?" Lilly asked.

"Nothing. I just think we should slow down." He glanced back at the tent. "I am glad you've made a decision about us, but I know you still want to connect with your father, and I'm no expert, but in my fifty-seven years, I haven't come across one father that was thrilled to come out and find his daughter making out with some guy."

Lilly sighed. "Always the gentleman." She slid off the truck, turned, and started walking away. She glanced back over her shoulder. "I'm not sure that's always a good thing," she said, slightly disappointed.

"Where are you going?" he whispered. "I didn't say you had to leave."

"Some of us still need sleep," Lilly smirked.

Tread shook his head as she walked away. "Women," he huffed. He heard Lilly stifle a giggle as she crawled into Lex's tent.

When the next morning rolled around, Lilly was surprised to find she wasn't the first one up. As she climbed out of her tent she saw her mom talking with Tread.

"I appreciate that," her mom was saying as she turned and walked back to the fire pit with a bundle of sticks in her arms.

She smiled at Lilly when she noticed Lilly looking at her.

Lilly walked over to her mother. "What was that about?" she asked, all the while following Tread with her eyes. He just smiled and raised his eyebrows in a knowing expression.

Her mother threw her bundle down. She smiled. "I know you really like him honey. I'm starting to understand a little more." She looked back at her and Dylan's tent. "A lot has happened. I know Tread did horrible things. A year ago, I probably would have tried to kill him. I would never have tried to understand him." She was silent for a moment. "I know I would take things back, do some things differently if I could," she said, looking meaningfully at her daughter. "I guess now I just understand more how our emotions can make us do crazy things."

"So you're really going to try with him?" Lilly asked suspiciously. She wanted to believe her mother but it was hard to just let go of all that had happened and trust her. She had only been held prisoner for three months and it was so difficult to even speak civilly with her mother. *Maybe it was asking for the impossible for her father and Tread to set aside their issues. How could she even begin to expect them to do something she still wasn't able to do? And her experience was so minimal compared to what Dylan and Tread had gone through,* she thought suddenly.

"We talked. Cleared the air so to speak." She hesitantly put her hand on Lilly's shoulder, waiting for her to shrink back. "I want you to be happy. I can see that he makes you happy. He adds something to your life that I can't give you."

"Thanks," Lilly said. She wasn't sure if she believed what her mom was saying, but she wanted to. Only time would tell.

Elaine went back to her tent, emerging a few minutes later with Dylan. They started packing up the tent and cleaning up their small camp.

Lilly figured it was time to wake up Adam and Lex too. A little over an hour later, all the humans in the group had packed up and had eaten breakfast.

Tread and Lilly loaded up the truck bed with the tents and bags as the others began loading up into the cab.

After a short discussion, it was decided that Adam would steer the truck while Tread pushed. Lilly would shift debris to the sides of the road, clearing a path for the truck.

It was slow going. If there had been three vampires in their small group, they would have made much better time. They needed one of them to push and one of them to clear the road, leaving them no other option but to have a human steer the truck.

Adam tried the best he could but he just didn't have the reflexes of a vampire. If Tread pushed too fast, Adam couldn't keep the truck on the road. So the pace was slow.

It was still faster than walking. They all hoped fuel would be easy to come by when they finally arrived in Nashville.

The weather was getting cooler, so it helped that the truck could keep out the wind and some of the cold. Lilly noticed that Tread didn't seem as agitated about the pace as he had been before. Pushing must have been enough of a distraction.

They had only been traveling for a few hours when they spotted a bridge.

"Please let there be a creek or river up ahead," Lex wished. "I would love to scrub some of this grime off me. Walking for days with no shower is not my idea of a good time."

"Tell me about it. I never thought I could miss my bathtub so much," Elaine agreed.

As they approached the bridge, they could see a small creek below them. It stretched out far in both directions, but with the lack of rain in the area, it wasn't too deep. But the water was clear, and hopefully, it would be enough to clean some of the dirt off them.

Adam climbed down out of the truck and stretched his arms up over his head. Then he arched his back and took a few steps, stretching his legs. He glanced around the bridge. "We should probably get a fire going first," he suggested, pointing up a small incline to a flat, open area carved out of the forest. "The water will be cold and we will want something to warm us up."

Elaine tugged at her shirt. It was fairly clean, thanks mostly to Tread's supply run the previous day, but even so it smelled. No matter how clean the clothes were, when you hadn't bathed in over a week, the stench would seep through. "Why don't you boys take care of the fire while we bathe?" Elaine suggested.

"Of course, ladies first," Dylan said as he pulled a tent out of the back of the truck.

"And no peeking," Lex added.

Lilly found a couple bars of soap and the girls headed down to the creek. They stripped down to their undergarments and started scrubbing from head to toe. Lilly finished in a few seconds.

"We should probably try and wash our clothes while we have water. Who knows when we'll pass another lake or river," Lilly suggested.

Lex was scrubbing as fast as she could. "Y-y-yeah. S-s-sure," she agreed through chattered teeth.

The water must have been pretty cold. Along with the stuttering, Lilly noticed a nice blue tint forming around Elaine's and Lex's lips.

Once the girls were done and had put on fresh clothes, they went to search out the fire. Lex and Elaine rushed to warm themselves up. They were shaking pretty badly. Lex reached her hands out, warming them against the heat of the fire. A pot of soup hung over the flames. Elaine started to pick up a bowl and a ladle when she heard Adam.

"The soup should be hot soon," he called back as the men headed down to the creek.

Elaine set the bowl down and huddled close to Lex beside the fire. Lilly found a sleeping bag, unzipped it and laid it over their shoulders.

Dylan put his foot in the water. "Dang!" he said, gritting his teeth as he stepped into the creek with his other foot. "This is freezing."

Tread tossed his shirt onto the bank of the creek and stripped down to his boxers. He followed Dylan into the creek and started lathering himself up.

"Must be nice to never feel anything," Dylan muttered.

Adam came down into the creek, cringing with each step.

"I may not be able to feel the cold, but I still have feelings," Tread admitted.

"Sure. Whatever."

"Listen," Tread began. "I've been trying to figure out how to say this. Waiting for the right time. But I don't think that's ever gonna happen. I just...I wanted..." Tread sighed and ran a hand through his now wet, soapy hair. He looked at his hand covered in suds and shook it off.

"Right time for w-w-what? What could you possibly have to say to me?" Dylan barked, as he tried not to back down.

Tread straightened up and looked squarely at Dylan. "I'm sorry," he apologized. "I know I can't undo the things I did to you, but I'm sorry."

Dylan looked at him, awestruck. He stood there for a moment not moving.

He laughed. "You're sorry. Ha! That's hilarious. Is this some kind of n-n-new game you've come up with?" He turned, facing his bare back towards Tread and then looked over his shoulder as best as he was able. "That's the best you've got. You're sorry." He scoffed.

Tread shook his head. "I am sorry. I don't expect your forgiveness—"

"I'd hope not," Dylan said, baffled. "Forgive y-y-... Oh, I get it n-n-now," he said, realization showing on his face.

Tread looked confused. "Get what?"

Dylan gestured back to the girls and the fire. "This is all so...some kind of act you're putting on for L-l-lilly. Some new sort of twisted revenge. You really are s-s-sick."

"What?" Tread asked, clearly shocked. "No. I'm doing this for me. Lilly helped me to see that revenge isn't the answer. It can't bring my sister back. I am doing this for me because I don't want to be that man."

"Man?" Dylan scoffed. "You're a m-m-monster. Leave Lilly out of this. Stay away from h-h-her," he demanded.

"I can't. I am in love with her," Tread explained in a calm, clear voice.

"STAY AWAY FROM MY DAUGHTER!" Dylan screamed.

"Knock it off already," Adam said.

"RAAWWRR!"

Dylan fell backward into the creek. Tread turned to see a huge black bear standing up on his hind paws, roaring just a few paces behind Adam. He had been so caught up in his heated argument-slash-apology with Dylan that he hadn't noticed the bear approach. And he'd given Lilly a hard time about not having any instincts.

The bear dropped down on all fours and stared directly at Adam, who had frozen in fear. The bear lifted one of his giant paws and swiped it at Adam.

Tread lunged forward and pushed the bear a few feet away.

The bear swiped a paw across Tread's chest, sounding more like it was hitting solid rock than flesh.

Tread leaned forward, fangs extended and a loud growl rippled through his teeth.

The bear hesitated for a moment, then turned and ran back up the creek.

Tread turned back to Adam. "Are you alright?"

"Yeah," he mumbled. He walked over and placed his hand on Tread's chest as if looking for something.

"What are you doing?" Tread asked uncomfortably.

"I mean, I've heard you're pretty much invincible. But hearing and seeing are two very different things," he said, still in awe. "I don't see a scratch on you."

"OK. Now that you see I'm fine," Tread said, gently removing Adam's hands off his chest, "you're kind of giving me the creeps."

Adam stepped back. "Sorry. Doctor, remember. Miraculous healing is kind of hard to believe."

They finished cleaning up and then began to walk back to the fire. Tread held back, staring at the creek.

He walked over to where he had first spotted the bear. He thought it was odd to see a bear this late in the year. They all should have been hibernating by now. Tread scanned the area and noticed that every few feet leading away from the woods it looked like the ground had been disturbed.

Upon further investigation, he found a small amount of a dark sticky substance at a disturbed area of ground closest to the creek. Tread rubbed his finger in the substance and smelled it. *Sap,* he thought.

He looked around. Although there were a few trees scattered along the creek bed, there were none close to this area. *How did the sap end up here?* he wondered.

Tread backtracked the bear's path until he was completely submerged in the woods. He paused and listened, scanning the area intently. After several minutes of hearing nothing irregular, Tread shrugged to himself and returned to camp.

When he arrived, the men were ladling soup into bowls as the girls were just finishing up.

Lilly smiled at him as he approached. She stood up and picked up one of the bags by her feet. "I'm gonna run down to the creek and wash our dirty clothes," she said once Adam and Dylan had gotten settled. Dylan was blowing gently on a spoonful of soup.

"I'll come with you," Tread offered, picking up a bag of dirty laundry.

"Maybe one of you should stay in case the bear comes back," Adam suggested in between mouthfuls of food.

Elaine snapped her finger, pointing at Lex. "See, I told you I heard a bear."

"Here." Lilly reached for the bag of laundry. "You stay here and protect everyone. I'll go wash the clothes."

"No I'll go," Tread offered.

She touched him gently on the shoulder. "It's fine. I'll be back in a jiffy," Lilly insisted.

"I'll come too," Lex offered, setting her mug of hot water down, and scampering down to where Lilly and Tread were. "I mean you can fight off a bear too, right?" she asked with a nervous laugh.

Tread glanced up. There were big, dark clouds overhead. "Don't be too long. It's getting darker earlier and it looks like a storm is rolling in."

"Got it," Lilly winked, as she looked up at the sky.

When they got to the creek Lilly made Lex sit on the bank, where she'd stay dry and warm, while Lilly started scrubbing clothes.

"That must be sooo cool," Lex said. "I can barely tell you are moving, but the pile of washed clothes keeps getting larger."

Lilly set the soap on a rock and turned to reach inside the bag of dirty clothes. "It is pretty awesome." She felt a breeze behind her and remembered Tread had mentioned a storm. She turned back for the soap and it was gone.

"Lex, do you see the soap?" Lilly asked.

Lex stood up on the bank to get a better view. "No, sorry, must have fallen into the creek."

Lilly hadn't heard it fall in. She knew she set it on the rock. It hadn't just gotten up and walked off on its own. She looked down and felt around the rock. The water was clear and the current didn't seem that strong, but there was no sign of the soap.

She pulled out another bar of soap and finished washing the clothes, assuming like Lex had suggested that the bar of soap had fallen in the creek and washed away.

As they walked back up to their camp, Lilly stopped and looked back at the creek. Everything was quiet except for the soft flow of the water running down stream and the murmur of conversation coming from their camp.

Lex noticed Lilly wasn't following her, and paused. "What is it?" she asked. "Forget something?"

Lilly shook her head. "Guess I'm just freaked out a little by the thought of a bear," she joked, turning back, her arms full of the wet, freshly laundered clothing.

"Why? Bears can't hurt you right?"

"So I've been told. But I've never put it to the test before," Lilly said.

"Let's hope you don't have to," Lex said as she looked around nervously.

When they got back to camp they hung the clothes over rocks and tree branches as best as they could. The wind started to pick up and the temperature began to drop.

163

"Guess we'd better call it an early night," Adam called through the wind.

"Night," Lex said as she crawled into the tent.

Lilly waited until her parents had gone into their tent before turning to say good night to Tread.

"Are you sure you never sleep?" she asked half-jokingly as she wrapped her arms around him. "I still can't wrap my head around that."

"Give it a few weeks after you turn nineteen and you'll wonder why you ever needed sleep." He leaned down and kissed her softly.

A huge clap of thunder crackled overhead.

"Lilly, get in here!" Lex called as she unzipped the tent and peeked out. "You know how thunderstorms freak me out. Oops, sorry," she added after noticing Lilly and Tread in an embrace.

Lilly rolled her eyes. "I better get in there; best friend duty is calling my name." She kissed Tread once more and then scampered off into the tent.

*   *   *   *   *   *   *   *   *   *

Each passing day seemed longer and longer. All they did was travel, sleep, and repeat. It was slow moving, pushing the truck. Hopefully they'd be able to get more gas in Nashville, or all this work would have been in vain. By the seventh day, supplies were dwindling and Tread and Lilly were getting hungry.

The last sign they'd seen about a day back was for some city called Pulaski. Tread said they were still in Virginia.

Lex sat down on a rock and stretched her legs and arms. She was tired of riding in the truck. She wished they could all just walk for a while, but that would just slow them down even more.

Lilly overheard Adam and Dylan grumbling about how there were only some pieces of beef jerky and granola bars left to eat.

Tread motioned Lilly over to the side. "I think I'm gonna have to try and go on ahead to Nashville and see what I can find. They are almost out of food and it's been over a week since we fed, and it wasn't like we had a lot."

"How long do you think you'll be?"

"At least a day there and a day back. Maybe longer. I don't usually spread my feedings out so far."

"OK. Try to bring back a little gas. Anything you could carry would be better than nothing," she requested hopefully. "And a cooler full of blood bags would be nice," she added, half joking.

"Sure, and I'll have Santa drop it here for us while I'm at it," Tread answered sarcastically.

"Let me just fill them in on the plan." Lilly walked back over to the group. "Tread's going to go on ahead and see if he can bring back some more food. I know we're all getting hungry and that should make the trip easier even if we have to keep pushing the truck."

"I feel so stupid. When Tread got the truck, that's the last time you ate, right?" Elaine asked.

"Yes," she nodded. "So we will all feel better when he gets back."

"Here, take some," Elaine said, stretching her arm out.

"What are you doing?" Dylan asked, horrified.

"Our daughter needs to eat. It's been too long."

Lilly pushed her mother's arm out of her face. "Mom, I'm not going to drink from your arm. I'm fine. I can wait till Tread gets back."

"No," Elaine said firmly. "You told me you were in pain when your feeding schedule was altered. Lilly, I can't undo what I did, but I can make sure you don't go hungry. Please," she pleaded.

The more she realized how close she was to the possibility of a meal, the more her hunger seemed to awaken. She could hear the blood pulsating through her mother's veins, making her want it even more.

"No," Lilly said again, shaking her head. "Besides I am not going to eat until Tread can."

"We are doing this," Elaine ordered. "We can go into the tent for more..." She noticed the look on Dylan's face, and didn't think he could handle watching. "...privacy."

"You can have some of my blood," Lex said to Tread.

Lilly stepped in front of Lex. "That's not what I meant," she insisted.

"I know. But seriously Lilly. We wouldn't survive without you guys, and if we want to make sure he makes it back..."

"Oh I'll make it back. I don't need your blood for that, I am not that hungry," Tread assured them.

Lex cocked her head around Lilly so she could look at Tread directly. "And would you be just as fast without my blood?" Lex asked. "Cause I am hungry and I am sick of beef jerky."

Tread didn't answer.

"Come on. I've given blood before, I am sure it can't be much different." Elaine pulled Lilly after her.

"Your turn Tread. At least this time I'm offering," Lex said, tapping him on his arm.

Tread cracked a smile and followed her into another tent.

A few minutes later Lilly and Elaine came out of the tent. Elaine had a small cloth pressed to her wrist.

A minute later, Tread came out of another tent.

"Where is Lex?" Dylan demanded. "If you hurt her..." he said, taking a few steps forward.

Tread glared at him and then turned back toward Lilly, Elaine, and Adam, who were checking Elaine's wrist to see if the bleeding had ceased. "She said she felt a little dizzy after seeing a few drops of blood. She just wanted a minute to lie down."

Adam had finished cleaning Elaine's puncture marks. "I'll go check on her," he offered.

"I'd better get going," Tread said. "I'll be back as soon as I can." He leaned forward and kissed Lilly on the cheek. "Keep your eyes open," he whispered.

He turned and disappeared off into the distance.

Chapter 12
Sabotage

The next morning, things got worse. Dylan came out of the tent and started looking for the bag with the water bottles.

"Hey, where's the water?" he asked as he glanced around the side of his tent.

Lex shrugged. She looked around and then saw the backpacks leaning against Adam's tent. "Over there," she pointed.

Dylan stretched and then walked over to the bags. He leaned down and unzipped the pack. He reached inside and started tossing bottles onto the ground.

"Hey, what the heck?" he snapped. "Who drank all the water? We had seven bottles last night and now there are only three."

He looked around accusingly.

Lex looked up from tying her shoe. "Wasn't me," she insisted.

"Well it wasn't Elaine or me."

Dylan yelled into Adam's tent. "Adam, get out here!" he barked.

Adam slowly unzipped the tent, yawning as he stepped out.

"What's with all the shouting?" he asked, rubbing the sleep out of his eyes. "Aren't we staying here till Tread gets back? I didn't think we needed to get up so early today."

Dylan threw a bottle at Adam.

Adam reached out and caught it. "What do I want an empty bottle for?" he asked.

Dylan took a few steps forward, glaring at his brother. "There are four of us here who need water. Don't you think drinking four bottles last night was a little excessive, not to mention selfish?" he asked as he chunked another one at Adam's head.

Adam ducked and then took a step back and pointed at himself. "I didn't drink these," he insisted. "I've been asleep this whole time." He looked around, hoping he persuaded the others of his innocence.

Elaine came out of their tent and Dylan filled her in on the missing water.

"Well, one of them is lying," Dylan accused.

Adam stepped towards Dylan. "Lying? Are you serious?" he asked in disbelief. "How dare you call me a liar. After all I've done for you!" He spat angrily, shoving his brother back.

"Adam," Elaine said, cautioning him to stop.

He looked to her and shook his head. "No. He's thought about no one but himself since he reappeared." Adam turned back to his twin. "I've thought of no one but you for the past twelve years. And you have the nerve to accuse me of being selfish."

Elaine walked over and placed her hand gently on Adam's arm. "Adam, now's not the time," she said consolingly. "He's been through too much. Just let it go." She said looking pleadingly with her eyes.

Dylan balked. "Is there something going on between you two?" he asked astonished, glaring at Elaine's hand on Adam.

Elaine turned back, surprised. "No—" she began.

"Yes," Adam said, gently pushing her to the side. "We've become a family. I put my life on hold to be there for your daughter, for your wife. I did everything for you."

168

"You have an affair with my wife and it's for me?" Dylan scoffed.

Adam sighed. "I never had an affair with Elaine. She's my sister. That's all she's ever been. I've been there for her as a friend, as a family member. I tried to be there for Lilly as a father since you weren't here. I thought of them and not myself. He pointed to Lilly and Elaine. Do you think I don't want a family of my own? I gave that up. For *you*."

"What do you mean?" Lilly asked, surprised at her uncle's revelation.

He stepped back. "Lilly, I love you. I wouldn't go back and change a thing. You have brought me so much joy. And it was always my choice," he began. "But this, a family of my own," he said pointing to her and Elaine, "it was never going to happen for me. I couldn't risk it. So yeah, I've dated. But anytime I started having feelings for someone, I'd end it."

"But why?" Lilly asked.

"Because he didn't want them finding out about you," Elaine answered, just realizing the truth for herself.

"And for you. They would have killed you too," Adam said. "And for you, you selfish jerk," Adam said, only half joking.

"I'm sorry, Adam. I never realized," Elaine began.

"Me too," Lilly said as she began to appreciate her uncle on so many more levels.

Dylan stood there silently, then turned and walked back into his tent.

"I'm not making excuses for him, but none of us can understand what he's been through," Elaine sighed.

"You're right. I shouldn't have said anything. I am glad he's alive and back. It's just hard to see him so bitter and angry. He's so different."

Elaine nodded. "I know. Just looking at the physical differences is hard enough. To know what he should look like," she said, smiling at Adam. "I can still see the family resemblance, but no stranger would guess that you two are identical twins." She turned and entered her and Dylan's tent.

169

Lilly could hear them talking quietly but she tried to distract herself from listening.

She walked over and picked up the pack. "There are three left," she said, looking at Lex and Adam. "You guys are just going to have to ration it. I'll hold onto the bag."

"Lilly, we passed that small creek yesterday. Can't you just zip down and fill them back up?"

Lilly shook her head. "Sorry Lex. I don't feel good about leaving you guys here alone. Something doesn't feel right. I agree with Dylan, it seems odd that four are empty, and the bag..." she said, feeling the bottom, "is dry." She walked over to where the bag had been sitting and felt the dirt. "And the ground is dry too. You'd think if they had leaked out there would be some remnant of moisture," she explained as she stood up and brushed her hand against her pant leg.

Lilly turned around, looking out over the vast landscape. There were too many trees to see much, even with her incredible vision. She looked around in a circle trying to come up with something that made sense, but she couldn't.

"So, Tread thought he'd be back in two days, maybe a little more," Lilly recounted. "So we should plan on three to be safe. That's one bottle a day between the four of you."

Lex sighed as she looked down the road. "Maybe we should keep going instead of waiting here. Who knows, maybe there is a river or stream close by."

Adam cleared his throat. "Just remember if we keep going we're going to be more thirsty and we may not find anything."

"I say we keep going," Dylan agreed as he stepped out of his tent with Elaine following. He gave an apologetic look to his brother. Adam nodded back. "I'd rather feel like I'm doing something than nothing. Do you think you can clear the debris for a hundred feet or so and then push the truck?" He looked at Lilly. "I think if we keep moving, it might be more of a distraction than sitting here thinking about how thirsty we are."

"Also, if we keep going, we'll be that much closer for Tread to find us," Elaine added.

Lilly looked down the road. There were several abandoned vehicles on the road along with a few fallen trees, and that was just what she could see before the road curved. "Sure. It will definitely be slower going, but if you guys are up for it, I am too."

"OK, let's pack up," Dylan ordered.

Lilly noticed Dylan was becoming more and more confident, albeit a jerk sometimes. She was glad to see him becoming more like the self-assured soldier her mother had always described.

With Tread gone, it was up to Lilly to do all the heavy lifting. She loaded up the truck, then started clearing the road while her family piled in the cab. Adam volunteered to steer again, and sat behind the wheel. Lex sat next to him in the front, while Dylan and Elaine climbed into the back.

As Lilly pushed them forward she kept getting a strange feeling. She would look around but never saw anything out of the ordinary, just thick forests on both sides of the freeway, mingled with the occasional abandoned car or the ruins of the occasional fast food establishment or gas station. She thought back to when they were washing the clothes in the creek. She had gotten the same feeling, but just dismissed it.

What if the soap really hadn't fallen in the creek? What if it had been swiped? And then someone had emptied the water out of the bottles. But then why not empty them all? Was someone or something messing with them?

If it were a vampire, why dump the water and not kill anyone? Even with her super speed, a vampire could have easily picked at least one of them off before disappearing back into the night.

It sounded crazy as Lilly thought it all out in her head, but then it also seemed like the only likely option.

By the time they rested for the night, they were exhausted and disheartened. There had been no sign of water throughout the day, and Lilly could tell it was taking a toll on her family.

A cold front was blowing in from the north, dropping the temperature rapidly. They had decided to stop at an abandoned gas station. The ceiling was caving in, and some of the windows were broken, but the walls seemed sturdy and offered some breakage from the gusting winds.

Lilly stepped inside and pushed some old shelving out of the way to make room for the tents. It smelled old and moldy, but Lex had said it was definitely warmer than camping outside.

They built a fire inside underneath an area where the ceiling had fallen in to try to add some extra warmth to their camp.

The night was cold and clear. They could see millions of stars up in the sky. When they finally called it a night, snow had begun to fall gently. They set out the couple of small pots they had in hopes of catching some of the snow and melting it later.

Lilly listened as one by one her uncle, mother, father, and best friend drifted off to sleep. She could hear their heartbeats and breathing slow to a nice, steady pace. She was tired too, but had vowed not to fall asleep. Something was happening. She had made herself a promise to figure it out.

A few hours later, Lilly was startled awake by a noise. She listened for a moment, trying to determine where the sound was coming from, angry with herself for drifting off. It sounded like a tent being unzipped. She waited. Maybe someone just needed to use the bathroom. She waited for the sound of footsteps but none came. Then she heard a quiet gasp.

She tore through her tent, not even bothering to unzip it. She glanced quickly between the two tents and saw that Adam's was partially unzipped. In the background, Lex was shouting, wanting to know what was going on as the tent collapsed down around her.

Lilly ran into Adam's tent and momentarily froze. There was a vampire drinking. His fangs were stuck deep into her uncle's neck. Adam was slumped down.

Lilly flew at the blond-headed vampire, missing by a mere inch or two. He released his grasp on Adam and tried to escape through the tent door. He was halfway out when Lilly gripped him by the leg, tumbling out of the tent with him onto the floor of the gas station.

They wrestled for a second, but he was much weaker than she. She pinned him underneath her after a brief struggle on his part.

He growled and tried to escape but it was a fruitless effort.

Lex, Dylan, and Elaine were all out of their tents by now.

"Check on Adam!" Lilly yelled to no one in particular.

Dylan and Elaine fumbled trying to find the opening to the now collapsed tent.

Elaine finally found the opening. Her fingers were shaking and it took her a minute to unzip it all the way. Then Dylan helped lift the tent up so Elaine could crawl in and check on Adam.

"I need a rag. Something...a shirt...anything. There's so much blood," Elaine sobbed. "Adam, Adam can you hear me?" she said quietly.

Lex turned to her tent. It was lying in tatters. She reached around frantically and found a pair of socks that had been folded together. She ran them over to Elaine.

"I can feel a pulse," Elaine called out.

A few minutes later Lex climbed back out of the tent. "I think we stopped the bleeding." She shrugged. "I don't know what else we can do."

Lilly nodded to Lex, slightly relieved for the moment, still holding the intruder in place. "What are you doing here? Who are you?" she demanded as she glared down at this young vampire. He didn't look more than fourteen or fifteen.

"What are you waiting for?" Dylan shouted angrily. "Kill him."

Lilly was taken aback. "What?" she asked, dumbfounded. "He's just a kid," she explained as she looked down at the blond-haired boy beneath her.

Dylan yelled again. "Kill him. For all we know he may have just killed Adam."

Lilly looked down at this adolescent. He looked so weak and helpless. Could she really kill him? He was just trying to feed himself. Maybe he didn't know there were other options.

173

Lilly locked eyes with him. "Look, I'm going to let you get up. Then I want you to leave and never come back. If you come back," Lilly warned, "things won't end well for you. Do you understand?"

The boy glanced around nervously. "I got it," he answered.

Lilly released him slowly.

"What are you doing?" Dylan screamed.

"Lilly, are you sure about this?" Lex said as she backed up into the corner.

The kid glanced to the door and then turned and grabbed Dylan, putting him in a chokehold.

"What?" Lilly asked, taken aback. "I just gave you the chance to leave. Let him go. I promise I won't hurt you."

"If you move I will break his neck," the vampire said. "I'm hungry. There's not a lot to eat out here and you interrupted my meal."

"If you kill him, I will kill you," Lilly promised.

"Here's what's going to happen," the kid sneered. "You're going to walk toward me, as I walk towards the door. I'm going to take a quick drink and then I'll leave him, and you won't see me again." He pulled Dylan closer towards him.

Lilly heard her father gasp.

"That's not going to happen," Lilly assured him.

"Ahhh!" Lex yelled as she ran toward the vampire with a stick in her hand.

The boy loosened his grasp on Dylan as he turned towards Lex. That was all Lilly needed; she grabbed him and put him in a similar chokehold. She wasn't sure what to do with him now. They couldn't tie him up. She couldn't trust him to leave and never come back. She tightened her grip as he continued to struggle. He became frantic, clawing at her. Lilly tightened even more. She was so angry. After she tried to show him kindness, he repaid her by going after her father. She tightened even more and he finally started to calm down.

At the same time, Lilly heard a ripping sound and then the vampire slumped to the floor. Lilly looked down and was horrified to see his body on the floor while she was still holding his head.

She felt disgusted. Dropping the head she ran outside, and kept running. She stopped after what seemed like a few moments. She looked around in a panic, surrounded by nothing but trees. She stopped and crumpled to the ground. She wrapped her hands around her knees and rocked back and forth. She had just murdered someone. It hadn't been intentional. She didn't realize how much stronger she was than him. That's why he had become so frantic. The pressure of the chokehold had been killing him.

She felt sick inside. Sick because of how easy it had been. Sick that because of her he was nothing, gone forever. She really was a monster. What was the difference between him and her? They both killed.

Lilly didn't know how long she stayed out there in the forest, lost in thought. She was jarred back to the present when she heard Lex calling her name.

It was faint, but clear. She had traveled into the woods further than she had imagined.

"Lilly...Lilly!" she called out. "Adam's awake! He woke up. Lilly!"

Lilly emerged through the trees, gave a meek smile to her friend, and walked back inside.

They had moved Adam into her parent's tent, as it was the only one still in one piece. He was sitting propped up in a corner, and Elaine was trying to get him to drink.

"I'm fine. I've had enough," he was saying. "We need to save the water."

"No. Adam Spencer Marsh," Elaine was arguing. "You are going to drink this entire bottle. You were almost killed. We will survive a day or two without water, but you might not. You've lost too much blood. Now drink it all before I have Dylan hold you down."

Adam rolled his eyes, but opened his mouth obediently and slowly took a few sips. With each sip he grimaced. A clean cloth had been tied around his neck.

After a few more sips he shook his head. "That's enough."

Elaine looked like she was about to say something but Adam continued.

"I will try and drink some more in a little bit. But really," he paused, looking like it was difficult for him to speak, "it's painful and I just think I should rest."

Elaine put the top back on the water bottle.

"OK. But I am leaving it right here. We'll revisit this in a couple of hours." She kissed him on the top of his forehead. "You had us so worried," she said, her eyes watering, fighting back the tears.

Her parents climbed out of the small tent so that her uncle could rest. Lilly stepped out behind them, looking at the scene in front of her. Two of the tents were destroyed and there were two pieces of a dead vampire in between the mess.

"You saved us," Dylan said as he clasped Lilly on the back in sort of a half hug. "I'm proud of you."

It was the most affection he'd shown her since they had met, but it disgusted her. How could his proudest moment be when she had ended someone's life and became a murderer? What kind of person congratulated someone for becoming a killer?

Lilly tried to distract herself by keeping busy. She built a fire and burned the body while the others went through the tents to salvage what they could.

When the body was finished burning Lilly threw more wood on the fire. It was wet but the fire had gotten big enough that it still burned even with the added moisture.

They still had a few hours till dawn. Lilly worried about the others getting frostbite or hypothermia now that they were down to one tent.

Lex walked outside to where Lilly stood. Her teeth were chattering and she was shivering uncontrollably.

"Weeee f-f-finished going through the t-t-tents," she managed to get out.

"Lex, get back inside. It's too cold out here for you," Lilly commanded. "At least get inside your sleeping bag. That'll help some, right?"

Lex nodded. "Are y-you o-o-kay?"

Lilly sighed. She had just murdered someone. She was anything but OK. "Yeah I'm fine," she lied. "Come on, go back inside and I'll see if I can find some wood that's not so wet. You guys need to stay warm."

Lilly looked around. She hadn't realized before how much snow had fallen. There were several inches on the ground and it was still falling.

She hoped it would stop soon. The snow would make it more difficult for them to travel and stay warm. But as she glanced around, she was grateful for it for now. She scraped off the top of the snow and filled one of their pots.

Now she could heat it over the fire and they wouldn't just have water to drink, they'd have something hot to drink, something to hopefully warm them up.

Once the snow had melted into a nice hot liquid, and Lex had stopped shaking so much, Lilly turned to check on Adam.

Elaine was inside the tent sitting next to him. She had barely left his side. She had changed his bandage again. The bleeding seemed to have stopped for the moment.

"How is he?" Lilly asked as she sat down on the opposite side of her uncle and took his hand.

"He's alive," Elaine said, relieved. "He seems to be drifting in and out of consciousness. I'm not a nurse. He lost a lot of blood, but for now, he's still here."

*　　*　　*　　*　　*　　*　　*　　*　　*　　*

It was two full days before Tread returned. Lilly had kept a fire going, trying to keep the humans warm and she had been able to keep them hydrated, but the food had completely run out yesterday, and before that there had only been a little bit of beef jerky.

Adam slept a lot, but when he was awake, he seemed alert, just weak from the loss of blood and lack of food.

Tread walked up loaded down like a pack mull. He had four containers of gas. They were tied together in twos and then slung over each shoulder. He carried two big duffle bags, one in each hand.

He set the bags down and then started to take the fuel off of his shoulders. "What happened?" he asked as he set the gasoline containers against the wall furthest from the open flame, looking at the tattered tents that were stuffed in a corner.

Adam was awake and was sitting by the fire, propped up by the help of Dylan and Elaine. He had a sleeping bag draped over him, tucked underneath his chin, encompassing his whole body.

Dylan hurriedly ran to retrieve the bags, digging through them quickly till he found a can of soup. "We were attacked," Dylan answered as he opened the soup and handed it to Elaine, who began feeding it to Adam without even heating it.

Lex walked over and dug through the bag, pulling out a can of chili.

"What?!" Tread exclaimed.

His eyes darted to Lilly who was sitting alone, staring out one of the broken windows of the store.

"What happened? Is everyone OK?" Tread asked, looking around the room more intently.

"Some bloodsucker got Adam, but he's recovering. Lilly took care of him, tore his head right off his body," Dylan smiled proudly.

Tread turned from Dylan and walked over to Lilly, who was avoiding looking at him.

He sat down beside her. "I'm so sorry," he whispered.

She glanced at him but didn't say anything.

"I should have been here. How are you?" he asked, noticing a slight tremble coming from her.

"She's great. She was awesome," Dylan said, talking loudly. "She snapped his neck like it was a tiny twig." He broke a small stick in half demonstrating the action. "Then she burned that vamp to a crisp. We didn't need you at all," he added smugly.

Lilly got up suddenly and ran out of the gas station.

"Where's she going?" Elaine asked, looking up.

Tread stood up angrily. "You really are thick," he lashed out. "Have you even talked with your daughter? She just killed someone for the first time. Did you even think to see how she was handling it?"

"She killed a monster, what's the big deal?" Dylan asked.

Tread stepped closer, and tried to calm down. "Lilly is trapped between two worlds. She's not human. She's not exactly a typical vampire. She wasn't raised around the violence I was. She just killed one of her own kind. She doesn't see a difference between you and me," he said, motioning between them and himself. "You just don't get it." He shook his head in frustration.

Dylan looked around. "What's there to get?" he asked. "She defended her family."

"Think back to how you felt when you ended your first life. Did it matter that he or she was an enemy? Did you not feel anything?"

Dylan opened his mouth to say something, then stopped.

"Tread's right," Elaine agreed. "We didn't think. She defended us and saved us. If she hadn't acted we would have died. We never thought about how it might affect her."

"You can't keep doing this to her. You can't pick one when it's convenient. You can't treat her like a human sometimes and a vampire the next. She's Lilly. She's unique, different, the best of both our worlds. Strong and fast and smart, but she's also compassionate, gentle, and hopeful." Tread turned to go after Lilly.

"Wait," Dylan called. He put a hand on Tread's shoulder, stopping him. "Let me go."

Tread looked at him astonished, first that Dylan had actually touched him, and second, that he thought he deserved another chance with Lilly.

"Please?" Dylan asked. "Give me a chance."

Tread threw up his hands in defeat and stomped over to the far side of the gas station and sat down. *He had better make this right,* he thought bitterly as he watched Dylan go.

The snow was falling steadily as Dylan followed Lilly outside. He shivered as he approached her. She was just standing, staring blankly off into the woods.

"I'm sorry," Dylan said.

Lilly turned and looked at him. She hadn't realized anyone had joined her.

"What?" she said, still half-dazed.

"I apologize. I haven't been doing a very good job of acting like a father. Tread gave me pause to reconsider some things." He hesitated, rubbing his hands up and down his arms for warmth. "When I found out my daughter was a vampire, it almost destroyed me. It felt like the final nail of torture in the coffin."

Lilly looked away, trying to hide her sadness.

Dylan reached and touched her gently on her shoulder. "I'm not trying to hurt you, I'm just trying to be honest. After seventeen years and a lifetime of listening to anti-vampire propaganda, all I felt for vampires was hatred."

A big gust of wind brushed over them. Dylan pulled up the collar of his jacket and blew into his hands, rubbing them together to stay warm. "Finding out that my daughter was one of these creatures I had been taught to hate..." he trailed off. "I just assumed you'd be the same, or that when push came to shove that you'd side with them. I'm sorry about my reaction after that vampire died. Seeing you put your family first just made me unbelievably happy. I never even thought about how it must have felt for you. But thinking back on my first kill," he shuddered as the wind began to pick up, "well, it didn't matter how justified the shooting was, it was difficult. I felt sick. I had ended a life. It took a long time to come to grips with it. It's not something you get past overnight."

He stepped forward, wrapping his arm awkwardly around her shoulders. "I'm glad you were here with us, and that you protected us, but I'm sorry that it ended the way it did."

Lilly turned and asked quietly, "How did you get over it?"

He thought about it for a moment. "It took time." He took her hand gently in his and squeezed it. "Talking about it helped, although it was difficult. And I really had to accept that what I did was necessary. It's a lot easier to say it than to actually believe it."

They walked back into the station together. Tread looked at Lilly. He started to get up and then stopped, unsure of what to do.

She smiled at him reassuringly, and then made her way over and sat beside him.

"I'm sorry. I should have been here," Tread repeated.

Lilly nudged him lovingly. "You know, you apologize an awful lot. You had to leave. We decided together. You can't always be here to protect me. I want to be strong."

Tread intertwined his fingers with hers, and held her gaze. "Lil, you are the strongest person I know." He rubbed her shoulder affectionately. "Still. I know what happened can't have been easy. How are you *really* doing?"

She looked down at their hands. "No, it was horrible. Realizing what my strength can do, what I can do, without even knowing it... Knowing that kind of power is in me... It's scary."

"You did what you had to. Lex told me you gave him a chance to leave. You tried everything you could to give him an out. He chose not to take it. That's on him, not you." Tread sighed and gently placed his hand on her chin, raising it up until their eyes met. "I know it may not make it any easier right now. But—"

"I know," Lilly interrupted. "Talking to my dad helped. Thanks for that." She smiled warmly. "It will just take time."

Tread filled the truck with gas, and then loaded the bags of food and the tent in the back. He had managed to secure four blood bags this time.

They drank them quickly. Then Tread helped Adam climb into the back of the cab with Dylan and Elaine. Lex climbed into the front with Lilly, leaving Tread as the driver.

As they drove away, Lilly hoped that leaving the ruins of the gas station behind would help her to move past what had happened in the last twenty-four hours.

Chapter 13
Alex

The drive to Nashville was uneventful. Adam slept most of the way. The snow had ceased falling and the temperature had warmed enough to keep anything from sticking to the roads.

The sun was just beginning to set as the Nashville walls came into view. The orange, pink, and red rays shining behind the wall made the city seem almost welcoming. Tread parked the truck about a mile from the wall, riding in on fumes. He managed to stop behind a fallen billboard that advertised chicken that was apparently "finger-lickin' good."

He helped Adam out of the truck cautiously. "I'm going to see if I can get more gas. It shouldn't be too hard. A vehicle is hard to come by, but gas," he moved his hands up and down like a balance, "well, not so much. If I can get the tank full, then we should be able to make it to Little Rock."

The color was returning to Adam's face, and his energy seemed to be increasing. He walked around the truck a couple of times trying to build up his stamina and then found an old stump to sit on.

"I think a friend of mine still lives in Little Rock, so maybe we can get some information on cities in Texas," Tread continued. "I think you should forgo the fire tonight," he added. "We're too close to the city, and they might send out a patrol if they see flames this close to the wall."

Lilly tugged on the front of his shirt, pulling him closer. "Be careful," she said, pressing her lips gently to his.

"You too," he said as he looked at her seriously. "You never know what's out here." He scanned the trees on both sides of the road.

"I will be." She looked back at her family. "But I'm feeling better now. I haven't gotten the feeling that we're being followed since we left the gas station."

Tread put his hands around her waist. "Good. But be careful anyway." He kissed her one last time and took off.

Lilly noticed her father had been watching their interaction. He still didn't appear to be happy. But she didn't see the same hatred in his eyes. Maybe they were making some progress.

Lex walked over and swung her arm over her BFF's shoulder. "So, seems like things are going well."

Lilly smiled. "I guess."

"So what's the plan?" Lex asked.

"Tread went to get more fuel," Lilly explained.

Lex shook her head. "No. I mean after that." Lex pulled out a granola bar from her pocket and took a bite. "What happens when we get to Texas? What if there is no vampire city? Or what if they just want to eat us? What then?"

Lilly sighed. "Honestly, I have no idea." She walked over and sat on the tailgate of the truck. "Mexico?" She shrugged. "I don't know. I know we can't stay in a human city in the states. You, my parents, and Uncle Adam would all be executed. I understand the fear that humans have for vampires. We are faster and stronger and well, you are very aware of our diet. But I just think if there really is a vampire city, four humans aren't going to pose a threat to that, right? I guess I think they can be reasoned with more easily than the humans can." Lilly shook her head. "I know I'm probably being naive. I don't have any idea of what's going to happen. I just know we need to stay together."

She looked across the road. There was an old speed limit sign bent almost to the ground, along with a couple of run-down cars, covered in a thick layer of dirt. She imagined how nice the world must have been before and wondered if it would ever become that way again.

"Well anything sounds better than being executed," Lex said sarcastically. "What does Tread think of this plan?" she asked, swinging her legs back and forth on the back of the truck.

Lilly paused. "I don't think I ever asked him."

"So he could think this is crazy and is just following it for you?" Lex observed.

"I don't know," Lilly finally admitted after several awkward moments of silence.

*   *   *   *   *   *   *   *   *   *

It was a dark night, overcast. The clouds were thick. Even with Lilly's incredible vision she could only faintly see the moon and she couldn't see any of the stars.

She glanced up as she heard movement. Tread was back sooner than Lilly had expected, and he hadn't come alone.

A middle-aged looking vampire of Indian descent had followed Tread, carrying several jugs filled with gasoline. He had a goatee and wore brown dress slacks with a short sleeve brown and white button-up shirt.

"This is Henry. He offered to help me bring the gas out of the city," Tread explained.

Lilly walked over and shook his hand. "That was thoughtful, thank you."

Tread chuckled lightly. "I wouldn't thank him too much. His reasons were more self-serving." He grinned at Henry. "I think he was more intrigued at the idea of me traveling with a group made up *entirely* of humans, than being courteous," Tread explained.

Lilly eyed him questioningly, hoping for an explanation later.

184

"Too true." Henry laughed. "The truth is, I didn't really believe him." He looked the group over. "So are you really traveling with him of your own free will?" he asked, astonished, as he set his jugs down by the truck.

Lilly had expected him to speak with an accent, but was surprised when he had none.

"Yep," Lex chimed in. "So far he's only tried to eat me once," she joked, eyeing him knowingly.

Adam, Elaine, and Dylan kept their distance, eyeing the newcomer suspiciously.

Tread walked behind Lilly and wrapped his arms around her, kissing her lightly on the cheek.

"So..." Lilly asked, attempting to sound nonchalant. "Have you ever heard of any cities where humans and vampires live together in harmony?"

He frowned slightly. "Sorry, Tread already asked me." He scratched his head. "I still can't believe you guys are making it work. Vampires and humans. Hmm." He turned to leave, but then lingered for a long moment, looking back at Lilly. "If you do ever find a place like that, let me know. It's an intriguing idea. One I think I'd like to be a part of."

"Thanks again for all the help." Tread said, shaking Henry's hand.

"Anytime. Any friend of Alex's is welcomed to whatever assistance I can provide." Then he nodded at Tread and sped away back to the city.

Tread began pouring the gasoline into the tank as the others loaded back in the truck. Lilly took down the tent that they hadn't needed after all.

She walked up beside him, handing him another container of gas. "What was all that about? Why'd you tell him we were all humans? Can't he tell I'm not?"

"You have a heartbeat Lil. If you don't move too fast or use more than human strength you blend in just as much to the vampires as you do to the humans. They can't tell you apart. I don't want anyone to know you are a Sunwalker. So if I ever have to come back again with another vampire, just act human."

They finished fueling up, and still had two containers full. Tread loaded them in the back along with the empty ones.

He drove so the others could sleep.

Around midnight Lilly awoke to a loud bang and a jolting sensation. She bolted upright and saw the others slowly doing the same.

The truck was shaking violently and slowly coming to a stop.

"What happened?" Lilly asked.

Tread stopped the vehicle and opened the door. "I think we got a flat," Tread said. Then he motioned for Lilly to join him outside. "I'm gonna check out the damage, you guys just go back to sleep."

Lilly opened her door and glanced down at the tire. It was completely shredded.

"What happened?" she whispered. "What's the big deal? So you got a flat. Why all the cloak and dagger?"

Tread motioned for her to join him. She walked slowly around the vehicle, and he pointed down. "I didn't just get a flat," he sighed. "I can see every pebble and rock for well over a mile, and I have wicked reflexes." He smiled and raised one eyebrow up, his signature cocky expression. "This was sabotage," he spoke so lowly, no one in the truck could hear him. "I was driving and there was nothing in the road one second and then the next there was a big spiky strip of metal and a black blur."

Lilly stood stunned into silence.

"I didn't want to worry anyone else, but this," he said gesturing to the tire, "this wasn't an accident. If I had glanced off the road for a split second, we'd probably be sitting on four flat tires."

Lilly slumped down onto the pavement, a defeated expression on her face. "I just thought it was over. I thought that vampire I had killed had been messing with us." She shook her head. "Obviously I was wrong."

Tread came and kneeled down in front of her.

"It's not over. I don't know who or what is messing with us. We're about fifteen minutes outside of Little Rock," Tread said as he looked down the road. "We have a couple of options to consider, none of which I particularly like."

Lilly looked back at the truck where Adam, Elaine, Dylan, and Lex slept, oblivious to everything around them.

"OK," Lilly said resolutely. "What are our options?"

"Well, first, I could leave and see if by some miracle I could find a new tire that actually fit this model. But I don't love the idea of leaving you alone here. We have no idea what this is."

"OK. So that's bad option numero uno, what's bad option number two?"

"Well, we could all walk there. It wouldn't take us that long to get to Little Rock, but the chances of us finding another car are slim to nil."

Lilly nodded. "Is there an option number three?"

Tread shook his head. "Not that I can think of."

Lilly walked around the truck, looking down at the few remaining strips of rubber that constituted the wheel. "Don' t these things come with spares?"

Tread chuckled quietly. "No, this thing is old and beat up. What you see is what you get!"

"Oh," Lilly sighed. "So you already checked. It was worth a shot."

"Well I didn't check, what's the point."

Lilly just glared at him. Apparently men in real life were just as stubborn as the men portrayed in movies.

"Fine," Tread huffed. He walked around to the back of the truck and leaned down to look under it. He muttered something so low even Lilly couldn't understand it. He slid under the vehicle for a moment and came back pulling out a dusty but functional looking tire. He stepped around the truck attempting to avoid eye contact with her.

Lilly smirked and turned, climbing back into the truck.

Tread changed the tire quickly and they resumed their drive.

"Good call back there," Tread said uncomfortably.

"Let's just get out of here," Lilly said, glancing around. "This place is giving me the creeps."

The drive to Little Rock was long and eerie. Although they made it in just over fifteen minutes, both of them were on edge.

It had been quiet other than the slightly labored breathing coming from Adam and the occasional snore from Elaine. But they were on high alert, unsure if anymore attacks would come their way from whoever or whatever seemed intent on following them.

Tread pulled over to the side of the road about a mile outside of the city, as he had previously done at each new city.

He opened the door quietly and Lilly followed suit as the others continued to sleep soundly.

Looking towards the city, Lilly scrunched up her face and turned to talk to Tread.

"Those walls are way taller than the other cities we've been to," she said, as she pointed toward Little Rock. "Why are they so high?"

"I haven't the faintest idea." He walked beside her and looked at the wall. "It's been a long time since I've been down here." He peered around cautiously. "Maybe they're paranoid, more so than the other cities. Or..." he added in a hushed voice, "maybe they have more of a reason to be."

He turned and cradled Lilly's face with his hand. "I'll be a little longer this time. We need fuel and I want to look and see if Alex still lives here. Maybe I can find out more about the cities if my friend is still around." He bent down and brushed his lips against her, so lightly she might almost have thought they hadn't touched.

He turned to leave.

"That's it?" Lilly huffed.

Tread chuckled quietly. "Just checking." He smiled as he cocked an eyebrow. He stepped swiftly back and pulled Lilly into his arms, lifting her off of her feet.

This time she didn't wait for him. She leaned forward, pulling him toward her. She hungered for him. She kissed him as if it might be her last. Things had been so crazy, she never knew what the next minute would bring.

Tread finally ended the kiss when he began laughing.

Lilly pushed him away with a shove. "My kissing is so bad that it's comical?" she asked, slightly hurt.

"No, not at all," Tread quickly corrected. "I was just thinking, I'm glad I don't need to breathe." He laughed one more time, gave her a peck on the cheek, winked and ran off toward the gate.

She shook her head as he ran away, trying but finding no humor in his comment.

*   *   *   *   *   *   *   *   *   *

The first to wake was Lex. She crawled out of the truck around six-thirty. She raised her arms up over her head, arched her back, and stretched.

"Man am I stiff and sore," she complained. "I sure miss beds." She yawned. "And pillows," she added, rubbing the back of her neck.

She took a few steps forward and spun around slowly. "So where are we?"

Lilly was sitting on a piece of broken guardrail up a little hill, looking off toward the wall. "Little Rock," she said without turning around, and then added, "Arkansas."

Lex stuck her head back in the truck and came out with a couple of Pop-Tarts and a bottle of water. She climbed up the incline and sat down beside Lilly.

"Did you get any sleep?" Lex asked.

"Some."

Lex opened her water and shivered. She shakily drank a few sips.

"Is it really that cold here?" Lilly asked. "I can't tell. It's easier for me to tell when there is snow on the ground. It gives me a clue to the temperature."

Lex shuddered and exaggerated her breath, blowing deeply in front of her.

Lilly laughed as she saw her friend's breath as Lex exhaled.

189

"OK," Lilly said, holding up her hands in surrender. "I guess it is cold." She darted to the car and was back with a blanket before Lex even realized she had moved.

"Thanks." She smiled as Lilly draped the blanket across her shoulders.

"That's what best friends who can move at super human speeds are for."

"Do you think you move as fast as Superman?" Lex asked.

Lilly looked at her funny. "Do I move faster than a made-up person? I wouldn't know."

"I mean, do you think you could stop a bullet if someone fired it? Are you that fast?" she asked, taking a bite out of her strawberry Pop-Tart.

Lilly shrugged. "I haven't been around a lot of bullets to test myself. As for darts, I've been struck twice. Granted, I didn't see them being shot at me, but I still wish I had been fast enough to avoid them."

"How do you turn someone into a vampire?" Lex asked out of nowhere.

Lilly leaned back, cocking her head, and looked at her quizzically. "What's with all the questions? How should I know?"

Lex looked at her with a hard look.

"What? It's not like I grew up in the typical vampire fashion. I didn't get an instruction manual. And as much as I've looked I never did find that Vampires for Dummies book."

"So you've never asked Tread?"

Lilly shook her head. "Nope. It actually never came up, never crossed my mind. Why?" Lilly asked. "Would you actually want to be one?"

"I don't know," Lex said, sounding surprised. "I'm just curious as to how it all works. I've never thought about becoming one," she said. "Living forever kind of gives me the creeps," she added hesitantly. "I guess I'm more surprised you've never asked."

Lilly reached down and picked up some small pebbles. "It's not anything I've even taken the time to consider," she said as she began tossing the rocks into the forest. "I mean, I know I'm going to

190

live possibly forever. I don't want to be alone. But you, Uncle Adam, my mom, and my dad are all perfect how you are, at least to me. You were born human. I've never really thought about changing it." She sat silently for a few minutes. "Now that you have mentioned it and I've kind of started to think about it, I wouldn't think any of you guys would be too keen on the idea. Saying it would be a huge adjustment is the biggest understatement I could make. Craving blood, not sleeping, the speed, the strength. Sometimes it's still a little overwhelming to me and I was born this way. I mean I'm sure it would have been easier to get used to had I been able to use all my abilities freely since birth. But I don't know. Not to mention you'd never be able to go out into sunlight again. That one I don't have to deal with, but I would imagine it's difficult to accept."

"For sure," Lex agreed, looking up at the sun. "Cravings, huh? Has it ever been hard for you? I mean were you ever tempted to..." She left her sentence hanging.

Lilly shoved Lex playfully. "To what, eat you?" She laughed. "No. Not really. As long as I feed frequently enough I'm fine. And the few times I haven't, well, let me put it this way." Lilly paused. "If you had really wanted a chocolate bar, but eating that chocolate bar would kill someone you loved, would it really be that big of a temptation?"

"No, I guess not...I mean depending on the brand," Lex joked.

Lilly turned around as she heard a noise coming from the truck.

"Looks like the rest of the gang is awake," Lex commented, finishing off her breakfast. "I'm going to go find something else to eat. Those Pop-Tarts weren't filling enough," she said, trying not to get her feet tangled in the blanket as she made her way back down the hill.

*   *   *   *   *   *   *   *   *   *

By noon, Lilly was beginning to get worried. She knew Tread had said he'd take longer this trip, but it had been over five hours. The sun was shining, and even though they were a mile out from the wall, she wasn't sure there was enough cover protecting her family from prying eyes.

Tread had parked behind a couple of decent sized oak trees. Lilly wondered if this city sent patrols outside the wall. Since the barricades around Little Rock were so much higher than the other places they had visited, it seemed likely there might be other security precautions taken.

It was several hours past dark when Tread finally arrived, and he brought company again.

Lilly almost ran and threw her arms around him but she stopped when she saw he was with a woman. She knew that being a Sunwalker was a secret that Tread thought should be kept.

He was walking with a tall, slender blonde. She had long hair that came several inches past her shoulders and bounced in the most perfect ringlets Lilly had ever seen.

She looked like a movie star. Lilly felt a pang of jealousy as she watched how at ease Tread was with her. She couldn't quite make out what they were saying yet. They were speaking softly, but appeared to be laughing and thoroughly enjoying each other's company.

A few minutes later they approached and set down several containers, filled with what Lilly could only assume was more gasoline.

Tread smiled. "Lilly, this is Alex."

Lilly smiled warmly. "Hello, Alex." She was slightly taken aback. She had always just assumed Alex was a guy.

"Thanks for dragging him back down this way. I was wondering when I'd see him again," Alex said as she shoved him playfully. "He's a great guy, but he's lousy at the keeping in touch part."

"Sorry," Tread apologized. "This one has been keeping me busy," he said as he reached across and grabbed Lilly by the arm, pulling her into his.

Alex shook her head. "I still can't believe you are serious about anyone, let alone a human," Alex scoffed. "No offense to you," she quickly amended.

Alex walked around them and turned her attention to the truck. "You really do have a whole group of them." She turned and looked back at Tread. "I really didn't believe you. Not that you've lied to me before. But this is really unbelievable, especially after all that happened with your—" Alex stopped herself and then appeared to try and change the subject. She looked back towards her city. "Are you sure you won't stay here? You're really headed to Allen?"

"No, I can't stay here. You said you've heard of a vampire city in Allen, Texas. I have to go check it out."

He felt Lilly tense as he spoke.

"I'm actually surprised you never went to check it out. I mean, you could make it there in an hour. How could you be so close and not take a peek?"

Alex laughed. "I'm good where I'm at. I have a nice setup here. Some things sound too good to be true. And like I said," Alex brushed some of her curls back behind her shoulders after a breeze ruffled her hair, "I know a few guys that went to check it out and they never made it back. Either it's paradise or..." She let her sentence trail off. She walked over and placed her hand on his shoulder. "Just be careful, Tread. Curiosity killed the cat."

He nodded. "Always."

"Well it was good to see you," she said as she walked past him. "Don't let it be seven years before I see you again." She turned to go but hesitated. "Tread."

"Yeah?"

"Either way, I'm not sure it's a great idea to check out a vampire city with a group of humans."

He nodded again. "I hear you. Take care, Alex."

She hurried off down the road and paused. "Let me know if it's paradise," she called and then took off.

"Will do," Tread said quietly.

Chapter 14
Mutiny

As soon as Alex was out of earshot, Lilly turned to Tread. "Allen? It really exists?" she asked, excitedly shaking him with both hands, practically jumping up and down.

"Supposedly. But try not to get your hopes up. I've heard all this before."

"But it might." Lilly smiled.

He put his hands up. "Maybe," he conceded.

Lilly grabbed his hand and started pulling him to the vehicle, where the others were already asleep. "Let's get going."

Tread pulled back lightly. "At least let me put the gas in the truck first." He stepped back and started picking up containers.

"So did you find out why the walls are so high here?"

"It's not just the walls," Tread explained. "It's everything. This city has much more security than any city I've been to, with the exception of D.C. maybe. The VAS presence is triple what it was in Harbor Cove. If I hadn't found Alex, I'm not sure I would have made a clean getaway. I barely got in. If Alex hadn't shown me a secret sewer passage that led out of the city, I wouldn't have made it out with anything."

Lilly glanced back at the city. "So what's so special about Little Rock? Why do they need all this extra protection? What do you think they have in there?" she wondered.

"Alex said she's heard rumors of humans disappearing. Not one or two like you hear about in other cities, but large numbers. Maybe they are just trying to protect the city."

He drizzled in the last few remaining drops of fuel and then got in the truck.

"You should try and get some rest," Tread suggested.

Lilly climbed in the front and leaned her head against the window. She closed her eyes and listened to the quiet symphony around her. Lex was breathing quietly beside her while her mother snored in the back seat. She wondered how Dylan and Adam could sleep with her in between them, but she could tell from their even breathing that they were asleep.

She awoke to a gentle shaking and Tread's voice.

"We're here," Tread whispered.

Lilly shot upright. Excitement and nervousness coursed through her veins.

"What time is it?" she asked quietly.

"A little after three."

Lilly peered out the windows. She was surrounded by trees and nothing else. "Where's the wall? I don't see any city?" she asked.

"We are about ten miles from the city. I found a park. Where people used to camp and stuff. It's secluded and I think this is a safe place to leave you while I check the city out."

"I'm coming with you," Lilly stated.

Tread opened the door and motioned for her to follow.

"No way," he said after he had closed the door.

"Yes I am," she insisted, walking around the car towards him. "This is a vampire city. Who knows how many vampires live there? I am coming."

Tread turned around looking into the trees. "Think about whatever's been following us. What if it followed us here? Or if it's waiting for us to leave your mother, father, uncle, and friend all alone?"

Lilly opened her mouth to speak and then stopped. She frowned slightly.

Tread leaned forward and kissed her on the top of her head. "Don't worry. I've been around awhile. I know how to keep myself out of trouble."

She sighed. "Fine. But be careful, and don't take forever. I will be going crazy the whole time you are gone." She rubbed his arm tenderly.

"I'll be back in an hour, OK?" Tread promised. "If I need to go back later I can, but I'll just do some quick reconnaissance."

He gave her a quick kiss and sped off through the trees, leaving Lilly alone with four sleeping humans. She wondered what he would find.

The next hour seemed to drag on forever. Every second seemed like a minute, every minute an hour. She walked around the truck impatiently, too anxious to sit. Finally, when Lilly thought she couldn't take it any longer, she heard a rustle and a few seconds later Tread emerged from the trees.

"So?" Lilly asked. "Is it there?"

"It's there..." Tread began.

"I knew we'd find a place," Lilly said, hugging Tread. Relief flooded through her.

"It's a vampire city. Pretty much how I envisioned it, but more sophisticated."

"So do you think they'll take us?" Lilly asked, taking a step back and gazing out in the direction Tread had come.

"Do you remember how I envisioned a city becoming?" Tread asked. "Lil, they breed humans just to feed off of them. They actually have it set up quite nicely."

"Of course they do," Lilly said.

Tread looked at her, baffled. "So you're just going to add your family to the mix?"

"No!" she said, shoving Tread hard, but quietly so as not to wake her sleeping family. "Of course not. But I expected it to be like this. I mean, it is a vampire city."

Tread looked at her and threw his hands up. "What am I missing?"

Lilly brought him over to a rusted picnic table and they sat down. "We just need to broaden their minds. Suggest other options and change their way of thinking," Lilly explained.

Tread held his hands up in a stopping motion. "So let me get this straight. You want to talk the vampires out of eating humans, and then, what, convince the humans to stay and live with the vampires who've been draining their blood for who knows how many years?"

"Yep." She smiled matter of factly. "So they aren't killing the humans, are they?"

He stood up and turned to face her. "How did you know that? Did you follow me?"

Lilly reached up and pulled Tread back on the bench beside her. "Of course not," she explained. "I just figure babies take nine months more or less to be born. It would take a lot of humans to keep a city going if you were continually killing the blood supply off. I mean the birth rate can't be too high."

"From what I could tell, the people are separated into groups, and the groups rotate giving blood. You should see the city, it's pretty impressive." Tread picked up a stick and started drawing a diagram in the dirt. "They have it walled off just like the human cities. The humans all live in this big building." He pointed to a square he had etched onto the ground. "I think it was a school at one point. There are ruins of what appear to be a big football stadium near it." He tugged at the hem of his shirt absentmindedly. "The walls all have covered glass walkways that appear to have some type of UV coating on them, so vampires can patrol day or night. There are also covered pathways throughout the city. There are huge gardens and several livestock areas," he said, pointing to other areas on his makeshift map. "I am assuming these are used to feed the humans. I bet they make them work and take care of the areas during the day. At least that's how I would have done it."

Lilly nodded in agreement.

"So, I think I will go back out and scout some more. I did—"

Lilly jumped up. "No," she said, putting her hands on Tread's shoulders and holding him in place. "You just got back. We need to come up with some kind of plan," she insisted.

"Like what?" Tread asked, but then continued before she could answer. "We need to get a better picture. I just skimmed the surface. I need more time." He carefully took Lilly's hands in his and stood back up. "I don't even know how many vampires are in there."

"I know. More intel is probably good, but I really think we need to get inside there," Lilly explained.

"Just walk up and bang on the door and see what happens?"

"I know this is going to take time. I'm not naive enough to believe I can just tell them to stop hurting humans and that will be that." Lilly heard a small thump. She turned back to the truck, and saw that Lex had shifted positions, and must have bumped something. "But I think," she continued, "if we try to infiltrate them, we can become friends with them and then slowly start planting ideas in their minds. Feel it out, see if anyone shares our beliefs."

Tread stood quietly for a minute. "Well I can try to get into the city today. It might take some time to build relationships, but I am sure I could sneak some supplies out and come back every few days and check on everyone."

"Really?" Lilly asked, raising her eyebrows. "You don't think my plan sounds too crazy?"

"Crazy? Yes." He laughed. "But if you told me six months ago I'd be traveling with a bunch of humans and drinking cold blood from plastic bags, I'd have said you were insane." He put his arm around her and squeezed her gently. "But crazy works for you."

She reached upward and kissed him on the cheek. "I'm relieved that you think you'll be able to get away every few days. I don't think I will be able to get away at all. Once I'm in, I'm sure it will be impossible to get out."

Tread stood up and faced her. "What are you talking about? I thought we both agreed I'd be going in."

Lilly stood up, looking eye-to-eye with Tread. "We did. I need you to go in and charm the vampires, make headway with them. I will be working with the humans, trying to convince them," she said, pointing back and forth between Tread and herself, "that not all vampires are evil."

Tread turned around and took a few steps away from her, shaking his head. "Lilly that's beyond crazy," he said as he stopped pacing and looked back at her. "They aren't going to be fooled. They're going—"

"I fooled Alex and that Henry fellow." She placed her finger to his lips to end his arguing. "You said it yourself. As long as I don't use my speed or strength, I just blend in. Vampires can't tell the difference. And I've been blending in with humans my whole life, so I am pretty sure they won't suspect anything."

He moved her hand away from his lips. "What about your family? We don't know if they are safe here."

Lilly sighed. "I know. You're right. But they won't be safe in there. Not until we change things. And they will be executed if they set foot in a human city. So our options are limited. I think leaving them here is the least risky option."

Tread shook his head. "I don't like this," he said.

She nodded. "I know. They won't like it either," she said, pointing to the truck. "I'm sure they will have plenty to say once they wake up and hear the plan."

Once Lilly's family was all up, she laid out their plan to them. Suffice it to say Elaine was adamantly against it.

"Lilly, it's too dangerous. We'll just keep going, find a human city in Mexico where they don't know us. Start over," Elaine pleaded.

"Mom..." Lilly began. She hadn't called her mother by that name in a while. It was difficult and felt awkward to her, but she was trying to work towards forgiveness. She knew if she kept calling her Elaine, it would only help her to feel less connected. "Mom, it won't work. I turn eighteen soon. In another year I will stop aging. People will notice. We can't just keep running."

"So let one of us go." Her mother motioned to Adam and Dylan. "We are the adults. We are human. We will be more convincing."

"No," Lilly said, pushing her mother back a step. "You can be hurt. You can die. It's safer this way. I can try to fight my way out, or run if things go south. You will have no recourse."

"Then let one of us come with you," Adam suggested. "We can help."

Lilly gave her uncle a hug. "Thanks Uncle Adam. But it will just put you in danger. Plus it's safer for you guys to stay together."

"So when will you leave?" Lex asked. She had been sitting on the hood of the truck quietly during the entire discussion.

"Tread will go now, and I will follow the day after tomorrow. We don't want to arrive at the same time. That might look suspicious. "

Dylan walked over to Tread. "We need to talk," he said as he stalked noisily off into the trees.

Tread followed him for a good twenty minutes before Dylan finally stopped by a small creek.

He knelt down and wet his hands and washed his face. Then picking up a few small smooth rocks, he started skipping them across the creek.

Tread stood there, waiting for Dylan to speak.

Finally, Dylan stopped and turned to him. "Listen, I don't like you. Despise still seems like an understatement to me. But I lo...I love Lilly. It sounds strange to say it out loud. I didn't think I ever would." He scratched his chin, seeming to surprise himself. "The more I watch her and see her...well Elaine's right. She's not a vampire. She's just our daughter. I can see Elaine in her, through her expressions, her temperament. I can even see my side of the family in her. She looks so much like my sister, only dark-haired instead of blonde. She is confident, loving, strong..." He looked up, embarrassed at how he was rattling on. "Look, just keep her safe. You do that and I'll work on getting past my hatred for you. I won't make any promises, but at least I'll try. Which is more than I ever thought I'd do."

He stuck his hand out toward Tread.

Tread studied it for half a second. Part of him wanted to swat it away. But he loved Lilly too. He knew this was what she yearned for. If there was a chance of making peace with her father, then he had to take it. He reached out hesitantly and shook his hand.

"I love her too. I give you my word. I won't let anything happen to her."

They walked back to camp in silence. When they stepped through the trees into the clearing where the vehicle was parked, Lilly was eyeing them questioningly.

"I'd better get going," Tread said. He bent down and kissed Lilly goodbye.

"So are you going to tell me what that was about?"

"Nope." He winked. "I think I'd rather it drive you crazy. See you in two days. Be careful."

He sped off through the trees, leaving her alone again. It would have been so much easier if it were just the two of them.

She wondered how she might have done things differently when she first met Tread. Maybe she could have avoided all this. If she had just left with him and joined a vampire community, things would be so different. Her family would be home, safe. Lex would be with her parents. But then, if Tread had never seen Adam, her father would still be locked up.

She sighed. Either way, things were messy. She couldn't go back in time anyway, so there wasn't really any point in second guessing her decisions now.

Lex walked up holding a backpack and a change of clothes. "Your dad mentioned there's a creek about a mile in. Want to take a stroll? I'm in desperate need of a bath."

"Sure." She smiled easily, glancing down at herself. "I'm sure I could use one too. Let me just grab some fresh clothes."

They walked through the trees in silence, with the crackling of fallen leaves underfoot and the occasional snapped branch as their only conversation.

"So..." Lex began. "Are you really going to just leave us here alone?"

Lilly paused and turned to her friend. "I think it's for the best. I think staying here is safer for you guys. I know it might be scary but—"

"Scary?" Lex interrupted. "I don't care about that. I don't think you should be going alone. I'm worried about you going in there by yourself. I don't think you've really thought this through."

"What do you mean?"

"You've blended in before, but you always had help. Your mom or me. We have always been there to help. Elaine took care of getting blood for you. I covered for you when you heard something you shouldn't have been able to hear, or saw something you shouldn't have been able to see."

"Well, I'm older now. I will be careful."

"Lilly, you need someone in there. I think it should be me," Lex said, stepping over a fallen log. "But if not me, then take someone. What are you going to do when they want to take your blood? When it's your turn to be harvested? Not to mention having two 'humans,'" Lex added air quotes around the word, "is going to make it a little more convincing when you try to sell your story."

"I don't know, Lex," Lilly said, shaking her head.

"That's the point. I know it will be dangerous, but if you don't take someone, even if it's not me...I'll just follow you after you leave. Sure it will take me longer, but I'll find the city eventually...or they'll find me."

"No Lex. You have to promise me," Lilly said urgently, shaking her friend. "I need to keep you safe."

"No Lilly, you don't. It's not your job. I'm eighteen, remember. I'm an adult. Heck, I'm older than you. I have to make my own decisions. And I'm not going to let you do this alone."

Lilly imagined Lex following after her. Scenarios flashed across her mind. She pictured Lex falling down a cliff, getting lost, being eaten by a bear. "Fine. You win. I'm not happy about it but you can come," Lilly finally agreed.

"Don't say it like you're granting me permission. You're not my mother. We've followed your lead so far, but that doesn't mean you are our General. I'm not committing mutiny by disagreeing with you," Lex grumbled.

Lilly put her hands up to surrender. "OK, you're right. I'm sorry. I didn't mean it like that."

Lex rolled her eyes. "I know. But sometimes that's what it sounds like. You've gotten to where you just tell us how it's going to be. I mean you don't even ask our opinions. I get that the vampires are stronger and faster, but that doesn't mean that we humans can't offer anything of value."

"OK. I am sorry," she insisted. "You're completely right. I didn't mean to make you feel like I value you less," Lilly said, holding a branch back as Lex passed. "I have just been so focused on everyone's safety, I didn't realize how it came off."

When they arrived at the creek, Lex found a dry rock for them to set their clean clothes on. They stripped down and scrubbed quickly.

Lilly could tell the water was cold by the chattering sound of Lex's teeth. The creek was shallow, only about a foot deep, but the water was clear, and it got them clean. As the dirt and grime washed away, Lilly felt like the uneasiness between her and Lex went with it.

It felt good to be clean and in new clothes. Things had been so hectic lately, bathing and changing clothes had been one of the last things on her mind.

* * * * * * * * * *

The next day passed by uneventfully. The weather wasn't terrible this far south. It was cold in the morning and evenings but manageable during the daytime.

Lilly had scouted around and found an old, gray, brick building that had at one point been a camp restroom. It wasn't much to look at. It was covered in long vines, growing along the outside walls and across the roof. Inside, grass and weeds grew up from cracks in the floor. There were a couple of broken sinks and two toilet stalls. The door to one was hanging by a hinge, and the second stall's door was gone completely. But the walls and roof were more or less intact, making this the most attractive place they'd stopped at yet.

Dylan and Adam had found a way to detach the back seat of the truck and folded it down to become a bed. They brought the sleeping bags, food, and other supplies down as well. There was more room inside the cement structure than in the truck, and they built a fire pit to keep them warm.

Lex and Lilly had discussed in length their exit from the group. They both had agreed on waiting until the last moment to inform Dylan, Elaine, and Adam that Lex would be accompanying Lilly.

The next morning they awoke early. Lilly made sure her family was set up the best she could manage before leaving.

Lilly gave her family one last hug and turned to see if she had missed anything.

"Remember, Tread will be back in another day or two. Until then, try to keep out of sight and take care of each other." She turned towards Lex. "Ready?"

"Let's go," Lex answered.

"Lex isn't going with you," Elaine called in a startled voice.

Lex turned back to Elaine. "I am. I'll be fine."

"No, Lex. You need to stay here. I have to protect you. It's too dangerous. I'd want Eric and Karen to do the same for Lilly if our places were reversed somehow." Elaine walked over and placed her hand on Lex's shoulder. "It's a city full of vampires," she said slowly, as if that hadn't occurred to Lex before.

"I know you are just trying to look out for me, Mrs. Marsh. And I appreciate it. But you aren't my mom. I'm eighteen and it's just me now. I have to do what's right for me. Whatever happens is on me, not you."

Elaine began to protest, but Dylan came and pulled her gently away. "She's right," he spoke softly. "It's her call. It's not up to you."

"But they're just kids," Elaine cried softly into Dylan's shoulder.

Dylan looked at Lilly and waved her on as he tried to comfort her mother.

Chapter 15
The City

It was early when they headed out. The sun was just beginning to peer up over the horizon.

Lilly missed Harbor Cove. It was gray and dreary in Texas. Everything here was dead. Back at home, it would be beautiful this time of year. There would be a white blanket of snow on everything, and many of the trees were evergreen, so they were vibrant all year long.

"So how far until we hit the wall?" Lex asked as she ducked beneath a low hanging branch.

"A few hours at least. Tread said it was about ten miles away," she replied as she hopped from a fallen log to a tree stump and then over a small ravine.

"That' so unfair," Lex mumbled. "Why couldn't I have super balance and speed like that?"

Lilly waited on the far side of the ravine for Lex . It took several minutes as her friend cautiously maneuvered her way down the steep incline and then climbed back up the far side.

By the time she finished the palms of her hands were beginning to get scratched and sore. "It might take us even longer if we have to travel through this forest the whole way there," she said as she stood and dusted herself off at the top of the ravine.

Lex stood and looked at herself. She had dirt stains on her knees. She'd snagged her jacket a couple of times on branches and had a few scratches. Although it was cool, she was beginning to get hot and sweaty. But when she looked at Lilly, she saw her beautiful friend completely put together, without a hair out of place.

She thought of picking up a handful of grass and twigs and throwing in on her. It would definitely make her look more human. But she thought better of it. She knew she was just frustrated with herself and it wasn't Lilly's fault.

They traveled for a couple more hours and then stopped. Lilly could tell Lex was tired, so they sat and rested while Lex munched on a granola bar.

"So," Lex said while chewing on a huge bite. "How do we get into the city once we find it?" A few crumbs flew out of her mouth.

"Um...first, gross," Lilly said, looking disgusted.

Lex started laughing and attempted to cover her mouth, but only succeeded in flinging more bits of granola bar out of it.

Lilly pretended that she didn't notice the pieces of granola raining down. "So... I've actually been thinking about this a lot. It doesn't exactly sound normal for two human girls to be wandering around outside in the open by themselves. But maybe they would risk it if their sisters went missing."

"So we're sisters?" Lex asked after swallowing a mouthful of granola bar.

Lilly shook her head. "No. We are two friends searching for our younger sisters. They went missing in Little Rock a couple of months ago and we heard a rumor that they might have been taken here. So we came looking for them."

"You think they kidnap girls from far off cities and bring them here?" Lex asked, finishing the last bite of her snack.

Lilly shrugged. "It makes sense to me. Alex mentioned groups of people disappearing. It sounds like that might be how they are creating their human population. Water?" she asked, noticing Lex was trying to reach the backpack but wasn't quite able to without getting up.

Lex nodded and Lilly pushed the pack closer.

"Kidnapping from cities in the vicinity sounds the most likely to me. How else are they going to do it? They need a lot of blood to maintain a city, which means they need a lot of bodies, right?"

Lex nodded, pausing between swigs of water. "OK, so how old are our sisters and what are their names? Do we need code names?"

"I think if we use our real names that will be the easiest. We are less likely to confuse our story if most of it is the truth. So we just need names for our fake sisters."

"OK, did you have a name in mind?"

"I don't know...I'm thinking Beth Marsh, age ten, for my sister. What about yours?"

Lex thought about it for a moment. "OK, how about Rebecca Crews? She's eleven. She should be older, since I'm older right?"

"Sure," Lilly said. "So can you remember Beth and Rebecca's names?"

"I'm not a vampire who never forgets, but I'm pretty sure I can remember two names," Lex said, jabbing Lilly in the ribs with her elbow playfully.

"OK, right. I think that's it. Now we just find the city, wander around, and wait to be caught." She stood up and brushed off the back of her pants, then added, "Oh and don't forget to pretend to be scared."

Lex choked down the last swallow of water bottle, spitting some of it out and coughing. "Who'll be pretending?" she asked, wiping off her mouth with her sleeve. "And what happens if they decide to eat us instead of taking us back to the city?"

"Then I guess they will find out I'm not really a frail little human," Lilly said with a wicked smile. "No offense," she quickly added.

Lex laughed awkwardly. "I think Tread may be rubbing off on you. I'm not entirely sure if I like that," she said, looking Lilly over.

Lilly laughed and looped her arm through her friend's as they hiked through the woods. She was glad there was no snow. Another reason heading to the South had probably been the right choice.

After walking for about another hour, the woods began to thin and they came to a hill.

At the top of the hill they were finally greeted with the sight they had been searching for.

"It looks like we're only about a mile out," Lex noted as she straightened up and arched her back in a huge stretch.

"It's impressive," Lilly commented.

From their hill they could see the whole city and beyond. The city was carved out of a huge forest. Lilly could tell that Allen had once been a much bigger city. Mingled in the forest were the remains of decaying houses and small buildings.

"What does it look like? Describe it to me. It just looks like a big, white wall and a bunch of tiny ants swarming around in a chaotic mess to me," Lex said as she squinted her eyes and strained to see better.

"Man are you guys blind," Lilly said as she nudged her with her hip. "From here I can see the main walkway that seems to run around the perimeter of the city. Tread was right; there is a dark coating on the glass. It must prevent the sunlight from penetrating the walkway. There are two vampires patrolling the northern wall."

"You can't really see all that, can you?" Lex asked, amazed.

"One is wearing camouflage pants and a black t-shirt and the other one has on blue jeans and a gray t-shirt."

Lex just stood looking at Lilly, stunned.

"Inside the old stadium appears to be where the livestock is kept. I can see younger kids in there, like maybe eight to twelve or thirteen. Some are milking cows, others are shoveling manure, some are feeding the livestock. It looks like they have some pigs and chickens too. I count about twelve chicken coops all lined up in the far-east corner.

Lilly continued, "Beyond the stadium are several fields. It looks like huge gardens; there's corn, lettuce, tomatoes, and some other plants I'm not familiar with. Teenagers appear to be working those."

"There are some other buildings and people moving around behind a massive brown building, but I can't really tell for certain what they are doing. Maybe some type of construction. I can't be positive."

Then realization dawned on her and she ducked down slightly. "If I can see them, they can see us if they look this way. So I better start acting human, and we should probably talk as if I am from now on," Lilly suggested. "Also I think we should wait here until dark, then we can use your flashlight and start fumbling around in the dark and really get their attention. What do you think?" Lilly asked, attempting to be more considerate of Lex's feelings.

"Fine," Lex said. "But I don't fumble," she huffed.

Once the sun had gone down and Lex had pulled out her flashlight, it didn't take long before they had company.

Two female vampires approached them, one from each side. One was a brunette with her hair cut into a bob, wearing jean shorts and a hot pink tank top that said "queen" in the center. She was obviously a vampire. No human would have been outside on a cold day dressed like that. And if that wasn't obvious enough, she was barefoot. The other had short spiky red hair. She wore black leather pants that were so tight, Lilly imagined they would have to be cut off. She was also wearing a white t-shirt and a black leather jacket with black boots.

"Whooo are you?" Lilly stuttered. "What do you want?" she asked, trying to imitate a tremble.

"Can you help us find our sisters?" Lex asked, shaking slightly.

The redhead stepped forward. "Where's the rest of your group?" she asked as she smiled warmly. "Do you two need help finding them?"

Lex took Lilly by the arm and huddled against her.

"No. Our sisters were taken. We heard they might have been brought down here. We came to find them," Lilly said.

The brunette took a few quick steps towards them. "Where are the others? Who else came to help you find them?" she asked, a little too eagerly.

"Everyone else thinks our sisters are dead," Lex sniffled. "So we ran away to find them ourselves." She buried her face in Lilly's shoulder, shaking slightly.

The brunette let out a loud eerie laugh. "Well aren't you two brave...or stupid," she spat the last word.

"Alright, let's just take them and be done with it," the redhead snapped impatiently.

"Take us where?" Lex asked, trying to cower slightly.

The brunette took a few more steps until she was standing right in front of them. "You'll see," she said as she smiled the creepiest smile they'd ever seen.

"We can do this the easy way or the hard way," the redhead began as she walked closer. "The easy way, is I throw you over my shoulder and we run back to the city. You don't scream, you don't fight, you don't get hurt."

"Or the hard way, which is my personal favorite, I just eat you now and we have one less human to populate our city," the brunette said as she took a step closer, daring them to make the wrong choice.

Lex shared an uneasy glance with Lilly.

"We'll take the easy way," they said together.

Lilly stepped forward toward the psychotic brunette. The redhead at least seemed slightly more reasonable. She'd rather Lex go with her.

Lilly held her breath slightly as the brunette swung her over her shoulder. She thought somehow her vampire nature would be discovered, even though Tread had reassured her no one would be able to tell, and she was relieved when it wasn't.

"Let's get out of here, Roxy," the brunette called to the redhead.

"After you."

Lilly watched the world pass her by as she hung upside down over the crazy vampire's shoulder. It didn't take long to get to the gate. The gate creaked open loudly as they approached. They ran past the football stadium and straight to the huge brown building, the one that Tread had thought was a school and housed the humans.

They dumped Lex and Lilly hard on the cement in front of a set of double glass doors.

"Ow," Lex said, rubbing her side and elbow where she had hit the ground. Her eyes were watering, but she fought back the tears, refusing to let them fall.

Lilly moaned and tried to mimic Lex as best she could. "Are you alright?" she whispered.

Lex nodded, not trusting herself to speak.

Roxy hit a buzzer on the door, and within a minute a young man opened it. He was tall and tanned from working in the sun for days on end. He had light brown hair, cut short like someone in the military. He was lean and muscular. He wore a pair of faded but clean jeans and a snug-fitting dark blue t-shirt. He looked tough, but he had a warm smile and his eyes softened when he looked down at them.

"We've got two new ones for you, Ethan. Show them the ropes and get them sorted," Roxy ordered.

The two vampires turned and left, but not before the brunette had time to give one last swift kick to Lilly's ribs as she sat on the pavement.

"Ow!" Lilly cried. She was glad she had received the kick and not Lex. It hadn't hurt, but she imagined it would have, had it been aimed at her friend.

Ethan reached his hand down to help them up.   "Sorry about that," he apologized. "Mary is just cruel. I'd avoid her at all costs. She has her favorites that she likes to terrorize and trust me when I tell you that you do not want to be on that list."

Lex reached forward and pulled herself up using Ethan to counter her weight.

"Sadistic is more like it," she grumbled, rubbing her backside.

Lilly got up and Ethan held the door open, ushering them inside.

They stepped inside to a wide corridor. There were several rooms on each side, with hallways branching off at various points. Each hallway and room was marked with a big streak of paint above it. Lilly glanced around and saw some red, orange, and black streaks. She wondered what the colors signified.

"So where are you gals from?" Ethan asked. "We normally don't get groups so small. Where'd they find you two?"

"We're from Little Rock. We were captured about a mile or two from here. We came down here to find our sisters who were kidnapped," Lex explained. "What is this place?" she asked as she peered down a hallway, trying to keep up with his long strides.

"It's the housing unit for humans, until more get built. I'll get you sorted, assign you a color, a working assignment, and if you tell me your sisters' names, I'll find them and make sure you get to see them." He paused and looked at them. "Although the earliest that will happen is tomorrow. It's too late tonight. Lights out at nine. And I'm Ethan, by the way."

"I'm Lilly and this is Lex. So where are you from?" she asked.

"Here," he said, looking around in a circle. "I was born here, in Allen, Texas. My parents came here from Houston."

Lilly noted eight colors altogether as they walked down hallway after hallway. They had passed markings of red, orange, yellow, green, blue, purple, gray, and black. "So how long has this place been here?" Lilly asked.

"I think about twenty-five years. My parents were among the first to get brought here." Ethan stopped in front of a door with a purple swipe above it. "Purple. That's your color, remember it. Unfortunately, purple goes to medical tomorrow, but it's not that bad. In fact, I think it's better to get it over with at the beginning. Then you don't have seven rotations to wait and dread about it."

"Wait. What happens at medical?" Lex asked, grabbing Ethan's arm as he turned to leave.

Ethan stopped and extended his arms. There were scars on both arms from where blood had been taken out over and over again.

"No. Please, we can't. Give us a different color." Lilly pleaded.

"I can't," Ethan said, shaking his head. "It's really not that bad." He turned around and started walking back down the hallway.

Lex looked worriedly at Lilly.

"Please, Lex, my friend—she was attacked. She lost a lot of blood. She shouldn't give blood this soon," Lilly lied smoothly.

He paused and turned. "You better not be messing with me. It's almost lights out and I had stuff I wanted to do."

"Just give us two seconds, please. Look at her wrist," Lilly implored.

He sighed and walked back down towards them and held out his hand. Lex placed her wrist in it. He looked down and saw the two puncture marks from when Tread had fed on her.

"You're right. They're what, a week old?" Ethan asked, examining the scar.

"Yeah, about that," she said.

"How did you get attacked and survive?" he asked, an edge of accusation in his tone.

"There were two of them. One attacked Lex, and started feeding on her. He didn't know I was there. There was a huge storm about to break and the wind and thunder were so loud. Then the other one started fighting the first one over who would get to finish her off. We slipped away then. We were near a river and got in and drifted down it a ways. But she was really weak and lightheaded for several days." Lilly thought back to Adam. "She kept coming in and out of consciousness, and I didn't think she was going to make it. I just tried to keep her hydrated, and I prayed she'd survive."

Ethan eyed Lilly suspiciously. "Fine," he huffed. "It's not like I have time left to do what I wanted anyway. Green. Green went last week so it will be like eight more weeks till it's green's turn again. They only take our blood about once every two months," Ethan said. "It used to be more, till we had an influx in population. But I'd better not hear any more excuses when your time comes up again. We all have to take a turn. It's only fair."

Ethan led them down a series of hallways as they talked. He explained the color system and how the work stations were assigned.

Ages seven and under didn't work. Eight to fourteen worked with the livestock. Fifteen to nineteen worked the gardens. Twenty to fifty worked construction, building more housing units for the humans, and more homes for the vampires. Those older than fifty rotated between working the kitchen, doing the laundry, cleaning, and providing childcare. A select few humans were picked as runners. These men normally ranged from seventeen to their mid-twenties. They ran messages from one vampire to another. This was the most prestigious job assignment. Runners got extra rations and one day a week off. Everyone else got a day off every two weeks.

They reached a door with a green stripe over it. "Just head inside and they'll get you set up with a bunk," Ethan explained. "Don't worry, it's not that bad. Just stay out of Mary's way."

Lex walked through the doorway, but Lilly waited.

"Something else?" Ethan asked.

"They're not all bad," Lilly said. "Vampires, I mean. It may be hard to believe but some are actually nice."

"I know," Ethan said.

"You do?" Lilly asked, clearly surprised by his response.

"I've lived here twenty years. Others have seen it too. Some speculate that since they don't kill us, they've begun to grow fond of us. Not all of them of course. Mary, Heath, Kevin...and..." he began to whisper. "Steel." He shuddered. "They are crazy. But there are others that are actually kind. Or at the very least indifferent."

"Do they ever try to help you?" Lilly asked, hope creeping in.

"No. Some have tried in the past. But Steel is the leader of this city. Nobody messes with him. Any who have tried ended up dead."

"Thanks for your help today," Lilly said.

"Sure. Don't worry. You'll do fine. Just read the rules and stick to them. Break the rules and it's game over." Ethan turned and left.

Lilly walked through the doorway into a room filled with bunk beds. It was a small room, a crowded room. There were twelve sets of bunks, most already had an occupant lying on them, or climbing into them. Lilly was surprised to see that there were a mixture of men and women in the room. Some looked as young as nine or ten and others looked to be in their fifties or sixties.

"Over here Lilly," Lex called from the back of the room. She was sitting on the bottom bed, leaving the top vacant for Lilly.

"Lights out in two minutes," someone called out.

"There are rules etched into a piece of wood on the wall." Lex pointed. "You should probably read them. The penalty for breaking them is pretty...intense," Lex added after a moment.

Lilly walked over to the wall. Hanging in the middle of it at eye level was a faded wooden plaque. It was carved, and the letters had been painted over in red. Lilly scanned it quickly.

RULES

1. No going outside after dark

2. No talking back to a Master

3. Lights out by nine

4. Be on time to work station

5. No taking extra rations

6. Must report any rule breaker

Penalty = Death

Lilly climbed up onto her bunk. "Well, at least it seems pretty straight forward."

The lights went off.

"Good-night Lilly."

"Night Lex," Lilly whispered.

Lilly laid there quietly thinking about all that had transpired. They'd made it. They had gotten into the city. She had gotten out of donating blood, at least for the time being. There were callous vampires. She'd been expecting that, although imagining and seeing were two very different things. She found out some of the vampires were kind.

She hadn't been expecting that. That was good news. Could Tread convince them to turn on Steel? *Tomorrow,* she thought. *Tomorrow she would find out more about Steel.*

They had a long road ahead but she decided that for tonight at least they'd celebrate all the little victories.

She closed her eyes and let sleep find her.

Chapter 16
Blending

Lilly awoke to the sound of a giant alarm going off through a PA system in the ceiling. The lights turned on automatically and everyone in their small room began climbing out of bed and quickly dressing.

Lilly glanced over to the clock on the wall. Five a.m. It would still be dark outside. *How hard did they work these people?* she wondered.

"Guess we'd better get up," Lilly said, hopping off the top bunk.

Lex crawled out of bed and made it up as she saw the others doing. "You seem way too chipper for this early," Lex grumbled. "No decent person gets up at this time."

A short blonde who looked to be around twelve walked up to them. "Aimee." She stuck her hand out across to them.

Lex shook her hand. "I'm Lex and this is Lilly," she said, motioning to her friend. "What do we do now? We don't have any other clothes to change into."

She waved her hand in front of her. "Don't worry about that. They'll sort that out at the end of the day. Follow me if you want to eat. There's a lot to get done in the morning. We have to be to our stations by six, so you don't have much time to eat. Less time the further out your work area is."

Aimee guided them down several hallways to a big open area with lots of tables. On the way, Aimee pointed out a couple of restrooms, a small library, and a room she referred to as the game room.

She showed them how to get food. Each person was assigned a pin number. They entered the pin number into a machine and they were allowed one meal at breakfast and one at dinner. Lunch was brought out to every work zone.

Lex pushed a tray through the line, piling on scrambled eggs and fried potatoes, then tossed on an apple and a glass of milk. Lilly pushed her tray through the line, unsure of what to get, but assumed getting nothing would draw attention. Finally, she scooped up some eggs and took an apple.

Aimee looked down at Lilly's plate. "You are going to want more to eat than that. We work ten hours a day, and the work is hard. Trust me, you should get more now while you have the chance. You can only go through the line once at each meal, so if you don't get enough, you're screwed."

Lilly looked down at her food. "I'm not really hungry." She picked up her tray and followed Aimee.

Aimee huffed as she led them away from the serving line. "You'll be sorry later, don't say I didn't warn you."

Aimee's plate was overflowing. She had eggs, potatoes, an apple, a banana, and two muffins.

They found space at a table and began eating. No one really talked. It was a little eerie how quiet it was in a room this large with a couple hundred people crammed into it. Everyone seemed to be in a hurry to eat.

Lilly scraped her eggs onto Lex's plate when Aimee wasn't looking. She wondered how Tread was doing, and if he'd had a chance to go check on her family yet.

Lex picked up her apple and started to take a bite.

"Save that for later," Aimee blurted out, her mouth full of eggs and potatoes. "You can eat that while you're walking or save it for a snack, but you can't take the eggs and potatoes with you."

Lex nodded and set the apple back down. She finished about half her eggs and potatoes before it was time to leave.

"You better learn to eat faster," Aimee suggested. "My work station is in another direction. Just follow that group over there," she said as she pointed to a group of about fifty guys and girls who were headed out a back door.

"Thanks, Aimee," Lilly called, as their guide rushed down a hallway with a group of younger kids.

They turned and followed the teenagers they had been shown.

"I'm glad I grabbed the apple," Lex said as she took a huge bite. "I'm still starving."

Lilly handed her the apple she had picked up from the line.

"Thanks," Lex said, stuffing the apple into a pocket. "The benefits of being your friend never cease to amaze me."

When they arrived at the fields, Lilly and Lex were separated. Lex was sent off to harvest potatoes, while Lilly was assigned to help till the ground for a new field.

It was hard for her to let Lex out of her sight. She wouldn't be able to protect her. But she knew the community wanted the humans alive to harvest their blood. She sighed and followed a girl named Ellen, who seemed to be in charge of their group.

For her work assignment, Lilly, along with a few other girls, was to mix manure in with the soil after the guys had tilled a section.

The stench was almost unbearable, but other than that, Lilly thought the job seemed pretty easy. She couldn't imagine breathing it in all day. Luckily for her breathing wasn't a necessity, and she could cease anytime there was an unpleasant smell. Lilly felt sorry for the others in her group who couldn't shut off their senses.

There were three other girls in her group. They all seemed to be about her age. One girl was tall, with freckles covering her face and dark brown hair pulled up into a bun. Lilly heard one of the

220

other girls call her Franny. Another girl was average height, brown hair, and had thick, black-rimmed glasses. Her name was Janet. The last girl, Ellen, who was either in charge, or just very bossy, had an athletic build with strawberry blond hair that was pulled up into a ponytail.

After a couple of hours of mixing the soil, Ellen called for a five-minute break. The other girls began to sit down and open bottles of water. Lilly paused to join them. She could have kept working, but she assumed it might look suspicious if she worked ten hours without stopping.

"So, Lilly, right?" Franny asked.

She nodded.

"Ethan said you were looking for your sister. What's her name?" Franny asked in between chugging down large swallows of water.

"Beth. Beth Marsh. She's ten. Do you know her?"

"No, sorry." She looked over at Janet. "Do you know her?"

Janet was quiet for a moment and scratched her head. "No. There is no Beth Marsh. Not sure what happened to your sister, but she didn't end up here. At least she has that going for her," Janet said.

"How can you be sure?" Lilly asked.

"Jan—" Franny began.

"Janet is our record keeper," Ellen interrupted. "She keeps track of everyone who comes here." Ellen downed the rest of her water, and then stood up. "Break's over," she announced.

Lilly noticed how quickly Janet and Franny jumped up. Picking up a bucket of manure, she shook it around a patch of earth and asked, "So how many vampires live here?"

"Way too many," Franny whispered. "They can hear from like twenty miles away."

I wish, Lilly thought.

Janet used a shovel to start mixing in the manure that Lilly had just dumped. "Enough to make sure we stay put. If you're thinking about trying to escape...DON'T. Even though there are only about twenty of them, it's more than enough," she whispered. "No one has ever made it out. Anyone who has ever tried has been executed."

"What do they do? Shoot you? Hang you?"

"No, wouldn't that be a nice change." Janet looked around nervously and then lowered her voice to barely a whisper. "They march you out in front of everyone and then it's a free-for-all. It's the only time *he* lets them kill us. They dart out from every direction, each trying to get a piece of you." She shuddered. "Imagine you, me, Franny, and Ellen each grabbing a doll by a limb and then pulling. It's kind of like that only with more red. It's horrifying. Once you see an execution it will cure any desire you have of trying to leave here."

They worked quietly for the rest of the morning. Lilly noticed that no one stopped unless Ellen did. Around noon, two older men (Lilly guessed they were in their sixties) came and brought sandwiches and fruit around.

"I'm surprised they go to so much trouble to feed us so well," Lilly noted. She put the apple in her pocket to save for Lex, and threw pieces of the sandwich into a trashcan when no one was watching.

"Apparently they tried just feeding everyone bread and water at first, but evidently unhealthy humans don't taste so good," Ellen said bitterly. She finished the last bite of her sandwich and then continued. "They also tried working us longer and harder, but after some of us started dropping dead in the summer, they shortened our work hours, and even give us a day off every two weeks to rest. It's all about keeping their livestock healthy," Ellen said cynically.

"Do you ever—" Lilly began and froze.

Walking towards them through the grass was a vampire, along with four human men. Two walked on each side, holding poles that draped a small tent-like object over the vampire. The tent was made of dark sheets of something that gave an appearance similar to plastic. It completely encompassed the female vampire, giving her plenty of room to walk and still be covered. If it wasn't moving, four people could have fit inside. The material was so dark that Lilly doubted the others could see which vampire was inside.

But Lilly could. It was Mary. The lunatic vampire she had met last night.

Ellen jumped up as she approached; she stood tall but with her head bowed down. Lilly saw the others do the same and followed suit.

"Slacking off like always," Mary sneered through the curtain.

"Sorry, Master," Ellen said, bowing. "We were just finishing our lunch. We'll get back to work now."

She bowed and started to turn back to the field.

"Hold on there," Mary demanded. "New girl. Find your sister?" she heckled.

"No, Master. She's not here," Lilly answered, mimicking Ellen's reply. She bowed lowly, but it took everything in her not to rip away the curtain.

"What a pity," Mary laughed. "You know, you don't look quite as dirty as the rest. If you don't work hard, you don't eat. Ellen, make sure she doesn't eat or drink for the rest of the day. We don't run a charity." She turned and left.

"I'm sorry," Janet said, patting Lilly's arm consolingly. "No food is bad enough, but no water." She shook her head slowly.

"The apple," Ellen said, stretching out her hand while pointing to Lilly's pocket with the other.

Franny looked appalled. "Really? Are you sure that's necessary? Couldn't you just pretend that you didn't see it?"

"Do you want to be on her list? I sure don't." Ellen said, stuffing the apple in her pocket and picking up a shovel. "Now let's get back to work."

"It's fine, really. Don't worry about me," Lilly said.

"Mary targets people and tortures them. If she's zeroed in on you, watch out. You won't be able to do anything right," Janet whispered. "I can't even remember the last time she's come out here. She hates the smell of the manure. They say that the stench is worse for the vampires on account of their heightened senses. Although, I've heard they don't even have to breathe. I think she

223

avoids this place because she thinks it's beneath her, just knowing that it stinks here."

Tell me about it, Lilly thought. "I haven't done anything. Why do you think she chose me?" she asked, picking up her shovel and mixing more manure into the soil.

"Your eyes. They're green," Franny explained.

Ellen and Janet looked at Lilly and shared a knowing glance.

Lilly pushed her shovel deep into the dirt and leaned against it. "What's me having green eyes have to do with anything?"

Janet paused halfway through filling another bucket. "Have you heard of Lord Steel?" she asked.

"I heard someone mention a Steel. I think he's in charge or something like that," Lilly replied.

"Lord Steel. Make sure that's what you call him," Janet corrected. "He wants a wife. Rumor has it that Mary wants the job. But he has a fetish for green eyes. Every few weeks we get a new group of humans. He rounds up everyone with green eyes and then picks the one he thinks is the most beautiful. Then he tries to turn her into a vampire," Janet whispered. She stood up and pulled a rag from her back pocket, wiping the dirt off. "I don't know what he's doing wrong but all of them have died."

Lilly thought about what she had learned as she finished her shift. What would happen if Steel picked her and then tried to turn her? There was no way she could sidestep that catastrophe without blowing her true identity.

She wondered about the twenty vampires. How many of them were open-minded? How many would they need on their side before they could start a coup?

As they walked back to the brown building, the mood seemed to lighten. Everyone was less rushed and Lilly actually heard laughing.

"Franny?" Lilly asked.

"Yes, Lilly," Franny answered as she opened up the door to the school.

"What happens if a vampire is in sunlight?" Lilly asked. "I mean I heard it kills them, but how?"

Franny glanced around nervously. "Poof." She held up her hands, closed them into fists, and then acted out a popping motion. "It's pretty instantaneous. It only takes a few seconds."

Lilly had never thought to ask Tread before. She had never really thought about it since daylight didn't affect her for some reason.

She spotted Lex wolfing down a tray filled with spaghetti at a table with two guys. She walked over, relieved to see her friend was still alive and seemed to be fine.

"Go get a plate," Lex hinted, tilting her head in the direction of the line.

Lilly sat down beside her. "Can't. I'm not allowed to eat by order of Mary." She made an apologetic look at Lex.

The two guys across from them shared a glance.

"This is Ryan and Justin." Lex nodded toward them as she took another giant mouthful.

"Lilly," Lilly said, introducing herself.

"Man, I don't have to guess where you got assigned," Justin said, waving a hand in front of his nose.

Lilly thought he looked like a Californian Surfer, from movies she had seen. The first thing she noticed were his teeth—they were perfectly straight and very white. He was tan, lean, and had blond wavy hair. The only difference between him and the surfer actors she'd watched on the big screen was the amount of product in their hair. His was a disheveled mess. She wondered if he didn't care or if it was because he just lacked the styling products.

Ryan elbowed him. "Be nice," he said, adjusting his glasses. His glasses seemed out of place with the rest of him. He was handsome. He wore a tight fitting t-shirt and Lilly could see the lines from his muscles beneath it. He wore a beat up cowboy hat and looked the part of a hardworking cowhand, except for his thick, black, horn-rimmed glasses. Lilly wondered if he lived somewhere else if he would have swapped them for contacts.

"We dug up and washed potatoes all day," Lex said. "I am beat. I don't think I've ever worked this hard a day in my life." She turned her hands over, and showed them to Lilly. "Have you ever seen so many blisters?" She pouted.

Justin shook his head and frowned. "Just wait until tomorrow. If you think the first day is rough, the next two will be even worse." He grimaced slightly, looking at her bloodied, beat up hands. "Tomorrow, you will feel ten times worse." He looked apologetic. "Just be prepared, tomorrow you will be so sore from squatting most of the day, and your hands will be even more tender. But," he gave a half smile, "your muscles will start to get used to the work and your hands will eventually callous." He raised up his hands as proof. "Things will get worse before they get better, but give it a week."

"Great," Lex mumbled sarcastically.

Ryan leaned forward, his elbows on the table. "You mentioned Mary? Where did you see her, anyway?"

"She came out to our field just after lunch," Lilly explained.

"She's a Sunwalker!" Lex said, choking on her milk and spitting some of it out onto her plate.

She said it a little too loudly, earning stares from multiple tables.

"No." Lilly shook her head. "She had some type of portable covering that a few humans carried."

"Humans?" Justin asked, staring at Lilly like she was from another planet. "Who talks like that?"

"Um. Vampires," Ryan said, looking at Lilly with the same weirded out expression.

"I'm just not sure how to talk here," Lilly sighed in frustration. "Sometimes you call the vampires Master, other times you use their first names. Some people say Steel, others Lord Steel. But I seem to get in trouble either way."

Justin nodded, seeming to believe her explanation. "It's Master to their faces and outside. I would always say Lord Steel. You don't ever want to mess with him. You think Mary is crazy..." He was silent for a moment. "The bloodsuckers never come in here. So we normally feel pretty comfortable in here."

"So are any of them friendly?"

"Annie is by far the nicest. She is gentle when she draws blood. And she even talks to you. Some of the others just jab you like a piece of meat," Ryan said, cutting a piece of his chicken. "Mark, Davis, and Jen aren't mean, but they don't really seem to care either. The new one though, Tread, I actually saw him help someone who fainted after giving blood. He seemed to genuinely care. He actually sat with her, and had a runner find her some fruit and bring it back."

"I wish we could just find a way to live together in peace," Lilly said.

Justin rolled his eyes. "Sure," he snorted.

Lilly glared at Lex.

"Oh, I mean, yeah," Lex chimed in, catching the hint. "Obviously not with that Mary chick. But I'm sure there are decent ones like, Tread, did you say?" Lex asked, trying to be supportive.

Ryan nodded, so Lex continued. "I mean, I probably wouldn't mind giving blood sometimes, if I were free and if we all got along."

"You're kidding, right?" Justin said, leaning forward. "Why would you do that, after all they do to us?"

Lex shrunk back a little, feeling less confident.

"Well, isn't it better to help each other and find some kind of peace, than to live constantly in fear?" Lilly chimed in. "What if we could go outside, take walks, go to the beach? Live in a world like before. Maybe it's possible. I mean the vampires are stronger, I don't think they are going away. Doesn't it sound better to find a way to live together?"

"It sounds crazy to me," Ryan said, running a hand through his hair. "It's a fairy tale. It will never happen. Not with vampires like Mary or Lord Steel."

"Come on, all humans aren't good either. That's why we have prisons. Maybe we need to come up with prisons for some of them too," Lilly proposed.

Ryan shrugged.

"How about prisons for all of them?" Justin suggested after he finished his last bite of chicken. "Sounds like a way better plan to me," he said as he wiped off his face with a napkin.

Lilly gave up arguing for the moment. She figured she and Lex had pushed it enough for today. She hoped Tread was making better headway with the vampires.

Justin and Ryan finished clearing their trays and invited the girls to try out the game room. They insisted it wasn't much but it was fun. Lex promised she'd join them soon. After they had walked out of the cafeteria Lex turned to Lilly.

"So how was your day really?" Lilly asked, looking sympathetically at her friend's hands.

"Long, hard." She sighed, then smiled bashfully. "Well, honestly, it wasn't all bad."

Lilly looked at her questioningly.

"Ethan was working in the potato fields too. He was really helpful and sweet."

"Oh really."

Lex shoved her. "Come on. I'm just saying he's nice. We talked the whole day, it really made the time go by faster, and he helped show me a few tricks he's learned over the years to make the work easier. I'm sure he was just being polite and helping me because I'm new."

Lilly changed the subject. "Did you learn anything useful?"

Lex swept up the last remnants of her spaghetti sauce with her roll. "No," she said apologetically. "Not really. All I really learned was that no one believes escape is possible and they adamantly tried to discourage me from ever trying."

Lex finished her last bite, then left to find Justin and Ryan. She was determined to start planting ideas about good, loving vampires to them. Lilly decided to head back to her sleeping quarters and try to meet more people. After all, that was the point of her being here.

As she turned the corner Ethan ran straight into her, knocking her down. She could have easily avoided him. It was hard for her not to just step out of the way with her speed instead of letting him run into her.

"Sorry," he said quickly, and then he took off in a hurry down another hallway, not helping her up or waiting to see if she was OK.

Lilly stood up and watched him go. *What a jerk,* she thought.

She didn't know why, but she decided to follow him. She wondered where he was going in such a hurry.

He rushed down a few hallways and then headed up a stairwell taking the steps two and three at a time. He stopped in front of a door with a white streak above it.

Chapter 17
Psychopath

No one had mentioned a white group. They weren't in the rotation to donate blood. She watched as Ethan stood in front of the door for a moment. He waited until his breathing leveled out, straightened his hair with his hands, tucked his shirt in, and walked inside.

Lilly crept closer and peeked inside the room.

She was surprised to find that the room looked like a big nursery. There were dozens of toddler beds lined up in two neat little rows. At the end of each row was a twin bed. Inside each bed was a boy or girl tucked in; most were asleep but a few were still awake. There were two lamps still on, and two older women were sitting up reading in each of the twin beds.

"He's been waiting," one of the old ladies said. "He was so worried you weren't coming. I don't think I could have handled it, seeing him disappointed two nights in a row."

Ethan frowned slightly. "I know. I wanted to be here." He stood there awkwardly rubbing the back of his head. "It just couldn't be helped." He turned and strode over to one of the toddler beds. A little boy who looked to be about three sat up as he approached, grinning ear-to-ear.

"Efan!" The little boy smiled. "I stay in bed. You come read to me."

He sat down on the edge of the bed and ruffled the boy's hair with his hand. "Of course I will, Lukey. Miss Evelyn said you've been being a good boy. I brought your favorite." Ethan reached into his back pocket and pulled out a small book.

He began reading, and Luke cuddled up against Ethan's chest, pulling the blanket over both of them.

"I love you across the river and over the hills, said Big Nutbrown Hare," Ethan read.

"And to the moon," Luke interrupted.

"Yes." He smiled as he tickled him lovingly on his tummy. "But I'm not at that part yet. You have to be patient."

The boy laughed and hugged Ethan tighter. "But Efan love Lukey to the moon," he said, pointing towards the window.

"Yes, Ethan loves Lukey to the moon and beyond."

He finished the story and gave the boy a hug and a kiss. "I love you buddy. Sweet dreams." He made sure the blanket was covering Luke, and turned to leave.

Luke yawned. "Efan be back tomowow?"

He stopped and kissed him once more on the forehead. "Tomorrow buddy."

Ethan walked out of the room and found Lilly waiting for him.

"Is that your brother?"

"Yes," he said shortly. He didn't seem too pleased that she had followed him—his face looked hard and angry.

"I'm sorry."

His face softened slightly. "Why?"

"That's what you missed yesterday," Lilly said. "When you had to deal with Lex and me. You mentioned having other things you had wanted to do. We made you miss reading to your brother."

"Yeah, well, it happens," he said as he started walking down the hallway away from her.

Lilly started following him. "Where are your parents? You said you were born here, right?"

Ethan stopped. He turned and looked angry. "Dead. OK?" he barked. "Anything else you want to know? Or would you rather just follow me some more?"

Lilly stopped. "You're right. I'm sorry, it's not my business. It's just...well you seem to be so content with this place. Not like everyone else. No one else wants to be here."

He sighed. "Look, I don't have the liberty of only worrying about myself." He peeked back longingly at the door where his brother slept. "Do I like being held captive? No. But I've been here a long time. I've seen things no one else has. Do I wish things were better? Yeah. Am I going to complain, push the limits, slack off? No. I'm all that kid's got," Ethan said, raising his voice.

Lilly placed a hand gently on his shoulder. "I'm sorry. I shouldn't have followed you. I hope someday things do change for you and Luke. He seems like a sweet boy. He deserves better than this."

"Yeah, he does. He deserved two parents, but they were stupid," he said bitterly. "They wanted a better life for him than I had been dealt. And now they're dead. What came from them stirring things up? Nothing." Ethan slammed his hand against the wall. "Now Luke gets the same crappy life, only without the two loving parents to help pull him through it all."

"Maybe things will change someday. Get better," Lilly said.

Ethan leaned against the wall and sighed. "Steel will never change." He rubbed his face, looking tired.

"You've lived here all your life. What is he like?"

"Twisted. Yeah, twisted would be a good word to describe him."

"Can I ask what happened to your parents?" Lilly asked, hesitantly.

Ethan sighed, studying her intently for a minute. "Somehow I don't think you're the type of person that takes no for an answer." He walked into an empty room.

There was a big, circular rug in the center of the room. It was a rainbow, made up of rings of different colors. It was probably bright and beautiful at one time. Now it just looked faded and sad.

There was a whitewash board on one wall, and the alphabet was written neatly on individual sheets of paper and pinned around the perimeter of the room near the top of the ceiling. There were small activity centers for the children; one with blocks, one with small plastic animals, and another with a few puzzles.

Lilly realized this must be a room they used for the children who were too young to work. There were a few toys in one corner of the room. A small table with mismatched makers and crayons made up an art station.

Ethan took a seat on the rug and sat with his legs criss-crossed. He motioned for her to sit in front of him.

"It's kind of a long story," he warned her.

She sat down across from him, crossed her legs, and waited.

"So, my parents are from Houston. It's several hours south of here. They were born there, grew up together, went to school together. They married right out of high school. My dad was good with his hands. He was a handyman-slash-mechanic-slash-engineer. He didn't have any official degrees or anything like that. He just always had this knack. He could take anything apart and put it right back together. He never needed notes or pictures to remember how something fit. He could just look at something and know right away what was wrong with it, even something he had never seen before."

He leaned back, putting his arms behind him to hold himself up and then continued. "He built himself a good business. People were hesitant at first to hire him because of his lack of a formal education, but word of mouth proved a powerful tool. He became so popular he had to turn down business.

"Life was perfect. They had been married a year. My mother didn't know it at the time, but she was pregnant with me. My father decided to do something special to celebrate their one-year wedding anniversary. They had always wondered what it was like outside the wall. My mother's favorite movie was *The Hustler*, some old black and white movie. The couple in the movie shared a picnic outside in a wooded area. My father hired two off-duty VAS soldiers, packed an elaborate lunch, and surprised my mom with a 'date to remember' outside the wall."

He laughed darkly. "Well she remembered it alright. They had just laid out their blanket when they were taken."

"My parents always said it happened so fast. No one had any time to react. One minute my father was spreading his blanket out neatly on the grass and the next thing he knew they were in a dark box, filled with other people. They didn't even get to enjoy their picnic." He glanced at his watch and continued.

"My dad used to tell me stories of how things were when they first began living here. No one lived at the school. This is like a castle compared to where they used to live. I was born in some old building with mold growing from the ceiling. There was no electricity or plumbing back then. People were all crammed together in a small brick structure, living in their own filth. Steel would come by occasionally and point to someone and they'd bleed them dry.

"My parents had fortunate timing." He reached up and rubbed the stubble on his chin. "Apparently the vampires had just started playing with the idea of keeping humans alive as a constant blood source. There was a human doctor here." He paused, closed his eyes, and squinted in concentration. "I can't remember his name," he said, shaking his head and opening his eyes again. "The doctor helped them set it up, anything to ensure his survival. He came up with the rotation cycle and the idea of siphoning the blood into bags to ensure human survival, instead of leaving it up to the vampire to stop in time. He was nice. He ended up dying of a heart attack, we think, when I was about five.

"Steel took a while to adjust to the whole feeding from blood bags idea. My mom told me that for the first few years, he would occasionally pick a person, usually a female. He would hang her in his chambers, and drain her slowly. He might slice her foot, or her arm and let the blood drain into a cup and then when it clotted, he would begin again." He cringed. "I think he did a lot more than that to them. My parents shielded me from what they could, but

234

they could never keep me from hearing the screaming." He shuddered. "I *never* want to know pain like that."

He looked down at the rug, pulling on a loose thread. "Anyway," he continued, "over time things got somewhat better. They improved things when people would get sick or start dying. They do what they have to in order to keep the *livestock*," he pointed at Lilly, and then back at himself, "in good health.

"Over the years we saw several escape attempts. My parents were always searching for a way out, but they didn't want to risk it unless it was foolproof. People were always punished in new ways once caught. I remember one getting his eyes gorged out. That was pretty gruesome." He shuddered at the memory. "But once he had recovered, well as much as he could, Steel fed on him anyway. I won't go into all the details of what he did to each person he caught. But the one that changed my parents' minds happened when I was ten."

He paused, and Lilly thought for a moment he was going to vomit. "I wish I could forget it," he said, shaking his head. "There was a young girl, about fourteen. She was new. We tried to warn her not to try anything, but a lot of those who hadn't seen Steel's cruelty didn't listen. She thought she could hide under a truck when the vampires went out for their next collection." He looked down at the ground, avoiding eye contact. "If she had told us her idea, we might have been able to stop her. Of course they heard her breathing, and they heard her heartbeat. She was caught and brought before Steel. I remember him saying what a *fun* idea he had for this one." Ethan stopped. He didn't speak for a long time. Lilly was beginning to think he wasn't going to finish the story when he finally continued. "He passed out spray bottles to several of his friends and made her stand in the center of them. Like most of his executions, he liked to put on a performance, and he made us watch. They started spraying her. She started screaming. We didn't understand at first, not until her skin started peeling, and she started bleeding. They were spraying her with acid." He shuddered again, and then got up and bolted to a small trashcan in the corner.

Lilly turned away. She could hear retching sounds, and something hitting the bottom of the trashcan.

"Sorry," Ethan said as he wiped his mouth on his shirt and walked back over to her.

Lilly stood up. "Ethan, it's okay, you don't have to finish. I don't want you to have to relive these horrible things."

Ethan held up a hand. "No, people need to hear these things. Realize what these vampires are really capable of." He paused, gathering his thoughts. "By the time they were finished," he began, tears welling up in his eyes, "there wasn't much left of her." He sniffled and wiped his eyes with his sleeve. "I think that's the only time I ever saw them not drain the body during an execution."

"After that, my parents didn't want to risk it. They kept their heads down, worked hard, donated their blood, and did everything they could to just go unnoticed. But that all changed when I was sixteen and my mom realized she was pregnant again."

Lilly walked over and hugged Ethan. "I'm so sorry, Ethan. Just stop. I shouldn't have asked."

He looked like he had the weight of the world on his shoulders. She couldn't imagine what it felt like to live everyday of your life in fear, not just for yourself, but for those you loved.

He shook her off. "No, it's fine. I don't want anyone else to go through what I have. You need to realize the type of maniac Steel is." Ethan reached down and picked up a small orange ball from a basket. He tossed it back and forth between his hands. "So, when my parents realized that they were going to have another baby, it relit the fire inside of them. They didn't want their second child to grow up the way I had. My mom told me that they had failed me, but that things were going to change for me and for my new sibling.

"My dad worked in a corn field that backed up against the western wall." Ethan motioned to the west. "He convinced two other men to escape with them. They took turns keeping watch and digging a small opening underneath the wall. A few days before they were scheduled to leave, my mother gave birth to Luke. They didn't think he was due for another three weeks.

"Well this slowed their timetable down considerably. You see, when a woman has a baby, they separate her from everyone else. They keep them quarantined for about eight weeks, to make sure the baby has a little time to build up an immune system." He laughed darkly. "It's all about keeping their food supply healthy. So after eight weeks they brought my mother and brother back to general population. My dad didn't want to wait any longer. I was seventeen then, and I refused to go with them. I begged them not to go. The original plan had been to sneak out during the daytime. That way, even if the vampires saw them, they'd have to wait until night to come after them. But once mom had Luke that became impossible. She wouldn't work until Luke had been weaned. So the only option was to wait close to a year and hope their hole wasn't discovered or to go then. So they left at night. My mom kept promising they'd come back and find a way to get me out," Ethan said as he fought back tears. "Obviously they were caught. It was a pointless risk. At night all the vampires were out. They didn't even make it anywhere near the corn field."

By now tears were streaming down his face. "Luke was spared. He was a baby and eventually he'd grow into another blood supply." Tears flooded down his cheeks but he continued. "My parents and the two other men weren't so lucky. Steel told the men it would be a fight to the death. There were two knives thrown into the center of a ring and when the whistle blew it was a free-for-all. Steel told my father that if he won, my mother's life would be spared. My father fought tooth and nail and although he lost a hand and had a couple of deep gashes on his arms and legs, he came out victorious."

Ethan stopped for a moment trying to reclaim control over his emotions. He half snorted, half cried, "Steel lied of course. As soon as my dad had won, he let my mother go to him. Right as they were about to embrace, Steel had Heath slit her throat. She dropped to the ground a foot in front of him, trying to speak as she grasped at her bloody throat. My father of course broke down on

237

the ground in front of his wife. After he had grieved for several minutes, Steel waved his hand and Heath finished him off as well." He tried to wipe the tears from his face, but they kept coming. He tossed the ball back in the basket and turned away from her.

She felt helpless sitting there listening to his life story. To be born a prisoner, to lose his parents in such a horrific way, and then to basically become the father to his little brother was more than anyone could handle. Yet he seemed to hold it together well. She was amazed after hearing his experiences that Ethan had grown into a man that was so caring and helpful, not a bitter, miserable soul as one might expect.

"He's the devil incarnate," Lilly said softly. "I heard once sometimes vampires fight each other for power or position. Maybe someone better will come along and challenge him," she added hopefully.

Ethan laughed cynically as he turned back to face her. He was no longer crying, but his face was red and puffy. "He's unstoppable. Not only is he an excellent fighter—I've seen him fight—he has a weapon that makes him undefeatable."

"What weapon?"

"Ever heard of dragon steel?" Ethan asked.

Lilly nodded.

"He has a sword edged with dragon steel. He carries it on his back all the time. No vampire will dare challenge him. A few have tried and they were all dispatched within a few seconds."

"How would he even get that? Dragon steel is said to be so rare that it's almost mythical."

Ethan rubbed a hand across his face and yawned. "Mythical or not, he has one. You'll see him soon enough. He has weekly meetings to remind us of how sadistic he really is, to keep us in our place. We're having one tomorrow night around seven. Right after we eat."

Lilly went back to her room and climbed into her bunk. Lex wasn't back yet. It was five minutes till lights out.

Lilly closed her eyes and thought about Ethan and Luke. How hard it must be to only see your brother for a few minutes every day.

It was one minute to lights out and Lex still wasn't back.

Lilly sat up. She was worried something bad might have happened when she heard footsteps in the hallway.

She could hear Lex panting as she ran. She burst into the room a few seconds later and dove onto her bed.

She made it with about ten seconds to spare.

"Cutting it a little close?" Lilly asked.

Lex was still panting. "South. Dumpsters. Outside. One a.m.," she said, barely in a whisper.

Tread had finally made contact.

Chapter 18
Dangerous Liaisons

Lilly climbed slowly out of bed a few minutes before one. It was dark inside the room, with the exception of the red numbers glowing on the clock that hung on the wall.

She crept between bunk beds, and slowly opened the door. She had left her shoes in the room, for fear they might squeak on the tile floor. The hallways were deserted, but there were lights on every
few feet. Lilly assumed they were there to light the way to the bathrooms.

She headed south, walking through the cafeteria until she found a side door in the back of the kitchen. She glanced around quickly before she pushed it opened.

She wasn't really worried about any humans seeing her leave. She could hear them coming long before she would see them. The vampires, however, were her main concern.

It was night now, so all twenty-something could be out anywhere. They could see her from afar. Especially if any were in the walkways that lined the city's perimeter. They'd have the advantage of being up high and having a clear outlook over the city.

She was down on the ground and had buildings and walls concealing her view.

She had to assume Tread had thought of that. She opened the door, prepared to sneak around the building as quickly as possible, but found the dumpsters immediately.

Tread had found a little pocket where the walls concealed them, leaving very little open space for prying eyes.

She walked over behind the oversized trash receptacles and saw him standing there.

He swept her up and kissed her quickly before setting her back down again.

"I don't have long. I feel like I always have someone watching me." He reached into his jacket and pulled out a blood bag.

Lilly took it and started to speak but Tread cut her off.

"You drink, I'll talk."

She sunk her teeth into the bag and began to drain its contents.

"I saw your family a few hours ago. They're worried but fine. I brought them some food and water." Tread began rattling off not stopping. "I've met two vampires, Annie and Davis, who like humans. They don't like how they are treated, but they are terrified to do anything about it. Mark, Jen, Randall, Keith, I think they could be convinced. Everyone is scared of Steel. He is the leader. I've only caught glimpses of him. Apparently he has no problem killing his own kind. The stories I've heard are disturbing to say the least."

Lilly's eyes widened. "That's an understatement if you've heard even half of what I have. What did they tell you about Steel?"

"Some other time. I really should get back. What's been going on with you? And you brought Lex with you," he said, sounding surprised. "How did that happen?"

"Another time," Lilly said dismissively. "First, Steel is supposed to be an expert fighter and he has a sword edged with dragon steel."

Tread nodded, recollection showing on his face. "That's why he carries it with him wherever he goes. I wondered why that sword seemed so important to him. But dragon steel—that definitely raises the value."

"Yeah. Well the humans are just as terrified of him. Have you heard how they are executed?"

"Yeah. It's pretty gruesome. Annie and several of the others don't participate. She said it's mainly his little posse. Heath, Kevin, and Mary."

"Mary has it in for me."

Tread sighed. "That's not good. Why?"

Lilly opened her eyes wide and blinked a few times. "Because I have green eyes, or that's the reason I've been told."

"I hadn't thought about that. Since you aren't human, it hadn't even crossed my mind that he might pick you." Tread hit himself on the side of the head. "I'm so stupid. Of course he'll pick you. No one else will hold a candle to you." Tread shook his head. "We don't have a lot of time. We are going out and getting a new batch of people next month, so that gives us five, six weeks tops," Tread explained. "Steel will give them a week to get settled before having anyone with green eyes brought before him for inspection. Then he will select one to be his bride."

"How does that even work? How do you turn someone? It obviously hasn't been working for him."

"It's a little complicated. I'll explain it—"

"Later," Lilly said, finishing his sentence in frustration.

He pulled her in his arms and ran a finger gently down her cheek, pushing a strand of hair out of her face. "Sorry. I really do have to go. I love you." He kissed her softly. "Keep working on them," he said, motioning to the building. "I'll do the same."

He left too quickly. She wished he could stay longer than two minutes, but understood the danger.

Lilly walked back to the building and looked around outside once more before slowly opening the door.

She heard him before she was able to see him. Someone was there. Lilly stepped through the door and saw Ethan standing there in a t-shirt and sweatpants. He had his arms folded and if she had an egg, she was pretty sure she could fry it on top of his head right now.

"I was just getting some air—" she began.

"Save it," he snapped. He walked over to the door, peered out, and then shut it. "Are you crazy?" he whisper-shouted. "Did you even read the rules?"

Lilly shrugged. "How did you even know?"

He looked flabbergasted. "That's it? That's all you have to say for yourself?"

She didn't answer.

Ethan covered his face with his hands and took a deep breath. "Rule number one: 'No going outside after dark.' It's the first rule. It's the easiest one to keep. What were you doing, and don't give me that bull about wanting air. I saw you," he sighed. "I knew you were here because we monitor the doors." He pointed to a miniscule black box at the top of the door that must have been motion activated. "Lilly." He shook his head. "I have no choice now. I have to report you."

"You can't report me," she said. "Please."

"I have to. Rule number six: 'Must report any rule breaker.' Lilly, they will kill me if I don't report it. Even if I didn't care about that, I have to be here for Luke. I'm all he has left. Why, Lilly? Just tell me why?" He paced around, shaking his head and looking disappointed. "What was so important you'd risk death? Didn't you listen to anything I told you today? I shared painful, personal memories with you. Just so you wouldn't do something stupid like this," he said, pointing to the door she had just entered.

"No one will ever know," Lilly insisted as she took a step forward and placed a hand on his arm. "Please, Ethan."

He looked torn. He let out a long sigh. "It doesn't matter anyway. If I don't tell, that vampire that saw you out there will. He's probably already told them."

Lilly stepped backed and tilted her head to the side surprised. "What exactly did you see?" she asked.

"I just saw you and that new vampire step behind the dumpster. What did he say to you?" Ethan asked.

Lilly avoided answering and asked another question instead. "Ethan. What would you give to be free? For Luke to never have to worry about getting executed?"

"Anything. Everything." He stepped forward. "But what does that have to do with anything? That is never going to happen. I'm sorry, Lilly. I like you and I really like Lex." A smile crept up on his face when he mentioned her name.

Lilly raised her eyebrows and smiled.

"Yeah, well we seemed to hit it off today at work." He blushed as he thought back. "I don't know, maybe I'm just imagining it. I guess it doesn't really matter, I know she'll hate me after this."

Lilly placed her hand on his shoulders and looked into his eyes. "Ethan, I promise you, that vampire is never going to tell anyone."

Ethan started to shake his head and tried to take a step back but Lilly wouldn't let him.

"Things can change, Ethan. We can make this place better. You can give Luke the kind of life your parents wanted for him. Please trust me," she pleaded earnestly.

"You're delusional," Ethan said, pushing her away from him. "That vampire's new. Just watch, he will throw you under the bus to get in good with Steel. There will never be a world like you imagine. Vampires just don't care as much as you do. They won't risk themselves. Their immortality matters too much to them."

"OK," Lilly said flatly.

"OK?" Ethan said. "That's it. You've given up, you're fine with being executed?"

"No!" She stepped back. "Ethan, look, I want you to trust me. I know I'm asking you to risk a lot. But sometimes you have to take major risks—it's the only way to change things. And..." she said, dragging the word out, "if I want you to trust me, then I have to trust you. I have to risk something too."

"What are you talking about?" Ethan asked.

"I'm a vampire," Lilly announced.

Ethan snorted and turned around. "Whatever. I thought—"

A split-second later, Lilly stood across the room next to a big rack with dishes on them. She picked a plate up and tossed it up in the air, catching it easily.

Ethan spun around back to the spot where she had been standing a second before. Then he turned back and she was still standing at the end of the hallway. "How did you—"

Now she was standing mere inches from him.

He jumped back. "You're a freaking vampire." He fell over and started scooting back frantically while trying to get back on his feet. "What? Did Lord Steel send you here to spy? I haven't broken any rules," Ethan explained frantically, holding his hands up. "I was going to report you. You have to tell him that."

Lilly knelt down next to him. "I am not a spy, at least not for him," she said reassuringly. "I came here to overthrow Steel and try to find a way for humans and vampires to live together peacefully, civilly."

Ethan kept glancing around, searching for others.

"I am the only vampire in here. No one knows about me," she said. "Well, other than Lex," she amended. "We've been best friends since we were five. Oh, and the vampire I was talking to, Tread. He's my...my...my boyfriend," she said, although she felt weird calling him that; it didn't seem like the right word.

"But you can go outside in the daytime," he said, astonished.

"Yes. A few of us can. I don't know if anyone else here can. I am a Sunwalker. I was born a vampire. My heart still beats inside my body. That's why none of the other vampires can tell I'm not human." She reached out to pat his leg, but he pulled it away.

Ethan sat there with his knees pulled up to his chest and his arms wrapped around them. He kept trying to push himself back further, as if the wall would suddenly give way and he could put more distance in between them.

"This just all sounds too crazy, I don't know if I can believe it."

"Let me get Lex," Lilly offered. "Sometimes hearing it from someone else makes it easier." She was about to leave when she thought better of it. "Don't move, Ethan. It will only take me about ten seconds to get to Lex and I'll be able to tell if you move. I'm not going to hurt you," she added when she saw the concerned expression on his face. "I just want to make sure you have all the facts before you make a decision."

"OK. I promise, I won't move." He looked up at Lilly, terrified.

Lilly wondered if it had been a mistake to tell him. *Would this just erase all the progress she'd made so far?* Well, there was no turning back now, the cat was already out of the bag.

Lilly rushed to Lex, woke her up and told her where to go, and then ran back to Ethan.

True to his word he was still sitting in the same spot. He trembled slightly, but seemed to be trying to pull it together.

He leaned to the right, tilting his head to see behind her. "Where's Lex?" he asked.

"She can't move as fast as I can. She's coming, but she is trying to be quiet about it."

It took about five minutes for Lex to make her way to them. She meandered in slowly, glancing around the room.

"What's going on?" she asked as she rubbed sleep out of her eyes.

"I told him," Lilly said.

Lex yawned. "Told him what?"

"Everything."

Lex's eyes opened wide. "Well now I'm awake." She turned to Ethan. "So Lilly told you she's a..." she trailed off.

"So you know," Ethan said, astonished. "And you're really friends with her? She doesn't have something she's holding over you?"

Lex laughed. "No, Lilly's not like that. She's not diabolical. She's quite the opposite. She has this crazy dream she's going to get us to all be friends." Lex sat down beside Ethan on the ground. She put her hand on his. "Look, I know it's a lot to take in. When she

246

told me, I didn't talk to her for a week. I needed time to process it all. Unlike you, I had years of friendship and memories to look back on."

"How do I know you're not a vampire too? Just pretending to be slow and human. Maybe you just don't want to blow your cover now that I found out about Lilly?"

Lilly stifled a laugh.

"Me, a vampire?" Lex asked, trying not laugh. "Well I'm not."

Ethan stood up and rolled his eyes. "That's not very convincing."

"Vampires can't eat. Well, human food anyway," Lilly explained. "You said you both worked together today. Did you see her eat?"

"Yes," he answered slowly as if he still wasn't sure. "So you're really not a vampire?" he asked.

Lex held up her wrist showing Ethan the puncture marks again. "No, I'm not. I don't think they can feed off each other either."

"So do you really think she can kill Steel?" he asked, stepping closer to Lex. "Because that's what it will take. And then even if she manages it, she can get us to live together? Peacefully?"

Lex smiled. "It sounds insane, right?"

"Those were the exact words I was thinking."

She looked at him seriously. "I don't know if all this will work. No one can make you that promise. All I know is that I have seen this girl do amazing things." She tilted her head up, gesturing behind her to Lilly. "She has brought people that hate each other together, working for the same thing. I'm here because I want what she wants. I've met amazing vampires. Vampires who care about humans, who even love them. Heck my best friend is a vampire. And if anyone can do it, it will be Lilly."

"It's just so much to risk," Ethan said, shaking his head.

"It is. But everything that's worth having takes some risk," Lex said.

"Alright," Ethan said in a resigned tone. "I won't say anything for now. I'll trust that Tread isn't going to turn his girlfriend in. But don't do it again. I can't risk Luke."

"OK," Lilly said, extending her hand.

He shook it awkwardly. "I still can't believe you are really a vampire. You've blended in well."

"I've had years of practice," Lilly smiled. "This isn't my first rodeo."

Lilly held back and watched as Ethan and Lex walked off together. She had her arm over his shoulder and was telling him about all the things she had endured to get here and what it was like growing up with a vampire for a friend.

*   *   *   *   *   *   *   *   *   *

The next morning went by quickly. Ethan and Lex sat together at breakfast. Lex had dark circles under her eyes, but seemed happier than Lilly had ever seen her. They must have talked all night because Lex never made it back to bed. They had invited Lilly to join them, but she wanted to give them some space. She sat with Ryan and Justin and was amazed at how open-minded Ryan was, no matter what the subject.

The day was bitterly cold. Lilly pretended to shake and shiver along with the rest of her work group, but she couldn't fake the blue lips that Ellen, Franny, and Janet had by the end of the day.

"Come on Lilly. Let's get something hot to drink," Franny said, as she dragged her towards a line.

Janet had saved them seats and was slurping up her soup loudly when they joined her. Ellen was sitting next to her, apparently trying to see how many green beans she could fit on one fork.

Ellen glanced up and tossed a roll to Lilly.

Lilly caught it and looked confused.

"Look, I know you guys think I'm bossy and mean. Sometimes I am. I just don't want to give them any reason to not like us. But I'm not completely cold-hearted. You must be famished, after not being able to eat. I can give up my roll for one meal."

"Ahh, she does have a heart," Franny laughed.

"Ha. Ha," Ellen said as she took a seat, glaring at Franny, who looked away quickly.

Lilly felt bad about taking Ellen's roll when she was just going to throw it away. She had to work extra hard to distract them while she got rid of her food.

She pointed out Lex and Ethan, laughing together and sitting a little too close to one another. She asked about the meeting they were having that night, and where it would be held.

Each time the girls would look another direction, Lilly would pour her soup in one of their bowls or toss her other food into a trashcan.

Lilly noticed Lex and Ethan disappearing down a hallway together halfway into the meal hour.

At about ten minutes to seven, everyone cleared their plates and headed out into the back field.

"Where are all the vampires?" Lilly whispered as she looked out on the open field in front of them. It was a clear night. Stars were shining brightly and the moon was full. It was cold too. Lilly could see little puffs of air every time a person took a breath.

"They like to make a dramatic entrance," Janet murmured.

Franny shuddered. "I wonder what's in store for us tonight," she said as she fidgeted with her gloves, pulling her jacket over the tops of them so that none of her bare skin was exposed.

It took a few minutes for everyone to gather. Lilly was informed they were all to stand with their heads slightly bowed until Lord Steel was introduced.

A few moments later a group of twenty-two vampires appeared in front of them, all dressed in black—probably to make them seem more ominous. Lilly, however, just thought they looked ridiculous. The people were terrified of them because of their actions, not because of some silly costume.

A white-haired male vampire who looked to be in his fifties stepped forward.

"Please give your attention to our beloved Lord Steel," he announced and then stepped back in line.

That wasn't much of an introduction, Lilly thought.

A tall slender man stepped forward. He had short, spiky, black hair. He didn't look more than about twenty-five, but he had a deep long scar running from underneath his right eye all the way down to his chin. And if that wasn't creepy enough, his eyes were black, solid black; there was no color around his iris. Demon was the first thought Lilly had when she saw him.

"Greetings, my humble servants. Today I have a treat for you," he began. His voice was high and squeaky and sounded too upbeat. "As you know, we have only a few rules in our beloved community. Someone has broken one, and tonight he will be punished."

Tread took a step forward. Lilly gasped. Then two other vampires stepped up from behind him, dragging a third. Tread had only moved to make room for the others to pass by. Relief flooded over Lilly.

She was stunned to see the man they were dragging into the center of the group was a vampire. He was an older man, maybe mid-forties. He looked Hispanic. He was shorter than most of the others. He was begging for forgiveness.

"Please!" he screamed. "Please forgive me Lord Steel," the man cried as he was dragged across the ground. "I will never do it again! I promise!"

"Commence with the execution," Steel said as he flourished his hand in a fancy wave. Then he turned back to the group of humans. He laughed shrilly. "This man stole from me. He took more blood than was his ration. Remember I am nothing if not fair." He looked blankly at them. His face gave no emotion away.

The screaming vampire was staked down with a thick, heavy-looking manacle that clamped around his neck. Another vampire stepped forward and doused him with a liquid he carried in a large canister.

All the while the man staked down was screaming, begging for his life. Lilly had to turn her head and look away several times. She felt pity for the man. He was terrified.

Lilly turned back around as a light caught her eye. Someone had lit the man on fire. His screaming was like nothing Lilly had ever heard. She could see how something like this might haunt her for the rest of her life.

As the man wreathed in pain, Lilly could hear gleeful clapping and chuckling from Steel.

Thankfully, it was over quickly. As Lilly had learned back at the gas station, vampires burned rather quickly. The whole spectacle lasted a few minutes. All that remained at the end was a pile of ashes.

Steel turned to face the other vampires. His voice was icy and determined. "That is what happens when you cross me. There is nothing lower than betraying your own species. Remember today. Next time I won't be so lenient." His dark, hollow eyes shone in the moonlight. He gazed at each of the other vampires and then was gone.

Chapter 19
Covert

A week had passed since Lilly had revealed her true identity to Ethan. He had been true to his word and had not turned her in; of course, she wondered if that had more to do with his obvious infatuation for Lex, over any loyalty to her. Regardless of the reason, Lilly was relieved.

She missed Tread. Keeping true to her word, she had not had any more secret rendezvous. Instead they had to resign themselves to leaving each other messages taped to the bottom of the dumpster. Their lack of meetings had brought on a new problem, one that Lilly had not foreseen when she made her promise to Ethan. She was hungry.

During their first—and only—secret meeting, Tread had brought her blood. Not being able to meet with him had eliminated that source of sustenance. She thought about leaving a note for Tread to leave her blood in a cooler, but that would be more obvious and easily seen by powerful, prying eyes. She thought about asking Lex to share a little with her, just to tide her over, but that was only a short-term solution. Lilly couldn't feed on her every week; that would kill Lex.

After careful deliberation, she decided to ask Ethan for help. After all, he was a runner; he could go freely over the grounds, and had access to areas she didn't dream of going.

After returning from working in the fields, Lilly's first order of business was to find Ethan. She scanned the mess hall and found him with Lex. They were both in line piling up mounding platefuls of spaghetti. Not wanting to disturb their meal, Lilly headed to Luke's hallway. She knew Ethan would eventually find his way there, as he did every night, to tuck his little brother into bed.

Lilly sat down and leaned against the wall. She could hear the little children getting ready for bed. They were changing into pajamas and listening to stories.

It wasn't long before Ethan turned the corner with Lex in tow. Her friend looked surprised but smiled when she saw her.

Lilly stood up as they approached. "Hey guys!" She smiled.

"We didn't expect to run into you here," Lex said, looking at her questioningly.

"I just need a word with Ethan." She saw Ethan's eyes dart to the door, missing his brother. "I thought we could talk after you put Luke to bed."

He smiled and she could see the relief on his face. She had made him miss this special moment before, on her first night here, and she wasn't about to do it again.

"Sure, just give me a few minutes," he agreed.

"Take your time. Really." Lilly reassured him.

Lex released Ethan's hand and he hurried into the room. She turned to her friend. "So what's up?"

"Nothing much, but I'd rather not go through it twice, so do you mind if we just wait for Ethan?"

"Fine," Lex huffed, clearly curious and annoyed she wouldn't be the first to know.

After about fifteen minutes, Ethan reemerged from the nursery. He motioned for them to join him across the hallway. It was the same room he had taken Lilly to before, when he shared his story with her. Lilly stepped into the room, standing on the faded rainbow rug. Lex followed, shutting the door behind them.

"So what did you need to ask me?"

Lilly contemplated how to begin. "So, remember how you made me promise that I wouldn't sneak out anymore?" she prompted.

"Yes," he said flatly. "And I'm not about to change my mind if that's what this is about," he added sternly.

"No, but..." she paused. "I didn't think things through all the way when I made that promise." It looked like Ethan was about to interrupt, so Lilly hurried on. "I'm not going to go back on my word. However, I seem to have eliminated my only source of food."

"Oh," Lex said. "I can help." She held out her arm.

Ethan gasped and stepped back, clearly unprepared for this gesture and possibly disgusted.

"It's fine." Lex smiled.

"No." Lilly shook her head. "Even if I did take some tonight," she watched as Ethan's eyes grew three sizes larger, "and I'm not," she added. "That's only a one-time fix. I can't keep feeding on you. It's not healthy for you."

Ethan stepped forward again, looking slightly more comfortable. "So what do you have in mind?" he asked.

"I thought," she began, glancing back and forth between him and Lex, "that I could leave a note for Tread telling him I need blood, and for him to figure out a way to get it to you."

"Me?" he asked, pointing at himself. "Why not Lex...or you?"

"I've never seen him anywhere near the fields. At least not during the day. Maybe they don't have enough tents, or maybe he's not allowed to go there." Lilly shrugged. "I don't know. But you, Ethan, well...you're a runner. You go inside their buildings. Sometimes you deliver messages or parcels. You have access."

"Wait," he said, putting his hands up. "Let me get this straight. So first, you want to write my name down in a note, that if found could get me killed. Then you want me to risk getting seen carrying blood back here for you, which could also get me killed. And third, you want me to risk them finding out about you, which would lead them back to me, and for the third time, get me killed?" Ethan asked, clearly stunned.

Lilly smiled meekly. "Well, on the bright side, technically I think you can only get killed once...I mean unless they turn you into a vampire...then maybe twice. But three times is really an impossibility."

Lex shoved Lilly hard. "You are not helping."

"Sorry."

"I can't." He shook his head. "They will catch me."

"Tread is smart. He's not going to just hand you a blood bag, he will figure out a way to conceal it, or give you a cover story."

Ethan crossed his arms and stared at her in disbelief.

"Just think about it. And let me see what Tread can come up with," Lilly pleaded.

He looked to Lex.

"It has to be your decision," she said. "I can't make it for you. You are the one that will be taking all the risk."

"Not all the risk," Ethan disagreed. "If they find out about Lilly, you'll be a target too because you arrived together, remember?"

Lilly took a few steps towards the door. "I'll just let you think about it." She slid out into the hallway leaving them alone.

*   *   *   *   *   *   *   *   *   *

The next morning on Lilly's way to work detail she taped another note underneath the dumpster for Tread.

Getting hungry. Still can't risk meeting face to face. Have a friend who might help. Think of ways he could get the blood to me if he can get to you. Be Safe. Love Always

She kept it vague, leaving out Ethan's name for the time being. She avoided specifics whenever possible. Lilly didn't want anyone knowing there was a vampire amongst the humans.

255

Hopefully Tread would come up with a plan which would minimize the risk for Lex's new boyfriend.

The next evening, a response was waiting. Lilly took it to an empty hallway and sat down to read it.

Don't worry. I am certain I know who the friend is and I can find him. He doesn't need to worry about finding me. I'll make contact tomorrow. If he is willing, I have a failsafe plan, although it might make things slightly uncomfortable for you. Yours Forever

She knew it was silly and the last thing she should be thinking about, but Lilly was always amazed at how much nicer Tread's handwriting was than hers. She read the note again, laughed quietly to herself, and stuffed it into her back pocket.

Lilly hurried to find Ethan. She went to the nursery first. The lights were dark and the children were already in bed. Lilly wandered the hallways and heard two pitter-pattering heartbeats coming from around the next corner.

As she turned Lilly spotted them. Lex had her back to the wall and had her arms wrapped around Ethan. He was leaning forward kissing her, and seemed to have forgotten that they weren't the only two people left on earth.

"Uhh, hum," Lilly said, clearing her throat awkwardly.

Ethan stepped back, looking down at his feet. Lex smiled at Lilly as she blushed.

"Um. Sorry to interrupt," Lilly said as she walked towards them.

Ethan rubbed the back of his head. "It's fine."

"Listen, I'm not trying to rush you or put pressure on you, but I got a response from Tread. He said he's going to find you tomorrow and if you are willing, he is sure his plan will work."

Ethan looked upset. "He's going to find me? I didn't even agree to anything."

"I know, and I'm sorry. I knew you wouldn't like that part," Lilly began. "I didn't mention your name, but he figured it out. Even if I leave another note telling him not to confront you, he won't get it until tomorrow night. It would be too late."

"So I really don't get a choice. You just drag me in deeper and deeper. I should have turned you in to begin with," Ethan said tersely, turning and leaving in a huff.

Lex watched him leave, then looked back at Lilly. "He's just nervous. I'll go talk to him."

"I'm sorry Lex. I just wanted to give Tread time to come up with some ideas, in case Ethan agreed. I wasn't trying to force his hand."

Lex hugged her. "I know. No worries." She smiled and then headed off in the direction that Ethan had gone.

That evening when Lex came back for bed, she told Lilly that Ethan was in. Lilly was relieved, but still felt bad for the way things had played out. She hoped Ethan didn't really think that she had tried to trap him into helping her.

The next morning, Lex and Lilly went off to their work assignments and Ethan left to meet up with the runners. Lilly worried the whole time she was working in the fields. Franny had tried to cheer her up, but it didn't help. Lilly was confident that if Tread had a plan it would work, but it was still hard to sit by while someone else took all the risk.

When she was walking back to the mess hall that evening, Lilly noticed Ethan standing off to the side. When he saw her, he motioned for Lilly to join him. Lilly sighed in relief. Even if he didn't get the blood, at least he was safe.

"Lilly, have you ever seen our herb garden?" he asked.
"No."

"Let me show you." He brought her around behind the kitchen and showed her a patch of earth that had all variety of herbs. Some weren't familiar to her, but she noticed basil, rosemary, sage, and cilantro.

"It's nice," she said, looking at him in confusion.

"Well, we take turns fertilizing it." He smiled and held out a bag. "I just picked this up today. I thought you could spread the manure around this time."

"Sure," she said, realizing what was in the bag. She reached for the bag, and was overwhelmed with the stench of it. She quickly stopped breathing. It really was manure. Then she thought back to what Tread had written in his note, about it being uncomfortable for her. She looked back at Ethan. "Thank you."

He nodded. "See you inside."

Lilly spread the fertilizer around the plants and at the bottom of the bag, she found the prize she'd been hoping for. Wrapped in several layers of plastic was a blood bag.

She walked over to the dumpster to throw away the manure bag, and ducked behind it, draining the contents of the bag in a few seconds. Then she tossed it into the dumpster, moved some trash to cover it up and headed inside.

When she walked into the cafeteria, Ethan and Lex were just clearing their trays. She walked with them down the hallway. Once they were alone, she spoke.

"So did everything go smoothly?"

Ethan glanced around. "Other than my near heart attack." He shook his head. "Tread found me easily enough. He gave me the bag along with the story. I was so nervous that I was sure I was shaking, but I took the sack and started running back here. I was about halfway back when I crossed paths with Mary." He shuddered as he said her name. "She was under a tent, so at least I couldn't see her. Anyway, she demanded to know what I was carrying. She had one her lackeys take the bag from me." He rubbed his face. "I felt like I was sweating bullets. Well I guess she opened it, or just smelled it. Mary threw the bag down, yelled at me to get going, and I did. I wasn't about to hang out with her any longer than I had to. I scooped up the bag and sprinted as fast as I could."

"I guess poop is disgusting no matter what you are," Lex laughed.

Lilly placed her hand on Ethan's arm. "Thank you, Ethan. Really. You have done so much for me. I hope to be able to return the favor sometime."

He nodded and Lilly turned and walked back to her bed, leaving them alone.

*   *   *   *   *   *   *   *   *   *

The next few weeks were uneventful. There were no new executions. Lilly fell into her new routine: wake up, work, sleep, repeat.

She had still only been able to contact Tread through the notes they left each other. Ethan had been bringing her blood every week. She was jealous that he had contact with Tread and she didn't.

Lilly ached to be able to see him, talk to him, hold him. She had to keep telling herself that this was only temporary. Soon, if all things went according to plan, they'd be back together, and then they could start a real life together.

Her family was restless. They were worried, but doing fine. Tread had only been able to sneak over there about once a week when he was out on perimeter check.

The weather was just beginning to warm up. There had been a thin layer of sleet covering the ground for the last few days, but it had finally all melted. Lilly and her work group had been moved to a new work detail to help with construction. The ground had gotten so hard, it had become mind numbingly slow work to till more ground. So they had been assigned to help repair greenhouses for the time being.

Lilly enjoyed a change in routine. Franny, Ellen, and Janet also seemed to prefer repair work over digging.

Ellen finished her last bite of oatmeal, and dabbed the corner of her mouth with a napkin. "We'd better get moving, we don't want to be late," she said, glancing at the clock.

259

Lilly looked up. "We still have a good five minutes, don't we?"

Franny shook her head. "We don't," she said, pointing to herself, Ellen, and Janet. "We are in purple." Then she smiled an exaggerated grin and added sarcastically, "Today is our day to give blood. Aren't we lucky."

Janet rolled her eyes. "Oh, yeah. We get all the luck," she said dryly, turning to nod goodbye to Lilly. "We'll see you out there in an hour or so."

Lilly followed some of the men in her group out to the greenhouse. The wind was howling as they made their way through the rubble-lined streets. She looked around and imagined how much nicer Allen could be if the vampires were to clean up some of the trash and debris.

Lilly was instructed to clean windows while some of the others began scraping off old caulking and reapplying new.

Erin, a girl Lilly had briefly met over dinner last week, was working inside the greenhouse watering plants and pulling weeds.

"Where's Ellen and the rest of the gang today?" Erin asked.

"It was their day to give blood," she answered while slowly using her fingernail inside her rag to scrape off all the dirt around the edges of the window.

"Ugh." Erin lowered her arm, exposing a bluish-green bruise. "My turn was last week. It's still sore. I don't have any medical training, but I bet I could do a better job." She rubbed her arm gently. "I mean some of them just jab it in so hard and far, I'm always surprised the needle doesn't coming jutting out the other side."

"I still have a couple of weeks before I have to go."

She gave a half smile. "That's the only good think about going—that I have six more weeks until it's my turn again." She sprayed her rag heavily with the cleaner. "Pray you get Annie. She is the nicest by far. But anyone is better than Heath or Mary." She shuddered when she said the last name and glanced around, looking paranoid.

Heath was the white-haired vampire who had introduced Steel at the execution, Lilly had learned. From all accounts, he was neck-and-neck with Mary to win psychopath of the year, second only to Lord Steel himself.

Lilly scrubbed slowly, trying to keep pace with the other two window washers. She had only finished about a dozen when Janet and the others made it to help.

Franny and Janet were laughing as they walked up to Lilly.

"So it looks like we are cleaning windows together. They assigned Ellen to try to patch some of the holes on the roof," Franny said, pointing to Ellen, who was getting a ladder and didn't look very thrilled.

Lilly dunked her rag into a bucket and wrung it out. "You two seem to be in a really good mood, especially for after giving blood."

Janet smiled. "That's because it was awesome." Then she added as she wet her towel in Lilly's bucket, "Or as great as it could go for someone getting their blood drained against their will."

Lilly looked at her curiously and then at Franny.

Franny extended her arm, showing a tiny little red dot from her donation. "That new vampire, Tread. He started helping out in the hospital this week and everything is different."

"Different how?"

"Well, he showed everyone how to insert the needles for one. Davis did mine, and while he's never been one of the vampires who seem to gain pleasure from our pain, he was never overly gentle either." She dipped her rag and started scrubbing the window next to Lilly. "They were all careful today. They even let us sit for about ten minutes after and gave us all a glass of juice," she said as she looked at her reflection in the window. "All in all it was a pretty pleasant experience. I hope it stays this way. But who knows once Mary sees it."

Lilly walked over to the corner and got a small ladder. She set it up next to Franny and climbed up to start on the higher windows. "It seems like the nicer vampires outnumber the really mean ones. Maybe more things will change," Lilly offered.

Janet sighed. "Maybe." Then she dropped her voice to a whisper. "But I don't see Lord Steel or Mary letting things change too much."

Janet handed a bucket up to Lilly. "Maybe they won't be here forever," Lilly said flatly, as she took the pail and began to scrub a new window.

Franny spun her head around. "Don't say things like that," she hissed quietly. "Or you'll get yourself on the chopping block."

"I'm just saying anything is possible," Lilly added and then turned back to her window.

They scrubbed in silence for the remainder of the day. Lilly smiled to herself whenever she thought about how Tread was making small but meaningful changes. She hoped the same could be said for herself.

As Lilly was assisting Michael, one of the men in her group, in putting the ladders away, she heard a gasp. Lilly turned and saw Mary coming in one of her fancy vampire tents.

Mary halted in front of the greenhouse and surveyed it, walking around it slowly. "This window is a disgrace," she announced hotly. "Who is responsible for this?" she demanded, as she stopped in front of a grimy window. She tried hard but unsuccessfully to suppress her smile. Lilly could tell that Mary enjoyed torturing them. Even through her cold, hard stare, Lilly could see the hint of a grin, and the evil smile in her eyes.

Lilly noticed that Erin was fidgeting and looking down at her shoes intently. She had seen Erin working over there but hadn't been paying too much attention. Based on her anxiety, she must have cleaned the area Mary was referring to.

Mary must have noticed too, because she spun and stalked towards Erin, pausing directly in front of her.

"I said..." she announced even louder, "who is responsible for that window? Do NOT make me ask a third time."

Erin started to shake and opened her mouth to speak, her lips quivering, but she seemed to struggle to come up with any words.

Lilly took a big step forward. "I cleaned that window," she announced.

Erin looked over, confused. She ceased shaking as Mary turned her attention towards Lilly.

The tent moved forward until it was almost touching Lilly's nose.

Lilly looked straight through until her eyes locked on Mary's. She saw Mary flinch, surprised at the eye contact.

Then, not wanting to make her suspicious, Lilly let her eyes begin to wander, so Mary would assume it had just been a lucky glance in the right direction, that Lilly really couldn't see through the opaque fabric.

"It looks like you don't learn too quickly here," Mary smirked. "One day obviously wasn't enough to teach you a lesson. So...hmm," she feigned deep contemplation. "Let's go for three. Three days no food or drink," she announced loudly so everyone could witness it.

Lilly heard a few people gasp, and even one quiet "no." She nodded to Mary.

"Oh and make sure you clean every window on that side of the greenhouse again before you leave. The rest of you can go."

Lilly grabbed a bucket and picked up a new rag as Mary disappeared behind another greenhouse.

She heard footsteps behind her as the rest of the group began to walk back to the school.

A hand tapped her shoulder lightly. "Why'd you do that?" she heard Erin ask.

Lilly turned the faucet and filled her bucket half way. Then she looked at Erin and shrugged. "You looked scared. Plus Mary already doesn't like me, so why not keep her attention off everyone else?"

Lilly walked past Erin and began rewashing the windows.

Erin picked up a rag. "At least let me help you," she offered, dipping her towel in the bucket.

"No. That will just make Mary even more mad." Lilly motioned in the direction of the cafeteria. "I'll be fine. Go. Eat."

Erin's eyes began to water. "How can I eat when you can't eat for three days?"

Lilly dropped her rag back into her bucket and turned to face her friend. She picked up Erin's hand and patted it gently. "Listen, there is no point in two people going hungry. What's done is done. It was my choice, not yours," she said, pointing to herself. "You didn't make me do this. I did it on my own. I'll be fine. I promise. I'm used to not eating as often as everyone else."

Erin wiped her sleeve across her face and lingered for another moment. "OK. I'll go. I'm sorry. Your family must have been pretty poor if you're used to skipping meals that often," Erin sniffed.

"I'll just say it was different." Lilly touched Erin on the back and nudged her gently. "Now hurry before you miss dinner too." She smiled warmly and waved as Erin ran down the path.

It was dark by the time Lilly finished. She was worried that someone could have been watching, so she cleaned the windows slowly.

She walked back to the school. The wind was still gusting but the night was clear. She never realized how windy Texas was. When she had thought of the South, the only images that had come to her mind were hot, sunny days.

The moon was nearly full and stars were shining brightly in the dark sky. As Lilly walked back, she kept hearing twigs break. She scanned the darkness and saw a figure watching her in the darkness of the trees.

The being was too far off for her to make anything out other than a silhouette, even with her superior eyesight.

With each step forward Lilly took, the figure matched pace. *Could it be Tread, keeping an eye on her, keeping his distance, afraid of being noticed? Or maybe that lunatic Mary, stalking her, waiting for Lilly to get her third strike?*

The individual never came any closer. Lilly peered into the forest every so often as she walked back to the school. Every glance over her shoulder revealed the same thing. The person trailed parallel to her but maintained distance at the edge of the woods.

Once Lilly was through the woods, the figure stayed concealed, but continued to watch her as she made her way carefully through the cluttered street back to the cafeteria.

Lilly entered an empty cafeteria. She glanced up at a clock; eight-thirty flashed in red. Lilly stopped dead in her tracks as she turned a corner and entered the main corridor.

Lex was leaning against the wall. She had her arms entangled in Ethan's embrace and was kissing him. The kiss must have been a good one, as they both seemed oblivious to the world.

Lilly waited for a few moments and then seeing no end in sight, she reluctantly began to clear her throat.

"Uh ummm."

Ethan jumped back and brushed the front of his shirt with his hands in an attempt to straighten it. His cheeks were turning a deep crimson.

"Uh, Lilly." He began rubbing the back of his head. "We were just waiting for you."

Lex smiled, and walked over looping her arm through his.

"Glad, you found something to occupy your time while you were both waiting," Lilly teased, causing Ethan's cheeks to grow even redder, which she hadn't thought was possible.

"Erin filled us in on what happened," Ethan explained. "That was either really stupid, or very brave. I'm not sure which yet."

Lex stepped forward. "I understand why you did it, but what will happen if you get a third strike? You have to take care of yourself too."

"I have a better chance of taking care of myself than Erin does," Lilly said, looking at them knowingly. "Besides, I have to do what I feel is right. I don't know any other way to live."

Lex slung her arm over her friend's shoulder. "I know," she said as they began walking back to their room. "You're a saint. Or you should be. Can vampires be made saints?" she asked, only half joking.

Ethan looked around nervously, hoping no one had overheard them.

"Whatever," Lilly said, disregarding her comment. "You know you would have done the same thing."

"Not for three days of no food and no water. I like living."

The next morning everyone was on edge. Steel had called for a meeting that evening. The workday was abnormally quiet, which made the day seem to drag on. Lilly tried initiating several dialogues, but the girls would just answer her direct questions, and made no attempt to keep the conversation going.

As they walked back to the mess hall at the end of their shift, Lilly began to get a little nervous. Rumor had it that a new batch of humans was being brought in tonight. That meant their time was running out. They had about a week left, two if they were lucky. Then they either went all in on their plan and Tread would challenge Steel, or her cover would be blown the moment Steel tried to change her. Assuming he picked her.

She wished she had been able to have more contact with Tread. She wasn't sure how much of a softening influence she had been in persuading people that vampires weren't all demons. She wondered how many would turn on her when they did find out the truth. Would they be able to overlook the deceit? Could they forgive her because her intentions had been honorable, like Ethan had seemed to do?

As soon as the sun had set, the entire brown building, with the exception of the kids and their caregivers, filed out and lined up in front of the field where Lord Steel held all of his meetings.

Lex stood to Lilly's right, next to Ethan, with Ryan and Justin flanking her left side.

"Is it wrong that I am actually glad when we get a new batch of humans?" Justin asked as he shifted his weight back and forth from one foot to the next.

Lilly glared at him.

He looked at her, his eyes open-wide. "Don't get me wrong," he said, holding up his palms defensively. "I feel bad for them. But the more people we have, the less the vampires feed on me," he said, looking at her as if that justified his feelings.

266

Ryan shook his head. "Just...Shut up. How many times do I have to tell you to think before you open up that mouth of yours? And yes, that kind of still makes you a jerk."

"At least I'm an honest jerk." Justin opened his mouth to say more when Ryan elbowed him, and pointed to the front.

Heath was standing in the center of the field, introducing Lord Steel, as he did at every meeting.

Lord Steel strode forward with exaggerated flare. He had attached a vibrant green cape to his ensemble, and it billowed out behind him as he walked.

He seemed quite proud of it. Heath retreated off to the side as Lord Steel took center stage. He stopped for a moment, adjusted his cloak, and smiled a wide, creepy grin.

"We have some new members to add to our family. Please make them feel welcome and help them acclimate into their new environment." He waved his hands dramatically and a crate was pushed forward and then opened.

People poured out. There were no children, just men and women ranging from their teens to mid-thirties.

"Get your hands off me!" a woman shouted.

Lilly froze. She would have recognized the voice anywhere. It was her mother's.

She turned and saw Mary coming from another direction, dragging Elaine as Dylan and Adam were being pushed and shoved by two other vampires she didn't know.

Lord Steel paused. "Well isn't this wonderful. Our family just got even bigger than I had planned." He smiled eerily.

Heath walked over and threw Adam and Dylan on the ground at Lord Steel's feet.

"Well done, Heath. It appears you were right. That was a campfire you saw last night." Steel turned to Elaine who was still struggling. "Kevin, bring out the rules. Let us inform our new servants what is expected."

Kevin, a weak-looking little lap dog of a vampire, bounded off and reappeared holding a sheet of paper.

Elaine had stopped struggling and was searching the crowd.

Kevin handed Heath the paper, and Heath read the Rules off to the new groups, attempting to make his voice sound more ominous than when he had introduced Steel. By the time he had finished, several of the newcomers were sobbing.

Lord Steel turned to Elaine. He grinned a sickly smile. "So do you understand what our expectations are?" he asked.

Elaine stood up straight, looked squarely into the black abyss that made up his eyes, and spit on him.

Steel let out a spine-chilling shriek.

Mary slapped Elaine across the face.

Elaine slumped to the ground and began crying, cradling her face in her hands. She tried to stop, but the mark on her face let Lilly know the hit had been hard.

When Lord Steel had composed himself, he looked back at Elaine. "I'm so glad you did that," he said, his voice sounding more disturbing than normal. "Now we get to show everyone what happens to rule breakers." He turned back to the group of vampires. "Form a square," he commanded.

The vampires immediately obeyed, forming a large square with their bodies.

Mary dragged the whimpering Elaine to the center of the square, twisting her arm backward until there was a cracking sound.

Elaine hollered out in pain as she was left in the center, standing, sobbing, her arm hanging unnaturally at her side.

Lilly watched in horror. She saw her father and uncle try to run to her aid, but they were quickly thrown back down.

She was about to run into the center when Lex caught the sleeve of her jacket.

"No," she whispered so lowly, only Lilly could hear it.

Lord Steel motioned to the square. "The punishment for breaking a rule is death. She was warned of the rules and the consequences and still she defied me. I sentence this human to death. Let the punishment commence on my mark. Three...Two..."

Lilly started to push through the crowd, while Lex feebly attempted to hold her back.

"Stop!" a voice called out.

Lilly paused.

Lord Steel looked around. "Who dares to interrupt me?" he asked, his voice laced with disdain.

"I do," Tread said, stepping forward.

There was a gasp among some of the vampires. "This is wrong," Tread said. "It's more than wrong, it's sickening," he said, disgusted. "These are people. They love, they hate, they hurt, just like us. Many of us were once human. How can we do this to them? There are better ways."

"There is only my way," Steel said, nodding at Heath and Kevin.

They began coming at Tread from both sides.

"I challenge you to combat," Tread announced loudly. "Just you versus me. Hand to hand. No weapons. Winner takes control of this city."

"What a fool," Lord Steel laughed as he gave a curt nod to Kevin and Heath.

They both came flying towards Tread. He sidestepped Heath, who arrived first, and jumped against his back, using the momentum to propel himself towards Kevin and fling Heath off to the side. The two struggled for half a second, and Tread landed lightly, Kevin's head dangling from his hand.

Heath turned to attack again, but Steel held up a hand to stop him.

"Very well," Lord Steel proclaimed. "I had to see if you were even worthy enough for me to waste my time on you. You have proven...sufficient. I will give you forty-eight hours to get your affairs in order. Then you will die." He turned and left, Heath and Mary rushing after him.

Tread turned to the vampires who were still there. "Annie, take this one to the medical quarters and patch her up."

He turned to the others. "Now is the time to start deciding whose side you want to be on. In two days time I will kill Steel. He has been a tyrant here for too long. Then you will be left with a choice. You can choose to change with the times and accept a new normal where we," he gestured to the humans, "live together as

269

equals, or if you want, you can choose to leave. The decision will be left up to you. But those are your only options. If you stay but choose not to change, I'll have another grave dug beside Steel's."

Tread turned and looked at Lilly. "You four," he said, pointing to Lilly, Lex, Ryan, and Ethan. "Go check on that woman. Make sure she's OK, and if she's up to it, bring her back to your quarters and make her comfortable. No one will bother you tonight."

"I'll walk with them," a female vampire offered. She was heavier set than the others, but was still beautiful. She had long wavy hair, and her eyes looked kind.

"Thanks, Jen," Tread said, patting her on the shoulder. He turned back to the group. "I'll be in my residence if anyone wants to come and talk about what the new future will be like."

Chapter 20
Cover-Up

Lilly rushed towards the medical building, dragging Lex behind her.

"Lilly slow down," Lex said, panting. "You're going to rip my arm off."

"Sorry," Lilly said, slowing down slightly.

Ryan jogged up beside them, catching up, with Ethan on his heels. "Do you know her or something?" he asked. "You seem awfully rushed."

"No," Lex answered jumping in. "Lilly just hates to see people in pain."

Ryan didn't push the issue, but Lex had a feeling he wasn't totally convinced. By the time they got there, Elaine had her arm bandaged up and in a sling.

Lilly burst through the doors a few seconds before the others.

"Are you OK, ma'am? I'm Lilly. What's your name?"

Her mother lay on a bed. Annie was moving around behind her, digging through a medicine cupboard. Jen, the vampire who had escorted them here, was sitting in a chair in the corner of the room looking bored.

Ryan was just behind her and looked back and forth between the two women.

Her mother sat quietly for a moment. She had a strange expression on her face and then it disappeared.

"I'm Elaine," she said, her eyes watering. "It was nice of you to come check on me. I'm sure I'll heal eventually. It hurts a lot," she said, fighting back tears. "I could use a hug."

Lilly hurried over and embraced her mother, carefully but in a long affectionate hug.

Ryan looked at Lex and rolled his eyes while shaking his head. "Really?" he scoffed.

Lex ignored him and walked over to Elaine, hugging her. "I'm Lex," she introduced herself, eyeing Ryan, daring him to contradict her.

Ethan and Ryan walked over, and Lilly introduced them.

"Do you think you can make it back to the building we were in front of m—Elaine? I think it would be safer for you to be there with all of us."

Elaine started to sit up. "If you help me, I can make it," she insisted.

The girls supported her as she carefully climbed out of the bed and winced at every movement.

"Give her these pain pills in four hours," Annie instructed. "It was a bad break. It is going to take quite awhile to heal. Try not to move her arm too much."

"Thanks for helping her, Annie," Lilly said. "I hope there are more like you."

"Me too," Annie murmured.

They walked back to the school slowly. Lilly could tell Elaine was trying to be tough. She didn't moan or make any sounds, but with each step Lilly could see her grimace.

When they walked back into the school the atmosphere was different. In a few minutes it would be lights out, but no one seemed to be in bed.

They walked by hallway after hallway of small groups of people talking and whispering about the events of the evening.

Ethan and Ryan helped Elaine into Lex's bed. Elaine was getting sleepy. She said Annie had given her something with a sleep aid in it.

The lights had gone out by the time they got Elaine into bed. A few other people were making it back into the room and into their beds.

Lilly and Lex walked back out into the hallway with Ethan and Ryan.

"Thanks for helping back there," Lilly said.

"No problem," Ryan said.

Ethan looked down the hallway. The majority of people were still out of bed. "I've never seen this before. Something is definitely different. I've never seen anyone out of bed after lights out, unless they were going to the bathroom." He shook his head in amazement.

Lilly turned to him. "Ethan. It's decision time. We only have two days."

He looked so lost and helpless when he looked up. "I don't know. I have to think about Luke. It's just not all about me," he sighed. "If I only had to think about myself, the choice would be easy."

She nodded, looking sympathetic. "Can you at least gather together those that you think might listen? I want to talk with them tonight. We can meet in the gym. We're running out of time," Lilly said.

He glanced at Lex, and she met his eyes and nodded.

"Sure, I guess I can do that much." He turned and started talking to a few kids at the end of the hallway.

Ryan stepped in front of Lilly, blocking her path. "What's going on? Running out of time for what? What's with all the secrecy? I'm not an idiot," he said, pointing inside the room. "I know you know her. She's your mother, isn't she?"

"There's a lot we need to explain," she said, hugging Lex and resting her head on her shoulder. "But I really only want to do it once. Can you wait another hour or so?" Lilly asked, closing her eyes for a second.

"When'd you sleep last?" Lex asked, stepping in front of her friend and really looking at her.

"A full night?" Lilly laughed. "When did we leave Harbor Cove?"

"Lilly!" she gasped. "You've got to take care of yourself."

Lilly slumped back over on her shoulder, "If this ever ends, I'm going to sleep for a full week. You have my word." She hugged Lex and then took a deep breath and stood up straight. "Ok, onward and upward."

"What's that mean?" Ryan asked.

"No idea, but let's get going."

Ryan showed them where the gymnasium was. It was one of the bigger rooms in the school, which would make the perfect gathering place for her announcement.

It took well over an hour for everyone to make their way there. People were talking and didn't seem to be letting up.

Ethan stood up, put his two index fingers in his mouth and whistled long and loud.

Many of the girls put their hands over their ears and glared at him, but he got his point across. Everyone shut up.

"OK. We are here to listen to Lilly, so let's give her the floor," he announced as he stepped aside, gesturing her forward.

Ryan came in and sat at the front next to Justin, eager to find out what was going on.

Lilly saw Ellen, Janet, and Franny looking at her strangely.

"OK," Lilly began, speaking up so that those in the back of the room would be able to hear her. "A lot went on today. I know I've heard people mention that although Lord Steel has been challenged in the past, this is the first time other vampires have ever started following someone new. I want to talk to you guys about what's been going on." She glanced over at Lex, who smiled encouragingly at her. "Please wait till I'm finished before you ask any questions."

"We have a chance to make major changes here," Lilly continued. "You heard Tread, the vampire out there. He wants to make this city a place where we can live together as equals."

274

"That's never gonna happen," someone from the back of the gym shouted out.

"Let her finish," Ryan interjected, standing up and looking around, trying to determine where the outburst had come from.

"I know change can be scary," Lilly continued, "but I think we all need to be thinking about what we'll do if Tread wins. Will we stay here? Will we try to make it work?"

"Why should we try? If they let us leave, which I don't think will ever happen, why would we want to stay?" Justin asked.

"There are vampires all over, not just in Texas," Lilly explained. "We live in fear, hide behind our walls, shut ourselves off from the beauty of the ocean, from the freedoms we once had. Wouldn't it be nice to not be afraid anymore? Wouldn't it be nice to not have to worry if you walk outside of a gate that you are going to be attacked?" She looked around the room, trying to read their faces. *Would they stay?* She couldn't tell.

Justin stood up to address the group. "That Tread is probably just saying what he thinks we want to hear, so things will be easier for him to control if he wins. Vampires aren't like us. They can't have rational conversations like this. They just want our blood," he said, thrusting his arm out, displaying scars and bruises from years of being forced to donate blood. "Why do you think they keep us separate? They can't trust themselves around us for more than a few minutes or they'd end up killing us all." He turned back and faced Lilly. "If they can't be around us for five minutes, how could they possible live with us?" he demanded.

"That's just not true," Lilly disagreed. "A vampire could be your friend and you wouldn't even know it, except for the fact that they drink blood."

"I'd be able to tell," Justin assured her. "If one was ever in the same room with me I'd know," he said, nodding to himself as he took his seat.

"So have any ever been in this school?" Lilly asked.

Justin shook his head. "Never."

"Most of you know I was picked up a few weeks ago."

She saw a few people here and there nod their head in agreement.

"What I didn't share was that I came here from Harbor Cove, New Hampshire. It took Lex and me awhile to get to Texas from there. We were out in the open, in the wild. We didn't have walls to protect us." She pointed to the walls of the building. "What we did have was a vampire."

There was a huge gasp. She heard someone say "no way."

"We traveled here with a vampire," Lilly said again for effect. "He was kind. He found us food and water. He protected us. Never in the entire time since we left Harbor Cove did he try and eat us," Lilly said, making sure she worded everything carefully. She didn't want to lie. She had misled most of them, but she hadn't outright lied to these people and she didn't want to start now. Some of these humans had become her friends.

"He saved us from a bear," Lex interrupted.

Lilly nodded for her to continue. She stepped back and let Lex take the lead.

"Why did he help you?" asked a younger girl, whom Lex hadn't met.

She approached the girl and patted her shoulder. "Because he cares," she said, looking into the young girl's face. Then she looked up towards the whole gathering. "He doesn't see us as food. He sees us as equals. We're different, but we are also a lot alike."

"If you traveled here with a vampire, how did you get captured?" Justin asked sarcastically, disbelief evident by his tone.

Lilly answered this time. "We didn't really get imprisoned. Not the way most of you did," she began hesitantly. "We intentionally got taken. We wanted them to find us so we could get into the city."

"Oh come on," Justin said, throwing his hands up. "Do you really believe any of this?" he asked everyone, although he was looking at Ryan.

"Yes, I think I'm starting to," Ryan replied. He turned his attention back on Lilly. "Tread. Tread is the vampire you were traveling with. He came in and then you two followed. But separately. So no one knew you were together."

"Exactly," Lilly smiled. "We came here to free you. But we also came with the hope that you might stay, that you might share our vision of the future."

Ethan stood up. "We still have to work tomorrow. I'm sure as much as things have changed in the last few hours, that fact won't have changed. I suggest we all go and sleep on this. We can meet again tomorrow and discuss things more if anyone wants to." Ethan took Lex by the hand and they left the gym.

After they left, people began trickling out in small groups as they whispered about the new revelations Lilly had made.

Ryan lingered, waiting for a moment to approach Lilly.

"So now do you understand why I don't want anyone to know that was my mom tonight?" Lilly asked, and then yawned. "If for some reason things don't work out, or anything goes wrong, I don't want them targeted."

"Them?" he asked, tilting his head inquisitively.

Lilly rubbed her eyes and yawned again. "The two men who were with them. One is my father and the other is my uncle."

"Ah," Ryan nodded. "Do you really think Tread can beat Steel?" he asked.

"I'm counting on it," Lilly said, placing her hand gently on his shoulder, pushing him gently towards the exit. "Come on, I think Ethan was right. We all need some sleep. We can talk more tomorrow."

*　　*　　*　　*　　*　　*　　*　　*　　*　　*

The next morning seemed to arrive too quickly. People took longer to climb out of their beds, and the rooms were quieter. Lilly noticed a lot of yawning and red eyes as everyone dressed for the day.

Lex had insisted that she stay with Elaine. People would realize if Lilly wasn't outside working, but Lex would be the one more likely to go unnoticed.

Adam and Dylan had yet to be seen. Someone must have sorted them while she was retrieving her mother last night. Lilly felt reasonably sure they were fine, but wouldn't be able to relax until she saw them both with her own eyes.

Hurrying into the cafeteria, she was relieved to see them sitting at a table with trays of pancakes, talking with Justin. As Lilly approached, she could tell they were deep in conversation. They hadn't noticed her.

"I have more reason to hate them than anyone here," her father was saying.

Lilly felt like she had been stabbed in the back. All her work and after all Tread had done and risked for them, he still couldn't let the hate go.

"So you understand," Justin said, leaning forward. "They can't be trusted."

"I understand better than anyone," Dylan agreed. "You're right. They can't be trusted." He cut a huge chunk out of his stack of pancakes and stuffed it into his mouth. "But as much as it pains me to say it," Dylan continued with his mouth full, "*he* can be."

"Wait, hold up. I thought you were on my side," Justin said, leaning back on his seat.

"Oh I am," Dylan assured him. "We have to be careful. We can't let our guard down. I don't think you should blindly trust anyone." He leaned forward. "But I've seen Tread. Believe me. I have more cause to be skeptical than you could imagine. I can't speak to his past. But his present character, I trust him." He shook his head. "You don't know how hard that is for me to say. I want to hate him. I have reason enough. I still don't like him, but I trust his motives are genuine."

Lilly came and sat down next to them, relieved to see her father was making some progress in letting go of his hate. "Hi. I'm Lilly," she introduced herself.

Dylan looked confused but Adam played along.

"Adam," he said, reaching behind Dylan and shaking her hand. "The slow one here is my brother, Dylan." He elbowed him lightly.

Dylan looked at Adam then back to Lilly. "How's Elaine? They wouldn't let me see her."

"She's doing better. She's in pain, but her arm's been set and she's resting. Lex is with her."

Dylan turned and hugged his daughter tightly. "Thank you. Thank goodness she's alright."

Adam walked over and hugged her too. "It's such a relief to know *everyone* is alright."

"You guys are awfully affectionate. You hug every stranger you meet?" Justin asked, making a strange face.

"Just the beautiful ones," Adam replied, letting Lilly go.

Justin began clearing his tray. "We better get going. Lots of potatoes to dig up."

Ryan walked over and nodded to Lilly.

"You ready?" he asked Justin.

"Yeah."

Dylan stood up and wiped his mouth off with a napkin. "Can't we go with you?" he asked Lilly.

"I think it would be better for you to go with them. Safer," she explained.

Dylan didn't argue. He hugged her once more. "Take care of Elaine."

"I will."

Justin rolled his eyes. "You guys are weird."

Ryan looked over at Lilly and winked at her. "Don't worry, I'll keep them out of trouble."

Lilly walked out with Ellen and the others. The sky was sunny, but off in the distance she could see big, dark clouds.

As they headed to their work station, Lilly saw Mary. She was sheathed in a black tent. Several men trailed behind her. As she walked through the fields she would pick a girl and the men would drag her off screaming.

"What are they doing?" Lilly asked.

Ellen turned to look. "They normally don't do it this soon," Ellen muttered. "Normally they wait a week after bringing in a new batch of people." She turned back to Lilly. "They're taking everyone with green eyes. Lord Steel must be ready to select a new bride."

Mary made her way toward them. She stopped about fifty feet from them and pointed to another girl. This time, a young boy who looked about fourteen stepped in front of her, protecting her.

"Stay back," the boy warned as he took a fighting stance and raised his fists.

"Todd, get her," Mary hissed. "We don't have time for this."

One of the men from Mary's entourage stepped forward and attempted to take the girl.

The boy drove his fist hard into the man's gut and then followed with another punch to the face. Todd went down holding his stomach.

Mary sighed. "Take them both," she ordered. "Bring him to me."

Two men dragged the boy toward the tent, shoving him inside.

He tried to escape but Mary gripped his arm hard and held onto him.

"I was denied an execution last night. You can make it up to me now. Slowly." She smiled an evil grin. "Which would you like to lose first, your right or your left arm?"

The boy stood there shaking, unable to speak.

"Can't decide," Mary sneered. "Right it is."

Lilly lunged forward, ripping a pole away from one of the humans carrying the tent. She flung the tent across the field, flinging the other pole carriers several feet in the process. Then she rushed back to her original position, hoping she was fast enough that no one could tell it was her. She turned back in time to see the boy staring in bewilderment, a pile of dust at his feet.

"What just happened? " Franny asked, looking around wildly. "Where did Mary go?"

Janet walked forward and pointed at the ground. "I think that's her." She looked up at the sun and turned back to Franny. "I mean the sun is out, that's got to be her."

The men who had been carrying the tent started getting up and dusting themselves off. The first one noticed the tent was in the field and turned back to the boy.

"What did you do?" the man yelled at the boy.

The boy looked around in a panic. "I...I didn't... nothing...I..."

Another of the tent bearers came up and looked around frantically. "We will all be killed," he added nervously.

Lilly stepped forward. "No one knows what happened," she began. "No one would believe us if we told them. Just go about your day. No one saw anything. No one knows where Mary went."

As she spoke, clouds started to blow in. "Put that tent thing back wherever you keep it. No one knows anything," she reemphasized as she turned to stare at each one. "Everyone else get back to work, this is just a normal day."

Franny, Janet, and Ellen just stood there looking stunned.

"Come on, we'd better get going," Lilly said as if nothing had happened.

Franny and Janet walked slowly, trailing behind, whispering about the boy and Mary.

Lilly walked ahead. Ellen ran to catch up with her. "I know it was you," she whispered. "But how?"

Lilly kept walking, looking straight ahead. "I have no idea what you're talking about."

Ellen glanced back over her shoulder. Janet and Franny were a good ten yards behind them and totally immersed in their own conversation.

"You moved the tent. You were there, then for a split second you weren't, and then suddenly you were back again." She looked back at the pile of dust. "I only noticed because I was about to warn you that you'd be next. None of the rest of us have green eyes."

Lilly didn't answer for a moment. "The less you know, the safer you are. Just drop it."

Ellen kept walking, keeping pace with her. "She was there. Then she was gone," she was muttering to herself. "You're a vampire," she whispered loudly.

"Shhhhh," Lilly scolded. "Do you want everyone else to figure it out?"

Ellen glanced around. "I don't get it. Why are you here? Why'd you just kill one of your own?"

Lilly looked at her with revulsion. "She was not one of my own. I have human parents. I grew up going to school with humans, playing with humans, depending on humans. "

"You did a great job fooling us all," Ellen said, reaching her hand out and touching Lilly. "You feel human." She studied Lilly for a moment, as if looking at her for the first time. "So if you had this great place with vampires and humans living together, why'd you give it up?"

"It's a long story, but no one knew I was a vampire. I hid it, like I tried to do here. I wanted people to become open to the idea of humans and vampires being friends. I knew if I told people right away that I'm a vampire, they'd only focus on that. No one would have listened to anything I had to say."

Ellen stopped suddenly, her mouth gaping open. "I can't believe I gave you my roll. I was hungry and you just, what, threw it in the trash?" Ellen accused.

Lilly laughed, and continued walking. "That's what you're mad about. Not that I deceived you but that I threw away your roll."

"Wasting food is not a joke," Ellen said seriously. "People lie all the time, it's not that shocking that a vampire would lie too." She picked up her shovel, and tossed another one to Lilly.

By the time they began working on the field again, the sun was long gone. Thick, dark clouds hung over them, threatening to pour down upon them at any moment.

They worked most of the morning in silence. Ellen would secretly smile or give Lilly a conspiring glance whenever she pretended to be tired and need a break.

Lunch came later than normal. The old man who brought it seemed especially nervous.

282

Dark clouds had covered the skies and it looked like any moment a storm could let loose.

"What's wrong, Gary?" Janet asked as she opened her brown bag and began fishing out her lunch.

He shook nervously. "They're everywhere," he whispered. "Searching everywhere. Mary never came back. I guess she went out and no one has seen her," he said anxiously. "Well I'd better get back," he said after he handed out the last lunch.

They ate quickly. Ellen stared, horrified, as she watched Lilly chunk pieces of her sandwich into the trash can.

Lilly smiled guiltily, but she was unsure what else to do with it. It was uncomfortable to have someone watching her every movement. Ellen seemed slightly appeased when Lilly slipped her the pear that had been in her lunch.

About an hour after lunch, Lilly heard footsteps approaching. She stopped, leaned against her shovel, and turned to see Annie and Tread come strolling towards them. Relief flooded through her. She was glad for the clouds, giving him an excuse to be outdoors.

As he walked up, the beginnings of a smile tugged at the corners of her mouth. He looked stunning as always. He was dressed in dark jeans and a fitted gray v-neck shirt.

"We're looking for Mary. Have you guys seen her?" he asked, glancing at each of the girls.

Franny and Janet looked down at the ground, not speaking.

"No," Ellen answered and went back to work with her shovel.

"We have until sundown to find her," Annie said. "If we don't find her, I don't know what will happen. Lord Steel is in a frenzy."

"I think he believes that I did something to her," Tread explained. "We may be fighting sooner than I thought." Then, looking at Lilly he said, "Annie is my friend. Do you really not know where Mary is?"

Lilly glanced toward Janet and Franny. They were both staring so hard at the ground that Lilly thought they might burn a hole in it.

Lilly exhaled. "You're not going to find her by tonight," she said, looking back apologetically.

Tread looked at Lilly skeptically. "Why not? Where is she, Lil?"

Lilly pointed at the field next to theirs. "She was over by the corn field, last I saw her."

"Well let's go check over there," Annie suggested, turning to leave.

Lilly continued. "By now, she could be blown halfway across Texas, maybe some of her even ended up in Oklahoma or Arkansas."

"She's dead?" Annie asked, covering her mouth in shock.

Lilly explained what had happened. That somehow the tent had been covering Mary for one second and the next it had flown into the field, leaving Mary a pile of ashes. Then she had explained how they had attempted to conceal it.

Tread looked knowingly at Lilly and then turned back to Annie and gave her half a smile. "Well I don't know what else to do. I guess we just play along," he suggested.

"I hear someone approaching," Lilly said.

"Several," Annie corrected.

A few seconds later seven vampires crested the hill.

Lilly recognized Jen from the night before along with the white-haired man named Heath.

Tread turned to the one on the right. "What's going on Davis?" he asked, directing his question to the man wearing a faded blue baseball cap. "Has someone found Mary?"

"Sorry, Tread, we've come to escort you back," Davis apologized. "Lord Steel said the fight is happening tonight." A gust of wind came up suddenly, blowing Davis's baseball cap off his head. He jumped up quickly and grabbed it, returning it to his head. "We are to lead you to your quarters and wait with you until six when the challenge will commence." He motioned for Tread to follow him.

"He thinks I did this, right Randall?" he asked, looking to another man in the group.

Randall nodded.

"Alright. Let's go," Tread said as he stepped beside Davis, as far away from Heath as possible.

"One more thing," Heath sneered as he turned to look at the humans. "Your work day is over. Return home, feed yourselves," he paused, looking at Lilly, "make yourselves presentable. All of you are required to attend. After Lord Steel dispenses with this rabble he will pick his bride, and you will all remember your *place*," he spat the last word.

As the vampires began to walk away, a mixture of rain and sleet began to pour down from the skies.

"Let's go," Ellen called out once the vampires were over the hill.

Chapter 21
Green-eyed

By the time they made it back to the brown building, everyone was soaked. Ellen, Janet, and Franny were shivering uncontrollably. When they walked in people were passing out mugs of hot water with lemon and honey mixed in.

Lilly left her friends to their drinks and headed off to change and check on her mother. Lex looked up when her BFF walked in, and held up a finger to her lips, signaling for Lilly to be quiet.

Elaine was sleeping soundly in her bunk. Lilly picked up some dry clothes and motioned for Lex to follow her out into the hallway.

"Just give me a sec," Lilly told her as she rushed into the bathroom and changed.

"Why are you back so early?" Lex asked as Lilly walked back into the hallway with her hair wrapped up in a towel. "I heard a bunch of commotion about vampires being everywhere."

"Tread is going to fight Steel tonight," she answered as she wrung her hair out with a towel.

"But I thought they were fighting tomorrow night."

"Everything has changed." She threw the towel on the floor and pulled out a comb from her pocket. "Steel is picking his new bride," she continued as she combed through her wet hair. "Then he will fight with her watching and if he wins, he will attempt to change her."

Lex placed a hand on Lilly's shoulder. "I'm sure it will be tough waiting here to find out who wins."

Lilly shook her head. "No, I'll be there. Watching. Everyone will be. Evidently there is a big warehouse they will use. Steel wants everyone there to witness his power, his domination."

Lilly glanced at the clock on the wall. It was three o'clock. "They are fighting at six. We are all heading over at five. It will take a while to walk there and then all of us lucky enough to be born with green eyes," Lilly said sarcastically, "will be lined up like livestock to be looked over and inspected." She rolled her eyes. "Will you stay here with my mom?"

"Of course."

Lilly gave her friend a hug and then hurried off to find her father and Adam.

She ran into Ryan as she headed back to the cafeteria. "Ryan. Is everybody alright?"

Ryan was sopping wet. A puddle began to form beneath him as he paused. "Oh yeah. We are all fine, just frozen." His bottom lip quivered as he spoke. "I just left Adam and Dylan. They were grabbing dry clothes from the laundry," he said, fidgeting with his wet shirt. "We are gonna meet up to eat before we head out. We said thirty minutes, so I'm not sure where they are at now."

Lilly leaned forward and kissed Ryan on the cheek. "Thanks for everything."

He blushed, looking away. "No problem," he said, trying to make his voice sound deeper.

She walked to the laundry but found no sign of her father or uncle. Then after scanning the cafeteria and still not seeing any sign of them, she began walking randomly through the school. Lilly turned down a hallway, only to find a little boy sitting down with his knees pulled up to his chest and his head bent down sobbing.

Lilly walked over and gently touched the boy's shoulder. "Are you OK?" she asked.

He looked up, tears brimming over his little eyes.

"Luke!" Lilly exclaimed. "Luke what are you doing down here?" she asked as she knelt down beside him.

"Who...are...you?" Luke asked in between sobs.

Lilly reached down and dried his tears with the end of her shirt. "I'm a friend of Ethan's," she explained.

He frowned, his lower lip sticking out. "I can't find Efan. I looked and now I can't find Miss Ef-lyn too."

Lilly swept Luke up in her arms, hugging him lovingly. "I will take you to Ethan. OK Luke?"

He wrapped his arms around her neck. "You find Efan!" he cried happily.

"I'll find him."

Lilly wasn't sure where to start looking for Ethan, so she headed in the direction of the room Luke slept in.

She hadn't made it far when Lex came running around the corner.

"Luke!" she cried out in relief. "Where have you been?" she asked as she hurried forward to meet them.

He turned and smiled. "Lex. You read more little red hen?" he asked.

"Sure," she reached out and took Luke from Lilly, kissing him on the cheek and ruffling his hair. "We've been looking for you, buddy. Ethan's been so frantic, where did you find him?" Lex asked, looking back at Lilly.

"In a hallway. You just left my mom?" she asked unhappily.

"Adam and your father are with her," Lex reassured her.

"Oh good. I was looking for them when I stumbled on this little cutie." She rubbed Luke on the back. "I should have known that's where they'd head."

She looked at Lex. Luke was so happy in her arms. He had his arms wrapped around her neck and was smiling and kissing her on the cheek.

"So when did you meet Luke?" Lilly asked.

"Ethan introduced me to him yesterday. We left dinner early so he could read to him. Ethan is so sweet. He reads to him every night." Her eyes seemed to dance when she mentioned Ethan.

Lilly laughed. "I was wondering where you two were sneaking off to."

Lex turned looking down the hallway. "Let's go find Ethan, Luke. He is worried sick about you."

Luke looked up. "Efan sick? I kiss him, make him all better."

Lex laughed. "You do that Luke. That's exactly what he needs."

They found Ethan a few minutes later, frantically running from room to room.

"Lukey," he called when he saw him.

Lex set Luke down and he ran to his brother, arms outstretched.

"Efan. I kiss you all better," he said as he ran to his brother.

Ethan swept him up in his arms and walked over to the girls. "I can't thank you enough," he said, clearly relieved to have his little brother back. "I thought something horrible had happened," he said, talking to both of them but with his eyes locked on Lex.

"Lex read more little red hen," Luke proclaimed happily.

"Well then we'd better get going," Ethan said, shifting Luke to one arm and wrapping the other around Lex.

Lilly watched them go. She was glad to see Lex was happy. She hoped Lex had found someone who would make her as ecstatic as Tread made her.

She made her way back to Elaine's room. She found her mother awake, propped up with pillows and being fed soup by her father. They were arguing. Her mother was insisting that she could feed herself, but Dylan wouldn't hear it.

It was a simple moment, but it hit her hard. These were the things she was fighting for. Simple, happy moments. Normalcy. That's all she had ever wanted.

"Hey sweetie," Adam said. He was standing against the wall, letting Dylan and Elaine have their moment. He put his arm around her and squeezed her tightly. "How you holding up kid?" he asked as he looked her over. "You look like you could use a break."

"Is that a nice way of saying I look like crap?" Lilly asked, nudging him lightly in the side with her elbow.

He looked appalled. "Not at all. You could never look anything other than beautiful." He leaned toward her and kissed her on the side of her head.

She smiled and rested her head against his chest. "I see I'm not the only one in the family who knows how to lie." She closed her eyes, resting them. "This is nice. I just need a few minutes of this, Uncle Adam."

Lex came back a few minutes later. Lilly glanced up at the wall; the clock showed four-fifteen.

"You guys better go eat." Lex said. "I'll stay with Elaine." She walked over and took the bowl of soup from Dylan, switching places.

Lilly begrudgingly lifted her head off Adam's shoulder. She sighed. "We'll be back as soon as we can."

"We'll be here," Elaine smiled.

Dylan walked beside Lilly and wrapped his arm around her. "Lilly, no matter what happens tonight, I want you to know I love you and I'm proud of you."

Lilly stopped and looked into Dylan's eyes. "I've been waiting to hear that for eighteen years," she said as she threw her arms around him. "I love you too, Dad."

"Eighteen? I thought you were seventeen," her dad said.

"I turned eighteen yesterday."

"Lilly. I'm sorry, I lost track of the date with everything that's been going on," Adam said. "Happy Birthday."

"Thanks. It's not a big deal. We've had a lot going on," Lilly said.

"Sometime we will celebrate it properly," Dylan said.

"Dad, it's fine. Really."

"No. I missed too many birthdays, I'm not missing anymore. We'll celebrate it soon. I promise."

Lilly sat at an empty table while Dylan and Adam went through the line. Ethan, Ryan, and Justin came and sat by Lilly. A few minutes later Ellen, Janet, and Franny came and asked to join the table.

The mood was light. Everyone was making small talk, but Lilly couldn't concentrate. She kept thinking about Tread. *What if he lost? What if Steel was older than Vanessa?* They had no way of knowing. She hoped that Tread being a Sunwalker would give him enough of an edge to beat him.

When it was time to head out to the warehouse, the sleet was barely falling. Everyone was grateful as they headed off to the fight.

The hike to the building took about twenty minutes. No one talked on the way there. It was a little eerie. Everyone was lost in their own thoughts, wondering about the future and what it would mean depending on the winner.

When they stepped into the dark empty warehouse, they were immediately sorted into two groups—the green-eyed girls in one group and everyone else in the other.

The bigger group was told to sit against the wall and wait for the fight to start.

The green-eyed girls were lined up to be presented to Lord Steel.

The warehouse was large with high ceilings. It was completely empty with the exception of two chairs that were set in the center of the wall, perpendicular to the wall where Dylan, Ethan, and the others sat waiting. There were lots of windows but they had all been covered in black paint. There were a few candles lit around the room, allowing plenty of light for her, but she wondered how much the humans could see.

Lilly glanced back at the two seats. She thought they looked like very pathetic thrones. They had jewels glued along the edges of the chairs. Beside them was a pile of broken bricks.

After standing for about ten minutes in the line, Heath, the white-haired vampire, the right hand of Lord Steel, came out.

He walked up and down the line of twelve girls and pointed to the ones he didn't think were up to snuff. When he had finished, Lilly and only three others remained.

Lilly wondered how they found so many girls with green eyes. It was the rarest eye color, and yet he seemed to always have a selection of women to choose from.

"You will kneel with your head bowed when Lord Steel approaches," Heath began. "If he taps you, you will raise your head for inspection. You will not speak. If selected, you will be grateful for this great honor."

When he finished giving instructions, he stepped back against the wall and nodded to a blonde vampire on the far side of the room.

The blonde opened a door and in stepped Lord Steel. He wore a dark black suit, with a black dress shirt and tie, along with an emerald green vest. The only other color he wore came from a single red rose in the lapel of his jacket.

He strode across to the four kneeling girls. Lilly dreaded looking at him. His black eyes made him seem even more the soulless, evil monster.

Lilly was third in the line-up. He tapped each girl quickly, gave her a quick glance and moved to the next. He stood in front of Lilly and tapped her once on her shoulder. She looked up, forced herself not to look away. He was horrifying. However, he did not move on quickly, but asked her to stand in his sick, high-pitched voice.

Lilly stood slowly, keeping eye contact the entire time.

He let out a high shrill squeal and turned to Heath, nodding.

The other girls were quickly ushered back to the group. Lilly could see the relief on their faces and in their posture.

Heath walked over and turned Lilly to the group. "Your new Queen," he announced.

"My lady," Steel said, "never has one so beautiful been brought home to us. As soon as I dispatch of this miscreant I will make you mine for eternity." He smiled crookedly.

Heath ushered her to one of the thrones and stood beside her. Lilly noticed Steel was carrying a sword. She wondered if this was *the* sword.

Lord Steel looked toward the back of the room. "Bring the degenerate in," he announced.

Another door creaked open and Tread came in, followed by what Lilly assumed were the rest of the vampires in this community.

He saw her and cocked an eyebrow, then resumed his attention to the front of the room.

Tread walked to the center of the warehouse but stopped several yards away from Steel.

He was wearing a white t-shirt and gray sweatpants. He turned and nodded to Lord Steel. "Shall we?" he asked.

Lord Steel ignored his question and took off his jacket, handing it to Jen, who stood near him. He tossed the sword across the room to Heath, who caught it easily. Then Steel took off his tie, dress shirt, vest and shoes, until he was left wearing just his black slacks and black socks.

"When the bell rings we will begin. Last one standing acquires the city."

Jen stepped forward, holding a bell and a small baton. She gave it one distinct ring and stepped back.

Steel began to circle to his right, as Tread moved to his left. Then they switched directions, both waiting for the other to make the first move. Steel feinted in several times, each time getting a little closer, and each time laughing in his shrill tone. Steel ran towards Tread, but this time he didn't pull back. Tread spun and grabbed him by the arm, swinging him in a circle before throwing him against a wall.

Vampires who had once been standing there scattered out of the way. Plaster fell and cracked around Steel. He brushed himself off, looking more shocked than hurt.

There was a clap from the audience, and Steel looked furious. He attacked again swiftly and powerfully. He managed to hit Tread on the right side of his face before Tread was able to get hold of him. Then Tread gripped him and he squeezed hard, making

293

Steel yelp. Tread tossed him over his shoulder, slamming him into the cement floor. Then he leapt quickly on top of him pinning Steel down with one of Lord Steel's arms trapped awkwardly beneath his body.

"If you yield now," Tread spoke loud enough for everyone to hear him, "I will spare you and let you leave, never to return."

There were several applauding now.

"You'll let me leave?" Steel asked, surprised.

He nodded. "If you give me your word you'll leave here and never come back, then yes," Tread said.

Steel looked around the room. "OK, fine. You win." Tread began to get up and release him as the people all began cheering and chanting Tread's name. He released his grip on him and was kicked across the room, slamming into a wall.

"You fool," Steel squealed. He turned to Heath, who unsheathed the sword and threw it to him.

Tread stood facing the now-armed Steel. "I gave you a chance," Tread reminded him as he dusted debris off his shirt.

They both ran towards each other, Steel with his blade raised high above his head. Tread dropped to slide underneath him when something whacked him in the head. Several bricks had been thrown at him in rapid succession. Lilly turned to see Heath dusting off his hands.

Tread leaned over, grabbing his head. His back was towards Steel. Steel raised the sword and jabbed it straight forward.

"No!" Lilly yelled.

Tread moved to turn toward Lilly. Steel thrust his blade at Tread. Instead of going straight through his spine it slashed through his side.

Tread screamed, falling to the ground as he grasped at the sword and landed on his uninjured side.

Lilly jumped up and threw Heath across the room into the midst of the vampires.

She saw Annie and another vampire restraining Heath out of the corner of her eye as she rushed forward. She barreled toward

Steel, as he yanked the blade from Tread and raised it to finish the job.

"You are a fo—" he began.

Lilly propelled into his side. They both went rolling and tumbling forward, the sword flying from his hand.

Steel recovered quickly, turning to see who had dared to attack him.

"My queen," he said, amused. "Here all this time I had a Sunwalker in my midst."

Lilly glanced at Tread. He was still hunched over, barely moving, clutching his side.

"What a pity," Steel continued. "I find a queen worthy of me and she falls for this reprobate who turned on his own kind."

He stepped towards Tread.

"Take another step and I will end you," Lilly snarled, her fangs extending.

She heard gasps from the spectators, apparently some of them were a little slow on the uptake and didn't realize she was a vampire until now.

"I will give you the same deal that Tread did," she offered. She could see the sword lying on the ground several yards behind Steel.

Jen was standing back, staring at the blade. If Jen would just toss her the blade she could end this for everyone. Hope flickered inside her for a moment, and then was doused just as quickly when she remembered Tread's words: "Everyone is scared of Steel."

Steel took another step toward Tread.

"Stop it. I'm warning you." Lilly hissed.

He ignored her and kept walking until he was straddling over Tread.

Lilly rushed toward him, stopping a few steps back, as Steel pushed Tread onto his back with his foot, and stepped on his gaping wound.

Tread cried out in pain.

"Stop it!" Lilly shouted. "Please," she begged.

He looked at Jen. "Toss me my sword so I can end this," he commanded.

Jen stepped forward and picked up the sword.

"Don't do it Jen. We can end his tyranny," Lilly pleaded.

Jen looked at the sword and then back and forth between Lord Steel and Lilly.

"Those who disobey will be punished, but those who are loyal will be rewarded," Lord Steel added.

Jen looked at the blade and lifted it up to throw it.

"You're a fraud!" Dylan said standing up. "What a coward *Lord* Steel turned out to be," Dylan called out, emphasizing Lord with as much sarcasm as he could muster.

Lilly froze, looking at her father. *What was he doing?* Fear overtook her momentarily, fear of what could happen to him—then she realized what he was doing.

Steel turned to look at the crowd. "I'll take care of you in a moment, you worthless—"

"So much for all powerful," Adam said as he stood up beside his brother. "You had to have a weapon to win." He looked at Dylan. "Man, what a sissy."

"How dare you?" Lord Steel wailed.

One by one, others began to stand: Ellen, Ryan, Janet, even Justin, along with others Lilly didn't know by name. Each one threw out some disparaging remark.

Lilly glanced at Jen. Their eyes locked and Jen tossed the sword in the air. Lilly jumped, catching the sword. She spun, bringing the sword down swiftly and chopped Steel's head off mid sentence.

"I'll kill all of yo—" Lord Steel's head went rolling as his body slumped to the floor.

Lilly dropped the sword and ran to Tread. She looked at Jen. "Burn the body."

"Tread, I'm here. You did it. We did it."

Tread shook his head. "No," he groaned. "You did it. You...are...amazing." He struggled to get the words out.

Adam rushed forward. "We need to get him to the hospital building."

"Annie," Lilly called, looking around, not sure where she was in the throng of people.

All the humans were hugging each other and shouting, celebrating the death of their longtime captor and tyrant.

"I'm here," Annie said, bending down beside her.

"We need to get to the medical center. Can you carry my uncle?" she asked, pointing to Adam. "He's a doctor. I'll carry Tread."

"Of course," Annie said, scooping Adam up in her arms, as if he were a baby doll.

Lilly picked up Tread. He grimaced. "Sorry," she said.

"Just go...fast and ignore...me," he gasped.

She ran fast, trying to run as smoothly as possible. Every little moan and groan was like a pin pricking her heart.

When they arrived, Adam was ready. He had a tray set up, lined with shiny instruments and a bottle of rubbing alcohol. He motioned to a bed near him that had been covered in a fresh sheet.

Lilly laid him down gently. "I love you," she whispered, stepping back to give Adam space.

He poured the alcohol all over the wound as Tread cringed, grasping the bed railings for support. When Adam finished cleaning the area he picked up a needle and thread. He noticed the huge dents in the rails Tread had been holding onto. He hesitantly began to stitch. "Lilly," he said, his voice choking slightly. "It's not working. The needle won't penetrate his skin." Adam explained, holding up the bent needle.

"Let me try. I'm stronger," Lilly said, pushing her uncle aside. "Bring me another needle."

"It won't work," Annie announced. "The needles will just continue to bend or break."

Lilly froze. She couldn't lose Tread. This wasn't supposed to happen. She should have been hurt, not him. They were supposed to live forever. A few months together wasn't enough.

"Do you have any of those dart guns?" She made the shape of a gun with her hand. "The kind the VAS use," she asked as an idea began to form.

Annie thought about it for a moment. "If we do they'd be in Steel's house." Annie placed her hand on Lilly's shoulder. "Wait here. I'll go look."

Waiting was agony. While Lilly waited, her dad, Ryan, and a few of her other friends had made their way to the clinic.

"He needs blood," Lilly said as she stroked Tread's hair. "Look around, see if there are any bags." She took a cool rag and put it on Tread's forehead. He felt hot to her. She didn't think vampires could get fevers, but then again, she never knew anyone who had been stabbed with dragon steel.

Lex and Ethan started opening cupboards and drawers, while Ryan began rummaging through closets.

"Lilly, there is nothing here," Ryan said disheartened. "I don't see any type of refrigeration. Doesn't blood have to be kept cold?" He looked around the room one more time, but to no avail.

"Here," Adam said, rolling up his sleeve. "He can take some of mine."

"No!" Dylan shouted, shoving his twin back away from the bed. "You are not giving him any of your blood."

Adam looked at his brother sadly. "Even after all of this, you can't let it go, can you? What else does he have to do for us?" he asked hopelessly.

"Adam, you could die," Dylan said forcefully. Who knows if you've even fully recovered from..." He was silent trying to think of the right words, and then sighed. "From being dinner." He shook his head firmly. "You can't donate blood. But I can." He took off his jacket and rolled up the sleeve on his shirt.

He stuck his wrist in front of Tread's mouth, and looked away trying to distract himself from what he was about to do.

"Drink," Lilly said, as she kissed his forehead.

"No. I can't," Tread whispered. "I've taken...too much...from him already," he added, struggling to keep his eyes open. "I can't take...anything else," he panted.

298

"Take it," Dylan ordered. "I don't love you," he said flatly. "I will probably never think you are good enough for my daughter. But if you die on her, if you break my baby's heart, I will hunt you down in the afterlife and you will never have a moment's peace."

Tread laughed weakly. "Even the impossible becomes possible around you," he said, reaching forwards and grasping Lilly's hand in his.

He leaned forward slightly and bit down.

Dylan grimaced at first and then relaxed. "It's actually not horrible," he said, and then added, "If you don't think about it too much."

"Dad." Lilly waited till he was looking at her. "Thank you. Not just for this, but for back there. You saved us too. That was really brave of you. If you hadn't distracted him, I'm not sure Jen would have had the courage to toss me the sword instead."

Dylan looked away, his face turning red, and nodded.

After a minute, Lilly tapped Tread on the shoulder. "That's probably enough."

Tread released him. "Thank you."

Annie came back about ten minutes later with a dart point in her hand. "I think this should work," she said excitedly. "I'm glad you thought of it."

Adam was able to stitch Tread up using the dart point as a needle. Annie showed Lilly where all the blood was kept and she had her uncle set up a blood IV while Tread rested.

Lilly sat in a chair beside him. "Can someone go fill Lex and Mom in on what happened?" Lilly asked.

Ryan stepped forward. "Ethan already went to take care of that." He placed something on a table in front of Lilly. It was wrapped in his jacket. She eyed it curiously.

He carefully unfolded the coat. "I didn't think that sword should be left lying around," Ryan shrugged. "Figured you could decide what to do with it," he added, fidgeting with his glasses.

"What about Heath and the other vampires?" Lilly turned, asking Annie, who had been coming and going the past couple of hours.

"Heath refused to leave or agree to stay and be peaceful. He's no longer with us," Annie said, looking down at the floor. "Jen is taking care of the others. She is explaining how things are changing and giving them the option to stay or go."

Lilly looked back at Tread, who appeared to be sleeping, even though she knew that wasn't possible.

"He'll pull through," Annie said reassuringly. "It's a good sign that Adam was able to stitch him up."

Lilly smiled. "Yeah, he's a tough one." She opened her mouth suddenly. "I almost forgot. Did someone burn the bodies?" Lilly asked in a panic.

Annie put her arm around Lilly. "Yes, it's all been handled. Just take care of Tread," she said, pointing Lilly in his direction. "I'll make sure the other stuff gets handled."

Chapter 22
Free

It was liberating in a way that Lilly never could have imagined. Everyone in the city knew that she was a vampire. There was no more hiding, no more lying, no more downplaying what she could do. It was a freedom like she had never experienced before. It was as if a weight she hadn't realized she was carrying had been lifted off of her shoulders.

It had been a week since Lilly had decapitated Steel. Things had changed drastically. Seventeen vampires had stayed. More than either she or Tread had imagined.

Tread was going to live. It was slow going but his wound was beginning to heal. He had gotten out of bed this morning and walked some.

The humans had stayed mainly inside the school. They had asked Lilly not to enter. That had been difficult, something she hadn't expected. She understood why, but it was still disappointing to be excluded from a place she was once welcomed.

Ethan had tried to reassure her, saying they just needed time. Time to discuss what had happened and to see how they wanted to move forward.

In a couple of hours, there would be a meeting. Ryan had suggested the warehouse, since it would have enough room for both species.

Lilly walked down to the stadium. The fields would survive a few days without attention, but she had worried about the livestock.

Annie had reassured her that things were being taken care of. Annie had been instrumental in helping so many of the vampires open their minds to a possibility of living side-by-side with the humans. But Lilly had worried that Annie might have forgotten about things the humans needed to survive.

Lex and Lilly had been making sure they were fed and taken care of. While Lex had also taken it upon herself to make sure the livestock was in good hands. Lilly had been coming to join her the last couple of days, now that Tread had really begun to make some headway on his path to recovery. She wasn't so nervous to leave his side.

Lilly pushed open the gate and heard voices at the far end of the stadium.

"Horseys!" she heard Luke exclaim happily as she headed down to see them.

Ethan was holding Luke up, showing him the different animals, and letting him touch them.

Lex stepped around the corner holding a baby chick she had retrieved to show Luke. She handed it to Ethan and then walked over to stand next to Lilly.

"Hey." Lex smiled. "Are you ready for the big meeting?"

Lilly brushed the back of a gray horse with her hand. It had taken her several hours the last two days to get the horses to calm down and trust her enough to let her get close enough to stroke them. They must have been able to sense that she was not human. "Not like there is anything I can do to get ready. Do you think they'll stay?"

"I haven't been to the meetings. Ethan's been so excited to spend some real time with Luke. And to take him outside. We've hardly been in the school."

Lilly nudged her with her shoulder. "You too seem like you've gotten really close." She eyed her expectantly, waiting for the juicy details.

"I know. It seems so fast. But he's amazing." Her whole face lit up when she mentioned him, even her eyes seemed to smile. "I know I probably sound like a silly school girl." She blushed and ducked her head, embarrassed, then turned back to her friend. "I always heard people say how when you have children you find different things sexy. Things you would never have imagined. It's true. I know Luke's not my child. But..." She glanced over at Ethan. He was pouring feed in Luke's little hand so the chickens could come and eat out of them. She smiled. "The way he is with him. So loving, so patient. I don't know. I just can't explain it. That and wow! Can he kiss! Like knock your socks off, fireworks. Way better than in the movies."

Lilly laughed. "So will he stay?"

Lex sighed, looking down at her feet. "I'm not sure," she said as she rolled a small stone around with her foot. "I've been too much of a coward to broach the subject with him." She looked up sheepishly.

"Well there's no time like the present," she said, pushing Lex in the direction of her boys. "Isn't it better to know one way or another, than sit here and dread about what if's?" Lilly squeezed her friend's shoulder. "I'm gonna head over and see Tread before the meeting. I'll see you there?" Lilly asked.

"You can count on it."

Lilly ran to the medical building. Running was one of her favorite things now. She felt like she was flying. She looked up at the sky and guessed she had about half an hour before the meeting.

She had met with Ryan earlier and arranged for him to find some men who would carry the tent poles, so all the vampires could make it to the warehouse safely. He seemed hesitant at first, but reluctantly agreed to figure something out.

Tread was out of bed when Lilly came in. He was walking a little and then speeding up for a moment. But when he sped up, he grimaced and held his side.

303

She whistled. "Looking good," she hollered from the doorway.

"Sure." He shook his head in disagreement. "Looking good if I were a one-hundred-year-old man. At least, that's what I feel like."

She walked up and gently put her arms around him, reaching around to kiss him on the cheek.

"That's alright. I don't mind. I'm finally faster than you."

He laughed. "Ow," he moaned. "Don't make me laugh. And don't get used to it. Running is the one thing I did better than you."

Lilly rolled her eyes. "Oh yeah, the one thing," she said sarcastically. "Anyway, I can't stay long. I've got to head over to the warehouse soon. We're having a meeting," she explained.

Tread took her hand, intertwining his fingers with hers. "I know. I'm coming with you, so we'd better leave now. I'm slower than Lex now."

"You need to—"

"Don't say rest." He held his hand up stopping her. "I've rested enough for two lifetimes. And if I can give you a piece of advice," he added looking serious, "never get stabbed with dragon steel. It's the worst."

They left the building and headed towards the warehouse. It was very slow going, but that didn't matter to Lilly. She would gladly go the slow pace for the rest of her existence. She was just glad he had survived.

"Lilly. I'm sorry. I never apologized before."

Lilly looked at him, confused. "What do you have to apologize to me for?"

He looked older again, his face ridden with guilt. "It's my fault everyone knows you're a Sunwalker. If only I hadn't given Steel a chance." He looked away. "I knew he was insane. I shouldn't have risked it."

"That's what I love about you. You've changed so much. You are always trying to do the right thing." She turned his head till he was facing her. "I don't care about that. It does—" She stopped. "You're out in the sunlight," she said, startled. "We need to get you back before someone sees you." She pulled on him but he wouldn't

304

budge. "Come on Tread. Hurry. This isn't funny. I will get one of those tents and come back for you."

"I'm not going to hide," he said, shaking his head. "Since they know about you, they are going to know about me too. I'm not gonna leave you with the only target on your back."

"No. Come on Tread," Lilly insisted. "You've kept this secret for fifty-seven years. I don't want to undo that." She tugged on his arm. She probably could have pulled hard enough to move him against his will, but she was worried about his injuries.

He pointed behind Lilly. Lilly saw four men about a half a mile away, carrying a tent forward.

"It's too late," Tread explained. "There's Annie." He waved.

Lilly saw the shocked expression on Annie's face as she saw Tread in the sunlight, and waved back hesitantly.

"No," Lilly frowned. "This is all my fault. I didn't even think when I brought you out here."

"You're right," Tread agreed.

Lilly looked at him, her eyes filled with sadness.

Tread laughed. "It's all your fault. I'm alive. I'm happy." He cocked his eyebrow up and smiled at her. "I am in love with the most incredible vampire in existence. It's all your fault." He laughed again and kissed her.

He kissed her again, until she started to kiss him back. She lost herself in the moment. She had to let things go. They were alive, they were safe, and they were together.

"Uh-hum," Dylan said, clearing his throat. "Come on. Do you have to do that in public where I can see it?" he complained as he walked up with Elaine and Adam.

"Well I just didn't want to take away all your reasons for hating me," Tread said.

Lilly and Elaine glared at him.

"Too soon?" he asked laughing, then moaning.

"You deserved that," Lilly said.

"No," Dylan said, shaking his head. "I think we have to joke about it. It'll help us move past it."

As they walked the remaining half-mile to the warehouse, Lilly couldn't help but contemplate on how blessed she was. She had her family and she had Tread, and best of all they were together. And they weren't trying to kill each other.

"There's one thing I haven't been able to figure out," Lilly said, leaning her head against Tread's shoulder as they walked.

He hugged her lovingly. "What's that? You seem to have it all figured out." He smiled.

She stopped and scratched her head. "I thought when a human becomes a vampire, the process heals them, even if its severe like being paralyzed?"

"Yeah, that's right," he agreed.

She looked confused. "Well than how did Steel have that scar on his face? Why wasn't it healed? Did that happen after he was made a vampire? What could do that? I mean even with dragon steel, you are healing, just slowly," she rambled on.

Tread waited a moment. "Are you finished?" He chuckled as she rolled her eyes at him, clearly not impressed with his attempt to be funny. "Steel didn't have a scar—" he began.

"What are you talking about it? It was huge!" Lilly interrupted, holding her hands apart to show the length of it.

Tread crossed his arms, looked at her and waited.

"Sorry," Lilly apologized, making an exaggeratedly sad expression.

"It looked a lot like a scar," Tread began, "but technically it was a birthmark. It looked more like a burn, but he was born that way. It wasn't an injury to be fixed. I guess birthmarks don't work the same way as typical injuries. Whatever changes in humans when they become a vampire, it doesn't recognize that as something that needs to be healed." He took her hand in his and started walking again.

"A birthmark," Lilly mused.

By the time they had arrived, everyone else had gathered. The atmosphere was tense. Lilly never understood the expression "you could cut the tension with a knife" until now. The humans all stood to one side while the vampires stayed on the other.

Lilly walked to the middle of the room and looked around. "So, I guess we should start. Steel is dead, and we need to see how we are going to proceed."

Ryan stood up. "So what will happen if we stay? Tread will become the new ruler? What guarantees do we have that another vampire won't just come usurp the throne from him? Or does it fall to you now, since technically you didn't issue that challenge, but you were the one that killed him?"

Several others murmured their agreement.

"I've been thinking a lot about that," Lilly said. "I've been talking with others too. Vampires and humans," she clarified. "Tread doesn't want to be a ruler. Neither do I."

Tread shook his head. "No, thank you."

"So what then?" Justin asked. "One of them?" He pointed to the vampires lined up against the wall across from them.

"Not exactly," Lilly began. " I think if we want this to work then we should form a council. A council made up of vampires and humans." Lilly took a few steps closer to the human side. "We'd vote on council members, three humans, three vampires. Then let them make the laws," she continued. "We'd all work. We'd all contribute. But anyone who wants to leave, can."

A woman Lilly had seen around but didn't know personally stood up. "If we leave these walls we're as good as dead. What kind of choice is that? We'd never make it to another city."

Lilly nodded. "That's where you have to at least have some trust in us. If you want to leave, we'll send you with an escort. We can't take you all the way into a city; that wouldn't be safe for any of us. But," Lilly added, "we can take you about a mile out from the wall of whichever city you choose and then you should be able to make it the rest of the way on your own."

"So how will the elections work?" Ryan asked.

"That's up to you guys," Lilly answered, waving her hand towards the entire human group. "Go back to the school and decide how you want to pick your representatives. We'll do the same. Then we can meet in front of the school tonight...if that will give you enough time, and form the council."

"That sounds fair," he said, looking towards his group. A few of them nodded in agreement. "And then whoever doesn't want to stay can leave?" Ryan checked.

"Of course."

Lilly watched as all the humans filed out. Her family and Lex went with them to do their voting.

Lilly turned back around. "I guess we should do our own voting. Any nominations?" she asked.

Randall stepped forward. "Annie," he offered, and then looked at Tread who was resting on an empty crate. "No offense, but she's been doing a pretty good job while you've been laid up."

Tread smiled. "I think Annie is a great choice," he agreed.

It was quiet for a moment and then Jen stepped forward. "I nominate Lilly."

Lilly was surprised. She didn't really know Jen; they had worked together to kill Steel but she hadn't had much contact with her since.

"Anyone else?" she asked, scanning the room.

"Mark," Tread submitted.

"Does anyone else have a recommendation?" Lilly asked.

She waited a minute and the silence continued.

Tread stood up and addressed the group. "Well I guess there is no point in voting. Let me be the first to congratulate our council members," Tread said. He walked forward and hugged Annie. Then he shook Mark's hand, and walked over and kissed Lilly.

"I'm proud of you," he said. "You are really doing it." He reached up and cupped the side of her face lovingly. Then he leaned forward and kissed her softly. "I just have one concern."

She waited.

"If you let all the humans leave, what's to stop them from turning us in?" he asked.

She shrugged and sighed. "Nothing. But forcing people to stay," she shook her head, "how does that make us any better than Steel? This isn't a prison anymore. We want people to have the desire to live here. Plus, humans need to trust us, so they need to see us put some trust in them too. I have faith in people. I believe they'll see that we are nothing like Lord Steel, and that will make all the difference.

Tread pulled her close and wrapped his arms around her. "You are amazing."

Lilly glanced around. "Hopefully I will be more thorough on the council." She smiled foolishly. "I just realized I sent all the humans away and we didn't leave any to carry the tents back. So I guess we're stuck here till it gets dark."

"It will give you a chance to get to know everyone," Tread said.

Of the fifteen other vampires in the room, Lilly only knew four by name. Tread introduced them one by one. Most didn't say much. Sam and Scott were introduced as a couple. They were friendly. Lilly thought she might come to like them. Sam had pink hair cut into a bob and was dressed to the nines. She had on black, strappy high heels, with a cute black dress that hit at her knees. Scott on the other had his hair neatly gelled, and wore a button-up flannel shirt with blue jeans. He wore thick, black glasses.

When Lilly asked why, since his vision was way beyond twenty-twenty, he had said he just felt naked without them. So he had switched out the prescription lenses for plain glass.

As soon as the sun went down, they headed for the school. It only took them a few minutes. Scott offered to piggyback Tread over.

Tread reluctantly accepted. He knew it would take him hours to get there on his own, and he didn't want to hold Lilly up.

Lilly heard someone from inside the school holler, "they're here," as they approached.

A moment later, a steady stream of men and women poured out of the building.

Ryan stepped forward when everyone was settled. "We have our council members. What about you?"

"Annie," Lilly nodded, and Annie stepped forward. "Mark," she called out, and he stepped forward, "And myself, have been chosen to be the council representatives," Lilly announced.

Ryan nodded. "We have elected Justin Granger, Lex Crews, and Ellen Miller," he announced, and each stepped forward.

"We'd like to try to meet tomorrow night to get things started," Lex said. She stepped forward and walked up to Annie and Mark, congratulating them.

Justin and Ellen followed her lead, though slightly more hesitant.

"That sounds great," Annie said.

"I guess that's it for now," Lilly announced.

Ryan walked forward.

"Some people would like to leave tomorrow. If that's still an option," Ryan said.

"Really? So soon?" Lilly asked disappointedly. She sighed. "I thought maybe they'd at least wait to see what kind of rules the council would come up with."

Ryan stepped closer. "Lilly, you have to understand. Some people haven't seen their family in years," he said patting her shoulder. "Also some think that this is all an elaborate ruse. I mean you infiltrate the humans, try to become their friends. They don't trust you," he said sadly. "They think you just want to become the next Lord Steel, only you're smarter about it. That you're making things look too good to be true, only to lure in more humans. Some don't believe that you'll really let any of them leave."

"I just want to make things better for everyone." Lilly shook her head. "I can't believe anyone could really think that's what I want." She looked back at the humans. Many were nervous, glancing around. "I wish they'd give us some more time, just to prove our intentions, but don't worry. I'll set it up. Whoever wants to leave tomorrow can go, but it will have to be after dark."

Ryan nodded.

"I was surprised you didn't get nominated for the council," Lilly said, poking him gently in the chest.

"I did. I declined." He looked away, out towards the wall.

"Why?" Lilly asked.

Ryan sighed. Then he looked Lilly in the eye. "I'm leaving tomorrow. So there wouldn't be much of a point."

Lilly stepped back. "Wow," she said, surprised. "I mean I just figured if anyone stayed it would be you." She shook her head. "Justin is staying and you are leaving. I would have never guessed that."

"We have to make changes everywhere. Not just here." He scratched his head. "I thought you were insane when you first pitched your vampire-human fairytale land." He laughed lightly. "But," he motioned around the city, "maybe I was the crazy one. If you can get it to work here, maybe we can get it to work in other cities."

"Be careful," Lilly warned him. "I never told you the whole story of how I ended up here. It's a long one. But basically my family is wanted for treason."

He looked at her inquiringly.

"Essentially it's because they didn't murder me when I was born." She made a cutting motion across her neck with her hand. "Lex too, because she was my friend. You start spouting vampire love...well, just watch your back. And remember not all vampires are evil. Tread's friend Alex in Little Rock for one. I bet she could be reasoned with. Vanessa too, last I saw her she was in my hometown."

He smiled. "I'll keep that in mind. And I'll be careful." He gave Lilly a hug. "You're pretty amazing. If I couldn't see how madly in love you are with that guy," he pointed to Tread, "I might have stayed for an entirely different reason. I'll try to send you word on how my efforts are going."

"Please do. I'll feel better knowing you're safe."

He smiled warmly. "Well I guess I should go pack. Not that I have much to show for my five years here." He winked, then turned and walked back inside.

*   *   *   *   *   *   *   *   *   *

The next evening, Davis, Jen, Scott, and Sam escorted about one hundred and twenty five humans, just under half the population, to Little Rock. They used two big eighteen-wheelers that Steel had acquired for the opposite objective.

Lilly was sad to see Ryan leave. She thought he would have made a great addition to their community. But regardless, she wished him well.

Watching to make sure the first group left safely made her late to the first council meeting. As she approached the warehouse, she could hear arguing.

"No," Justin was saying. "How is that any different than when Lord Steel was in charge?"

Lilly walked in and took the empty seat at the table. She looked around the room, trying to get an idea of what was going on.

"This will never work if you don't agree to it. We can't live here and never eat," Annie said calmly.

"What if we make it voluntary?" Ellen suggested.

"That won't work," Mark argued. "Not enough people will volunteer. We need everyone. We can't take blood from someone that often. That's why the rotation works."

Lilly placed her hands on the table. "Look. There's not a lot that's non-negotiable but the two things that aren't is one, we have to eat, and two, you have to eat. It is voluntary—"Lilly began.

Mark threw up his hands. "Figures she'd side with the humans." He slumped down in his chair, folding his arms across his chest looking upset.

Lilly ignored him. "It's voluntary in a sense, in that you can choose to live here or not. If you live here then you are volunteering to donate blood. It's the only way this can work.

She noticed Mark seemed to sit up a little taller and almost smile.

"So day one on the council," Justin began, holding his index finger up to indicate the number one, "and you are already telling us how it has to be. So this is just a dictatorship in disguise," he argued.

"Come on guys," Lex said. "They have a point. This community can't work if both sides don't eat. What if we came up with some guidelines, on how often people give blood. Age limits. How many times they can miss their turn, like if they are sick."

Justin looked like he was about to argue some more when Ellen interjected.

"Yeah that sounds fair. I mean, come on Justin. What did you expect when you decided to stay? How do you think they are going to eat? I mean we'll benefit from it too."

"Whatever," he said waving them off. "Just don't be surprised if more people decide to leave tomorrow or whenever we announce this."

The council meeting lasted several hours. Tread waited outside as one by one everyone exited.

"So how'd it go?" he asked.

Lilly smiled. "Well, we had some heated moments. I'm sure we will have more," she explained as she took his hand in hers. "We have a lot of work to do and I'm sure there will be plenty of obstacles."

"More than we can imagine," he said as he glanced around at their newly acquired town. "Lil, I know you have high hopes for this place, but there are just so many factors up in the air. I just keep wondering how long we can keep this place a secret. What will happen if all those people we let leave lead the VAS right back here? Or they could just drop another bomb right down on us. What if the vampires we let go find someone more powerful to come and challenge us? The ones that left may not know about me but they all know you are a Sunwalker." He paused and looked at her. "I'm not trying to diminish all that you've accomplished here, but I mean we are basically running a city now. I'm sure we can't even begin to imagine half of what this will entail. Shelter, food, clothing, quality of living...I mean it was difficult for the six of us for a couple months, let alone for a couple hundred. Not to mention getting vampires and humans to really live together and trust each other, like with Lex and you." He shook his head. "I just think we have our work cut out for us."

Lilly wrapped her arms around him and kissed him, first to shut him up and second because they deserved an unrushed, uninterrupted moment. Between all the chaos of transitioning to a new city dynamic, and all the stress of Tread's recovery, there hadn't been time for just a minute of pure happiness. She slid her hand behind his head, and pressed him closer as her need for him seemed to take control.

She finally released him and took a step back. He was smiling at her, with his cocky one eyebrow up signature move, as if he knew he was irresistible.

"You're probably right," Lilly agreed. "We have a long road ahead of us. I think it will be a long time before we see each other as individuals rather than 'them versus us,' but we are making progress." Lilly smiled. "And for today, that's enough."

A gush of wind whipped across them, and Natalie, an older vampire, appeared beside her.

Lilly had only talked to her for a few brief moments over the past week. She had been helping Annie make some plans and improvements for the layout of the city. She was quiet and soft spoken.

She stopped directly in front of them. "You need to come to the south wall now. There is something you need to see."

Tread released Lilly's hand. "Go ahead. I'll just slow you down."

Lilly sped off, following Natalie through the streets and across several fields. They stopped in front of the southern gate.

"What is it?" Lilly asked. "I don't see anything." She looked around. She saw Randall up on the catwalk patrolling.

Natalie waved at Randall, and he began to open the gate. "It's outside. On the wall." She motioned to the right.

Lilly stepped outside cautiously and turned the direction Natalie had pointed.

"Randall noticed the red spots a few minutes ago," she said quietly. "He said he is certain it wasn't here before." She motioned to a red liquid on the dirt. "He was watching the wall, then heard a noise to the east. Randall said he turned for less than a minute. When he didn't see anything he turned back around and noticed splotches of red on the ground. That's when he called down to me. I

314

was walking past," Natalie pointed to where she had been walking, "and he asked me to check it out. That's when I found this."

Lilly knelt down and rubbed her finger in the red substance. She lifted her finger and sniffed it. "It's blood," Lilly said, stunned.

She looked at Natalie, who was standing in front of the wall. Only then did she see what Natalie had brought her out here for. In big, drippy letters painted in blood were the words:

I'm Coming for You

Acknowledgements

First and foremost, I want to thank Courtney Johansson. Not only did you edit my book, more than once, you also designed my amazing cover, and helped in countless other ways.

Thank you to all my beta readers. Your input was immeasurable. It helped to shape my book into what it has become. A special thanks to my harshest critic, Jessica Deragon. A few times your comments stung, but overall they helped to make the story better.

Thank you to Karen Drake. I know you might doubt your contributions, but your input helped more than I can put into words. Your encouragement helped me to finish it. Without it, I am not sure if Sunwalker would have ever been finished.

Mom and Dadd, thank you. You have always been there for me. Mom, you have encouraged me, and helped me to become a better writer. You have read everything I have written. I wouldn't have gotten here without you.

Of course I couldn't have done any of it without my husband. Thank you Armando. Thank you for working so hard, so that I have time to do something I enjoy. I love you!

And finally, thank you to everyone who takes the time to read Sunwalker. I hope you enjoy the adventure, and come to love the characters as much as I do.

Keep up with the latest in the Sunwalker Trilogy at
http://sunwalkertrilogy.blogspot.com/
https://www.facebook.com/SunwalkerTrilogy/
or email me at **sunwalkertrilogy@hotmail.com**

Made in the USA
San Bernardino, CA
01 December 2017